ON LINE

Red in Tooth

and Claw

Red in Tooth and Claw

Twenty-six Years in

Communist Chinese Prisons

Pu Ning

Grove Press
New York

Published simultaneously in Canada
Printed in the United States of America

FIRST ENGLISH-LANGUAGE EDITION

Library of Congress Cataloging-in-Publication Data

Wu-ming-shih, pseud.
Red in tooth and claw: twenty-six years in Communist Chinese prisons / by Pu Ning.—1st ed.
Includes bibliographical references.
ISBN 0-8021-1454-7
1. Wu-ming-shih, pseud.   2. Authors, Chinese—20th century—
Biography.   3. Political prisoners—China—Biography.   I. Title.
PL2824.Z5Z84   1993   895.1′351—dc20   93-12025

Design by Laura Hough

Grove Press
841 Broadway
New York, NY 10003

10 9 8 7 6 5 4 3 2 1

This book is dedicated to the freedom fighters

who lost their lives, in Tiananmen Square and elsewhere,

as well as to all the other heroes and brave spirits

who carry on the struggle for freedom in mainland China.

Acknowledgments

I would like to express my heartfelt thanks to the following people, without whom this book would not have been available to the English-speaking world: Professor Tung Chung-hsuan of Chung-hsing University for the translation, Tad Ferris for the first revision of the Chinese, and Walt Bode and Allison Draper for the final revision and editing of the text. I would also like to thank Professor C. T. Hsia for the Foreword.

Acknowledgements

Contents

Foreword

by C. T. Hsia

In the English-speaking world, most books about mainland China since 1949 have been written by Western journalists and scholars, but in recent years two kinds of Chinese authors writing about China under Communist rule have also found favor with the public. The first consists of those who are not professional writers but feel the urge to tell the world about their ordeals and those of their relatives and friends. Among these, those who write English well or have found ideal collaborators can score huge successes with the public. Thus Nien Cheng's *Life and Death in Shanghai,* Jung Chang's *Wild Swans,* and Liang Heng and Judith Shapiro's *Son of the Revolution* have all been best-sellers and gained worldwide influence through translation into other languages, including Chinese. The second group consists of professional writers who write in Chinese and who, while less well known in the West, are steadily gaining ground.

Practically all such writers require the services of translators to reach the public, and many of these translators use their discretion to delete or condense what they believe to be duller passages. But since the death of Mao Tse-tung in 1976, and especially since the Tiananmen massacres of June 1989, more Americans are reading contemporary fiction from the mainland and Taiwan, and highly qualified translators are dedicating themselves to the task of introducing the best works of Chinese fiction to the American public. Major newspapers and news weeklies have responded with articles and reviews, with the result that readership of Chinese fiction in this country has increased. Thus through translation the novels of Chang Hsien-liang (or Zhang Xianliang, as he is known according to the pinyin system of romanization) have received much critical attention. John Updike, who has been for years a regular reviewer of world fiction for the *New Yorker,* has found in Chang a Chinese novelist of interest. Updike, in fact, included his review of Chang's novel *Half of Man Is Woman* in his latest volume of essays and criticism, *Odd Jobs* (Knopf, 1991).

Even though he couldn't know that the translation is full of mistakes, Updike does express some reservations about *Half of Man Is Woman:* "The novel's virtues—its penetration, candor, and lyricism—are accompanied by some clumsiness and awkward reticences. The author and the hero almost never express the indignation to which their undeserved sufferings would seem to have entitled them" (*Odd Jobs,* p. 587). This is certainly true even though, at the time of its publication in 1985, the book was greeted as a very bold work both for its intellectual courage and for its adult treatment of the sexual theme. Chang is a gifted writer with much to tell us, having served in prisons, state farms, and labor reform camps for twenty-two years. But he cannot tell the whole truth if he intends to write and publish in the People's Republic. Those who want to tell the whole truth about China and retain their creative autonomy must stay silent and cunning in ways unimagined by James Joyce.

Pu Ning, the author of *Red in Tooth and Claw (Hung sha;* literally, *Red Shark,* 1989), is one such rare writer who, despite constant surveillance by the local police and short periods in prisons and labor camps, managed to complete a multivolume project without at all compromising his own integrity as a novelist. Nor did he serve the government in any capacity while living with his mother in Hangchow until December 19, 1982. On that day, having been granted permission to visit his elder brother Pu Shao-fu, a distinguished journalist in Hong Kong, he flew to Canton and a few days later arrived at his destination. With the help of numerous friends throughout China, he had earlier mailed the complete manuscript to his brother in thousands of letters. Known under the collective title of *Book Without a Title (Wu-ming shu),* this most ambitious work by a writer known to his readers as Wu-ming Shih (Man Without a Name) was eventually published in its entirety in Taipei in 1984, even though revised editions of some component parts came out later. The work

comprises six consecutive novels in seven or eight volumes (depend-
ing on the edition used), and only the first three novels—*Beasts (Yeh-
shou, yeh-shou, yeh-shou), The Siren of the Sea (Hai-yen),* and *Golden Nights
of the Snake (Chin-se te she-yeh)*—had been published in Shanghai from
1946 to 1949, prior to the founding of the People's Republic. Whatever its ultimate position in modern Chinese literature, *Book Without
a Title* was certainly the most magnificent undertaking by an individual writer to be completed on the mainland during the Maoist era.

Pu Ning left the mainland to settle in Taipei in March 1983 and
started a new productive career there at the age of sixty-six. By so
doing he has joined that group of Chinese writers, both natives and
immigrants, who have left China for a life of greater intellectual and
artistic freedom. Since the Tiananmen massacres many Chinese writers then abroad, such as the journalist Liu Pin-yen (Liu Binyan in
pinyin) and the poet Pei Tao (Bai Dao), have chosen permanent exile
to protest their government's tyranny. The defectors prior to that
event were far fewer in number, but their company was certainly
distinguished. In 1952 Eileen Chang was the first major writer to leave
for Hong Kong, where she wrote two novels in both Chinese and
English about life under Chinese communism: *The Rice-sprout Song
(Yang-ko)* and *Naked Earth (Ch'ih-ti chih lien).* The former was published
by Scribner's in 1955 to critical acclaim. Because anti-communism
was not then in fashion, the book's commercial sales languished, but
the novel, along with a few of her own translations of her stories, has
been for years required reading in courses on modern Chinese literature in many American universities. Ch'en Jo-hsi, a native of Taiwan,
who in 1960 had founded with several of her college classmates the
influential magazine *Modern Literature (Hsien-tai Wen-hsüeh),* flew with
her equally idealistic husband from Canada to China in 1966, during
the full-scale launching of the Cultural Revolution. After suffering
through this national upheaval, she and her family (they now had
two sons) finally left China in 1973, and she began writing a series
of short stories that would form the collection *The Execution of Mayor
Yin and Other Stories from the Great Proletarian Cultural Revolution (Yin
Hsien-chang,* 1976; translated into English in 1978). Just as *The Rice-
sprout Song* is the first authentic novel about Maoist China, so are

these the first authentic stories about a country gone mad with revolutionary fervor.

While Ch'en Jo-hsi continued to write about Chinese communism in novels, stories, and memoirs, Eileen Chang appeared to have lost interest in that topic upon the completion of her two novels and returned in her writing to an older China that had been the subject of her stories of the forties. In contrast to these two women writers, now long settled in America, Pu Ning is much more knowledgeable about communism, dating from even before the Communists assumed control of the mainland. He has continued to be engrossed in the topic, as evidenced by the short stories, poems, essays, memoirs, and exposés of Communist atrocities he has produced in recent years. It is not without reason, therefore, that along with other critics, Mr. Huang Wen-fan, the translator of *War and Peace* and the full text of *The Gulag Archipelago,* has saluted Pu Ning as China's Solzhenitsyn. *Red in Tooth and Claw* alone, despite its much smaller size, deserves comparison with *The Gulag Archipelago* for showing the disregard for human lives in Communist China and the full range of horrors in its prisons and labor camps.

Pu Ning (b. 1917) and Alexander Solzhenitsyn (b. 1918) share a passion for documenting the evil deeds perpetrated by the Communists; they are also both serious literary artists. Assured of worldwide fame when he won the Nobel Prize in 1970, Solzhenitsyn had begun his literary career with *One Day in the Life of Ivan Denisovich* in 1962, and he is only now engaged in the writing of his major work. Pu Ning is luckier in that what he regards as his principal work—*Book Without a Title*—is already published. He started his literary career at a much earlier age, and two of the novels he published in 1944—*Romance in the Arctic Region (Pei-chi feng-ching hua)* and *Woman in the Pagoda (T'a-li te nü-jen)*—have remained perennial best-sellers. The cost of this early success has been quite high, however, since many serious readers still identify Pu Ning with these youthful works and have never bothered to examine his subsequent novels of greater seriousness and achievement.

Pu Ning has always been a diligent student of Western literature, music, and art, and these youthful novels can be seen as attempts to make use of the Byronic hero in Siberian and Chinese settings. The core situation in each novel is the lover's deliberate, premeditated attempt to win the heroine's heart, a task at which he persists until she loses her pride and confesses her unconditional love for him. At this point, with or without a delirious honeymoon, the lover denies her any further happiness by abruptly leaving her or, worse, consigning her to a totally unworthy suitor to ensure her misery and then leaving. The Korean hero of *Romance in the Arctic Region* discloses in his diary his great admiration for Julien Sorel, the calculating lover in Stendhal's *The Red and the Black,* and he could have cited Pushkin's Eugene Onegin or the hero of Dostoevsky's *Notes from the Underground,* who deliberately spurns the prostitute Liza after having cunningly aroused her love and her compassion for his pitiful condition. What is of interest to a serious student of Pu Ning's literary development is his early identification with that cold lover and the influence on the construction of his novels of certain European works of the nineteenth century, particularly the younger Dumas's *La Dame aux Camélias.*

I have confidently attributed to Pu Ning a reading knowledge of certain Russian works not explicitly mentioned in the two novels, as he attended the Russian Language Junior College in Peking after finishing high school in his native city of Nanking and would certainly have read the major novelists of nineteenth-century Russia in Chinese translation, if not in the original. He has clearly also read many major English and French novelists of the nineteenth and early twentieth centuries. In the perspective of the present time, both Pu Ning and Solzhenitsyn are rooted in the nineteenth century and would be identified as cultural conservatives. Though he has not yet seen it, I am sure Pu Ning would have applauded Solzhenitsyn's recent attack on twentieth-century literature and art, "The Relentless Cult of Novelty and How It Wrecked This Century" (*The New York Times Book Review,* February 7, 1993), as he did Solzhenitsyn's earlier speeches deploring the spineless liberalism of the West. As a new arrival from a Communist country, Pu Ning was as much lionized in Taiwan as Solzhenitsyn in the United States, the two men being admired both for their resolute stand against communism and their personal fortitude. But readers in Taiwan are now too materialistic to care about the issue of communism, and there Pu Ning suffers the same fate as does the reclusive Nobel laureate in the United States now that the initial welcome has worn off: he is highly honored and respected but, in the absence of enthusiastic backing from the press, not as widely read as he would like. Solzhenitsyn's disillusionment with the liberal West is now well known. Similarly, Pu Ning has not been very happy with the political and social developments in Taiwan. In the Chinese preface to *Red in Tooth and Claw,* he admonishes the young for their dual pursuit of money and mindless excitement.

This pursuit of wealth and entertainment is a recent phenomenon in Taiwan, though today even the coastal cities of China are gripped with a passion for material wealth. Because China had always been poor, communism, with its promise to eradicate poverty and injustice, had an irresistible appeal for a great many intellectuals and writers. By the early thirties, the leftist faction of Chinese writers was dominant, and few serious writers were openly anti-Communist, excepting those in the employ of the Nationalist Party or government. Lao She, who had mocked the Communists and leftists in some of his early novels, by the late forties was diplomatically avoiding the issue of communism and glorifying anti-Japanese patriotism in his trilogy *Four Generations Under One Roof (Ssu-shih t'ung-t'ang).* In this postwar period the Communists gained ground steadily, until in 1949 they won control of the mainland. Pu Ning appeared to be a far more serious novelist than Lao She in his planning and composition of the first volumes of his gigantic *Book Without a Title.* It features a Faustian hero named Yin Ti whose attempt to serve China plunges him into politics; his subsequent search for a more meaningful life leads him through romantic love, sensuality and demonism, and religious and philosophical contemplation, utilizing both the Eastern and Western traditions. In the last volume, after all the seeking and questing, Yin Ti returns to his true love, Ch'ü Yung, and settles with her and their young son on an idyllic farm. Ch'ü Yung's reciprocal confession of undying love for Yin Ti at the very end of that volume constitutes the rhapsodic high point of the entire work.

Pu Ning has called *Book Without a Title* a roman-fleuve *(chiang-ho hsiao-shuo),* as did Romain Rolland his multivolume *Jean-Christophe* (1903-12), a work little read in America today but very influential among Chinese novelists of the thirties and forties. That work's influence on the *Book Without a Title* is manifested in its similar construction as a long chronicle of the life-enriching adventures in mind and body of an individual hero. Dostoevsky's influence is similarly explicit, especially in the author's depiction of politics in *Beasts*. Pu Ning was also inspired by Thomas Hardy and Joseph Conrad in his use of elaborately rich and sensuous prose, although he read these writers only in Chinese translation. Indebted to particular authors for their contributions to form, thought, and style, *Book Without a Title* is a summa in fictional guise of Pu Ning's understanding and appreciation of the earth, sun, and moon, of human history, science, and art, and of religion, philosophy, and all varieties of human love. It is thus a work of unprecedented ambition and scope in modern Chinese literature, far superior to the famous trilogies of the acknowledged leading writers, such as the aforementioned *Four Generations Under One Roof* and Pa Chin's *Turbulent Stream (Chi-liu).*

The first volume of *Book Without a Title, Beasts,* deals with the Communists on the Northern Expedition against the warlords in 1926-27. The hero, Yin Ti, leaves his final term of high school in Nanking for five years of self-study in Peking, in the fashion of the author himself. Already a member of the Communist Party, he returns home briefly before joining the expeditionary forces in Canton, like so many of his Communist comrades. After the Shanghai massacre of Communists in April 1927, Yin Ti goes into hiding but is arrested, again like some of his friends. He refuses to disclose his identity and is subjected to torture and maltreatment in prison. He is finally released through the good offices of his father, a respected professor of biology, but what sickens and infuriates him most upon regaining his freedom is the total distrust of his former comrades, who demand that he confess his errors and crimes before applying for readmission to the Party. It is now apparent to Yin Ti that these men must have maligned him in his absence to serve their own interests and that, in defeat, the Party is using all manner of unscrupulous means to regain political power. Yin Ti is thus awakened to the perfidy and treachery of his erstwhile comrades and to the hideous truth about a party that professes democracy but demands total obedience from not only its members but all people under its control. Earlier novelists, notably Mao Tun, have written about the disillusionment and despair of individual party members during this period of political setback, but no novelist of any importance before Pu Ning has so unambiguously denounced the Chinese Communist Party and so eloquently illustrated the thesis that its very struggle for survival has sowed the seeds of its inhumanity and corruption. The author's knowledge of things Russian surely includes the ruthless careers of Lenin and Stalin.

Only a few years after the publication of *Beasts* Pu Ning had ample opportunity to observe the Communists and their henchmen in action in the city of Hangchow. Moreover, he was detained in a labor camp by the sea for over a month in 1958, and in another camp for fourteen months in 1960–61. He was also imprisoned for over a year starting at the end of June 1968, during the Cultural Revolution. Thus Pu Ning had much to write about his own tribulations once he was free to do so. *The Scourge of the Sea (Hai te ch'eng-fa,* 1985) is a memoir of his life at a labor camp in 1958, and *To Calvary I Go (Tsou-hsiang Ko-ko-t'a,* 1986) is an account of the events leading to his arrest and imprisonment in 1968. Both are now available in English as booklets published in Taipei.

Red in Tooth and Claw was first published as a book in September 1989, following its serialization in a leading newspaper. Unlike *Beasts,* a fictional work with autobiographical overtones, and his personal memoirs, *The Scourge of the Sea* and *To Calvary I Go,* this work is the author's retelling of events recorded and recalled by Han Wei-tien. Han was a former Nationalist military officer serving as a secret agent for Chiang Ching-kuo when he was arrested by the Communist security police in Shanghai in March of 1951. First placed in a Shanghai prison, Han was transferred in August 1952 to a prison in the province of Chinghai (Qinghai), where he began his ordeal as a member of the construction team building a highway linking Chinghai to Tibet. Nicholas D. Kristof, the *New York Times* correspondent in China, described the province as follows:

Qinghai Province, the northeastern part of what was once Tibet, is a sparsely populated region of prairies and mountains, 10,000 feet or more in elevation, with few trees or shrubs, and bitterly cold winds that leave cheeks dry and cracked. Soon after the 1949 Communist revolution, it was made the centerpiece of China's gulag: the site of harsh, remote labor camps where "counterrevolutionaries" and criminals fought for survival and often lost.

Though a lucky survivor in the fall of 1954, when he was released from the construction team to go to the Telingha Farm in Chinghai for further reform through labor, thirteen years later Han Wei-tien received a punishment of extreme cruelty: he was imprisoned at the bottom of a dry well for almost two years. In 1976 he was finally freed, along with all other higher-ranking Nationalist officers and bureaucrats in captivity, because the Peking government had adopted a new policy to please Washington. But Han insisted on going to Taipei, and it was not until November 1978 that he arrived there. Pu Ning first met him in April 1987, and became greatly interested in his story. After reading through Han's memoirs of his years as a prisoner and laborer undergoing reform and interviewing him at great length, Pu Ning proceeded to write *Red in Tooth and Claw*.

Even for those who have systematically followed books containing shocking disclosures about Communist China, *Red in Tooth and Claw* is an astonishing record of extreme human relevance. Its recurrent scenes of mass suffering and death involve thousands or tens of thousands of victims. We have all seen on television or read about the massacre of students at Tiananmen Square, but who would have thought that the Communist authorities in Hsining, the capital of Chinghai, would, from eight in the morning to three in the afternoon, machine-gun an unceasing parade of protesters against the government, leaving seven to eight thousand dead and ten thousand wounded, and arresting the remaining twenty or thirty thousand? Who would have thought that some six hundred men with bare legs would be ordered to form concentric circles in an icy river so as to obstruct the current and allow other workers to lay the foundation for a bridge in the relatively dry area at the center? Among the designers of this bridge, who would have known that the legs of many such men long immersed in the icy water would literally break off at the knees once exposed to the warmth of a fire? Among these same primitive engineers, who could have foreseen that a bridge so built would, only a year later, collapse, as would a three-story department store on the bank of the same river? And who would have anticipated that, a few years later, a jerry-built reservoir would crash down and drown an entire village, sparing only three hundred of its two thousand inhabitants?

In reading such grim accounts and statistics, we are not merely shocked by the wanton cruelty of the Communists in charge and by their utter disregard for the welfare of the workers; we are also exasperated by their stupidity and wastefulness, which entail needless deaths and avoidable ecological disasters. And the prisoners, the workers on the highway and at the Telingha Farm, strike us as overly docile and meek. The marchers in Hsining are certainly tragically misguided to have sacrificed themselves merely in the hope that their story would be broadcast to the rest of China and the outside world. The massacre was, of course, not reported and would have remained unknown but for Han Wei-tien's disclosure to our author. In fact, the horrendous story of the construction of the Chinghai-Tibet Highway, which is so memorably retold here, remains to this day practically unknown to the people in mainland China.

In this book, there are only a few instances where maddened convicts retaliate by killing some cadres or innocent people. Practically all the others just go to work undernourished and chronically hungry, and work day after day until they drop dead, still uncomplaining. This is the saddest discovery about the condition of Maoist China. Only in 1951, and then only in Shanghai, does the author report an organized protest, in a maximum-security prison. The ringleaders of this protest are three Western-style doctors who are themselves prisoners but who also serve the other prisoners as physicians. In the end thirty-four demonstrators were shot and fifty-eight had their sentences lengthened. But this was only 1951, when professional men and women in Shanghai were not yet cowed. As the story progresses, we see less and less of this spirit of rebellion among the convicts in Chinghai, who would suffer any humiliation to stay alive.

In retelling Han Wei-tien's story, Pu Ning does far more than serve as a reporter. Though Han had an extremely retentive memory, during his years of imprisonment and penal servitude he was out of touch with the world and knew little of what was going on in the country. He didn't have books to read, and he was not a modern intellectual. The rich descriptive style, the large vocabulary, and the penchant for certain modes of rhetorical emphasis here are typically Pu Ning's. But Han is very much a Pu Ning protagonist. In *The Scourge of the Sea* and other memoirs, Pu Ning often emphasizes his cunning and resourcefulness in besting the Communists despite his puny strength, and the hero of *Red in Tooth and Claw* enjoys a similar advantage. Thus while the highway builders and their overseers suggest thousands of Sisyphuses repeatedly pushing colossal boulders up hills only to have them roll down to kill and maim the men in their paths—the overseers included—the hero himself manages his affairs better than most prisoners. Pu Ning begins the book with an account of the hero's worst ordeal, when he was condemned to live at the bottom of a dry well for nearly two years. This emphasizes not so much his despair and impotent rage as his optimism and resourcefulness. Though without the divine protection of an Athena, he is still an Odysseus, able to widen the tiny living space at his disposal and separate the area where he relieves himself from that where he eats. His health steadily deteriorates in this well-cell due to poor nutrition and lack of sunlight, but there is always a sense that, while he can still cope, he is winning the battle against his tormentors by surviving.

In Chapter 3 of the main narrative, moreover, the hero, while working on the highway, enjoys a romantic interlude with Yelusa, a Sino-Tibetan woman from a nomadic family of great wealth. She visits Han Wei-tien regularly from the fall of 1953 to the summer of 1954, when he is assigned to the Telingha Farm and can no longer see her by the highway. But for almost a year, the young woman's presence among the road workers means a much improved diet for the hero, his select friends, and the Communist cadres as she regularly brings them freshly slaughtered sheep. A bucolic atmosphere is sustained as the two fall in love and the company is regaled with meat. For a while the reader cannot believe that things have improved so spectacularly for the hero. The story unfolds in a way reminiscent of *Romance in the Arctic Region* and *Woman in the Pagoda,* where the heroine is far more in love than the hero and languishes when he departs. Yelusa appears an even nobler woman than her fictional counterparts, as her deprivation of the hero's company eventually prompts her to organize a guerrilla band to fight the Communists. She dies of battle wounds in 1959, and the hero, finally hearing of her death from her younger sister, is disconsolate. The bearer of the sad news also brings along Yelusa's dying gifts for him: two braids of her hair and two pillowcases she had embroidered with words pledging her perpetual service to her lord. Thus, though she is a contemporary figure involved in the Tibetan's uprising against the Chinese Communists, Yelusa, with her exotic traditionalism and sentimental regard for her Chinese lover, appears at the same time as a heroine from Ch'ing dynasty fiction.

While this love episode is of special interest to connoisseurs of Pu Ning's fiction, to readers previously unacquainted with his work it shows how in his view love ennobles and enriches life even in the bleakest circumstances. Our author also praises life itself with fervor. In his world, the restoration to health and freedom of anyone afflicted with a disease or serving a prison term is always an occasion for the joyous affirmation of human existence. Even the man in the dry well, his eyes going blind and his flesh rotting away, is resurrected like Lazarus, and relishes life all the more keenly because he had lived unwashed in darkness for almost two years. Thus in *Red in Tooth and Claw* the graphic descriptions of Communist hell are counterbalanced by the author's ineradicable optimism and highest regard for the precious gifts of life and love.

Rightly valued for its haunting images of the senseless cruelty and stupidity of the Chinese Communists, *Red in Tooth and Claw* should also be appreciated as the work of a major literary artist who has dedicated himself to Chinese letters for over fifty years. It is to be hoped that with the publication of this book the name Pu Ning will be better known not only among Western readers but also among

Chinese readers, who have customarily identified him as the Man Without a Name,* and that more of his works will be made available in English, until someday even the *Book Without a Title* will acquire a new English title for his readers in the Western world.

*The name Pu Ning translates as Mr. Anonymous.

Prologue:

The Secret of the Cave

by Pu Ning

I have read quite a few Western short stories, some of which have left very deep impressions on me. There is an allegory by the modern Spanish writer Unamuno Jugo, called "The Cave of Silence," about a cave from which you can never return. Even if you are tied to one end of a rope and have someone outside hold the other end, you still cannot be pulled out. Once you pass a turn in the cave, the rope will automatically loosen itself. According to the story, many wise people have tried in vain to solve the mystery of the cave.

I had never fully grasped the meaning of this allegory, but after thirty-three years of life in Red China, I have come to associate it with the China I knew in the fifties. China during that horrible period was indeed a cave of silence, permeated with an atmosphere of terror as oppressive as Robespierre's Reign of Terror, or George Orwell's *1984*. Slaughters occurred everywhere, every day in that cave, yet it was as silent as a tomb to those outside, because no news of the secrets inside it seemed to be able to reach the Free World.

In May of 1962, waves of refugees rushed to Hong Kong from China. For the first time the Chinese cave of silence roared, as if a volcano were erupting a flow of indignant people toward Hong Kong. The impression the event left on the outside world, however, was short-lived. People of the Free World were quick to forget.

In the years of the Great Cultural Revolution, 1966-76, the Chinese cave of silence again erupted lava and ashes in the form of persecuted people. But all the same, very few people outside the cave paid enough heed to the continual extraordinary howls. On June 4, 1989, with the Tiananmen Square Massacre, the Chinese cave of silence once again became the focus of the world's attention. The cries of aggrieved souls were heard clearly, and many of the cave's mysteries were disclosed. The world began to understand the real situation of the miserable mainland Chinese and the ruling style of the Chinese Communists.

Why has it taken so long to learn the real character of the Chinese Communists? Because they propagandize as craftily as they wage guerrilla war. In the fifties, for instance, after killing many rich old landlords, they arranged for an eighty-year-old gray-haired Moslem to represent them at an international conference so as to refute the rumor that they had intentionally persecuted old men. The Communists are also good at the art of controlling people. Within the Chinese cave of silence, they organize various groups and place them secretly in the worlds of literature, the arts, journalism, politics, philosophy, and so on, to defend communism and conceal its secrets. Outside the cave, as well, they bribe people and convert "comrades" to talk for them and watch over those who are liable to be their enemies.

Finally, most people are forgetful, especially of that which does not concern them directly. The Czechoslovakian writer Milan Kundera once said that the "struggle against power is memory's struggle against forgetfulness." Some conscientious outsiders may have seen the inhumanity in the Chinese cave of silence, but it did not hurt them directly. After a time, they forgot. Who would care what had once happened to a billion other people if he or she were safe in the sunshine or had problems of his or her own?

I wrote this book to remind conscientious outsiders not to forget the injustice of the Chinese Communists. After the Tiananmen massacre, after we have come to grips with the brutality of the "Scarlet Predators," will we again become as unconcerned as we did after the Cultural Revolution? Are we to keep the cave silent forever?

I started writing this book almost two years before the Tiananmen massacre, and I did not anticipate it. But the events in this book show the appalling and absurd continuity of the recent slaughter with the past. In building the Chinghai-Tibet Road, for instance, the Communists relentlessly abused the people and their rights. I can't help but think that that road resulted in more senseless deaths than did the construction of the Egyptian pyramids or the Great Wall of China.

I am happy that I could collect enough information to write this book. I hope it can serve as further proof of what the Chinese Communists have been doing in their cave of silence. And I hope that those who care about human rights and dignity will do something to help break the cave's silence after they have learned its secrets.

Man, her last work, who seem'd so fair
Such splendid purpose in his eyes,
Who roll'd the psalm to wintry skies,
Who built him fanes of fruitless prayer,

Who trusted God was love indeed
And love creation's final law,—
Tho' Nature, red in tooth and claw
With ravin, shriek'd against his creed.—

Who loved, who suffer'd countless ills,
Who battled for the True, the Just,
Be blown about the desert dust,
Or seal'd within the iron hills¿

—Alfred, Lord Tennyson, from *In Memoriam* (1833)

Red in Tooth

and Claw

In the

Well-Cell

The cell was twenty-odd meters deep. It was cylindrical, about one meter in diameter and walled with bricks made from yellow clay. On its top was a one-inch-thick round wooden cover divided into two even sections. Each section was joined to an iron chain, the other end of which was fastened to the brick balustrade surrounding the cell.

Early in the winter of 1967, four ganbu* and three guards took me to the well from an interrogation room of the prison house at Telingha, in the Tsaidamu Basin, where I had been cross-examined for a long time. I remember thinking it was already as cold as deep winter.

The well was in a large fenced yard. At each corner of the yard a fully armed cadre stood guard over the well and the prison house nearby. As soon as I was brought to the well, one of the cadres who had been irritated by my answers during the cross-examination angrily commanded the guards, "Drop him down!" Then he turned to me and said in a tone of warning: "Reflect well on what you've said while you're down below! We'll come back later to ask you more questions."

A basket was brought, made of willow branches strung with four thick cords and tied to a thick rope more than twenty meters long. Willow baskets are a traditional craft of the peasants of the North. It was to be my personal elevator. I dared not hesitate, but

---

*In the Chinese Communist personnel system, a ganbu is a cadre who often acts as the leader of a unit or as the superintendent of a task.

stepped into the basket slowly and sat in it without stirring. At one point I risked giving the commander a cold smile. However, I knew I could dare no more than this if I meant to live. A guard then came with a key, opened the lock on the iron chain of the wooden cover, and lifted the cover. Another guard came and unfettered my hands. With a third guard, they grasped the long thick rope tied to the basket and began to let me down slowly into the well. But when I was yet some meters above the bottom, they let me drop—purposely, I guessed. With the shock of the fall, I passed out.

When I regained consciousness, my whole body was aching, but I thought I was lucky to be still alive. I knew I was to be imprisoned at the bottom of the well until I was willing to tell the Communists what they wanted to hear. Now, as I looked around, I found that darkness had enveloped everything: they had again covered the well.

I had neither matches nor a lighter. I was trapped in the dark. After considering my plight for a while, I began to crawl, groping. Then I sat up to think again. Suddenly, I noticed a foul smell. I studied the smell uncomfortably for a time before I realized that it was only the smell of urine and feces. This well had been a cell for other prisoners before me. They had eaten, slept, and excreted all in the same place. I reached out my hands and touched the ground to "see" if I had crawled into anything unmentionable. I had, and I had already rubbed my clothing in some of it.

The bottom of the well was like a cave. Near the surrounding wall, I could not stand up without hitting a protrusion, but I could stand upright and jump as high as I was able in the central part, where the shaft of the well rose up to the top. Estimating with my groping hands, I guessed my living space was about two meters in diameter. This made me a bit thankful to the designer: If the space had been any smaller, I might not have been able to stretch out comfortably when I lay down.

Fortunately, the well was dry. I cleaned my hands by rubbing them against the wall and then lay down for a long rest.

About two hours later I heard noise coming from the top of the well. Then half of the well-cover was lifted. Some light shone down, enabling me to see that the bottom was covered with pebbles and broken pieces of stone in sand. As the light was dim, I supposed it was getting dark outside.

Then I saw a basket being let down from above. When it reached me, I found there was a mug inside. It was my evening meal. I took the mug out of the basket and looked at its contents: some rice gruel with boiled Chinese cabbage. But I found no chopsticks. This was probably to prevent me from killing myself by swallowing them. Before I could finish the thought, the basket was lifted up and the well was covered again. The dim light had been with me for no more than five minutes. Suddenly very hungry, I finished the food at once. While eating, I held the mug all the time. I never put it on the ground for fear of what it might touch.

I didn't feel too bad that afternoon and evening. I believed that they probably wouldn't keep me imprisoned there for a long time. Besides, I was too tired for any quick or appropriate response to my situation. As I lay on the ground, I felt the pebbles and broken pieces of stone hard and uncomfortable underneath my body, but the thick cotton clothes I wore prevented them from hurting me. The most unpleasant thing was still the smell. I wondered why the former occupants hadn't tried to keep the cell cleaner. Was it because they came for such a short time? Were they so disheartened by their plight that they had no will to do anything? Or were they so weak that they had no strength to stir at all? Before I finished puzzling this out, I realized that I had lost any sense of the smell, though the disgusting atmosphere had entered deep in me.

On the whole, my first night in the well-cell was full of ease compared with my nights above, which were full of pains, both physical and mental. For fourteen years I had either been sick or forced to labor like an animal. I had had very few days at the prison when I did not feel the pressure ready to crush me as surely as a huge rock. Now I was alone in the cell. I thought I might be able to get a good long rest if they did not bother me. In this dark world, I thought, I would be free from the weary life outside and even the struggle to maintain my dignity. No one, I believed, could understand how I cherished this chance of having someplace entirely to myself.

That night I slept soundly. I even had the sweetest dream of my life. I dreamed I had been released and led by a divinity to a new world, a new Arcadia. When I awoke the next morning, I still fancied I was enjoying my life in that blissful land, until a dull pain intruded. But still, even though I was not in the world of my dreams, just to be away from the Communist leaders' whistles and whips, from having to labor in chilly weather was enough compensation for the lightless imprisonment.

Sometime the next morning, another succession of noises came from the top of the well. I was given a mug of gruel for breakfast. Again, I had about five minutes of daylight while a basket was let down and then lifted up through the half-open cover of the well.

After finishing breakfast, the first thing I did was try to clean the ground of my "home." I rid my garment of the dirt which was stuck to it, then used my hands as brooms and gingerly swept the floor. I collected all the filth in one corner. When the work was done, I scooped up a handful of sand and scrubbed my hands with it. I finished by rubbing my hands on the wall, to make sure that they were as clean as possible. It was a pity that I had nothing to dispel the unpleasant smell emitted from the corner of filth, which I decided to use as my temporary "toilet." After cleaning the ground, I found I could further improve it by removing the jagged stones to make it smooth. As I had time to spare, I took great care in carrying out my improvements. Finally, I had a little space which I could call both my seat and my bed and which I believed was tolerably comfortable for one used to the meager comforts of prison life.

In my school days I had read the adventures of Robinson Crusoe, and the Englishman's plight on the deserted island naturally came to mind. I was, like him, isolated from the outside world, but I was even more alone than he. He had at least had a dog for a companion, while I had nothing but dirt and stone. What made me, the "well-bottom Crusoe," even more miserable was that the space in which I dwelled was too limited to allow me any real activity at all. I saw no daylight except during the few minutes when they brought me my meals, but I could not spend all the long hours of endless night in sleep. I spent most of my time thinking. Very often this mental exercise carried me very far into the past.

In that year, 1967, the Cultural Revolution was still raging. The previous year the Communist Guards were revolting everywhere in China, seemingly turning over every stone in every corner of the distressed country. This year the party chiefs at Chungnanhai* were taking measures to end the tumult. They now waved, for instance, banners reading "Support the Peasants" and "Exploit the Frontier," and accordingly sent the "little generals" into the countryside, where they were made to "munch" stones and "eat" clay for exercise. The more unlucky guards, who had "committed serious errors" or "belonged to the class of dissenters," were treated even more "impolitely." They were sent to labor correction farms such as Telingha. Once in the Gobi desert labor camps, the young heroes began to exert their influence on the farms. An atmosphere of tension grew and their collective rebellious attitude wound its way, directly or indirectly, into each farm laborer's mind.

On one of the farms there were many big heaps of wheat grain which the "criminal laborers" had just harvested. Each heap was as high as a two-story building and was about ten meters in diameter. All the heaps covered nearly 300 meters, including the distance between each heap. It was estimated that all that grain might weigh more than four million jin.†

One night a fire broke out on the farm. For two hours it burned fiercely, making the drying yard as bright as day. The flames devoured all the hills of grain in the most shocking event in the history of the farm.

The Party commissioners held urgent meetings day and night. They decided that the fire was set on purpose by some rebellious inmates. Naturally, thorough investigations began immediately, and soon it was determined that Cheng Ching-yu (a former chief of the Communist Radar Station at Tinghai) and Shen Fu-ying (a former platoon leader of the Communist Army) were the responsible arsonists. Both had been imprisoned for being malcontents: they had "unduly" criticized their Communist chiefs and had been delivered

*Mainland China's equivalent of the American White House.
†2.4 million kilograms.

to the farm for proper "corrections." They were cross-examined and given severe penalties for three months before they were tried.

The day they were brought to public trial in a square on the Pa Yin River, its audience included two thousand "criminal laborers" from Telingha Farm. Half were "positive members" or "members with better thoughts." I also attended the prosecution. I had been lifted from the bottom of the well and brought to see how the Party leaders and "positive members" prosecuted the criminals. At the end of the trial, Cheng, Shen, and three accomplices received death sentences and were immediately executed. Each criminal had a placard hanging from his neck, on which was written ANTI-REVOLUTIONARY.

After the trial, the Communist leaders continued to investigate the arson. They believed there were still some "plotters" hidden among the rest of the prisoners. Since I had been considered one of the few "stubborn malcontents," I was suspected and interrogated. I had gotten wind of the arson plot, but I had not involved myself in it. I was cross-examined all the same, and as I would not confess my guilt, they kept torturing me in a dark room. There were some ten dark rooms on the farm, designed for the special purpose of putting suspects on the rack. Each of the rooms had a corner "furnished" with some straw for a bed, and a heap of sand for a "toilet." Any suspect brought to one of these rooms was likely to be tortured there for days, or months, if he would not confess anything. I had been put on the rack there four times before, the longest time lasting almost four months and the shortest time about two weeks.

This time I was in the dark penal room less than two weeks. I was interrogated by the vice-chief of the Correction Office. He was from Chiangsu Province in the North and was of average height, with a square face and a loud voice. "You die-hard anti-revolutionary! You'll see what I can do, you bastard, if you're not frank with me!" he barked, pounding the table with his palm. I knew that if I admitted I had even heard anything beforehand about the arson, my brain would not be long for my head. For me, then, death meant eternal darkness, and although I knew that to some it seemed a good means of salvation, I still wished to live. I preferred staying in the dark penal room to entering eternal darkness, so I refused to talk. Consequently, I was severely punished.

corner, I had only gravel to clean myself. The air in the well was never fresh. Three times a day a guard would come with the meal and open the lid of the well. If the guard was kind-hearted, he would come earlier and open the lid for thirty to forty minutes, so that some fresh air might reach the bottom of the well. Otherwise, the lid would be open for only five minutes or so while my new mug of gruel was sent down and the finished mug from the last meal was lifted up.

There was a small round hole in the lid of the well. It was through that hole and the gap along the seam of the two planks making up the lid that a little fresh air could come down to the well. That was how I was able to live on in that cell.

I guessed I was the only "well-bottom man" in the world. Was it a glory? I thought not.

"What should I do?" I kept asking myself. After thinking and lamenting a thousand times, I had only one piece of advice for myself: Manage to survive. I knew I couldn't lie motionless all the time. To sit or to sleep without exercise would expedite my death, just as being melancholy would. I knew that to live I had to move, to keep in motion, to be constantly active. But what could I do? In such a limited area I could not even crawl like an insect. How could I get enough exercise?

When I was thinking about this question, the story of the Count of Monte Cristo suddenly came to mind. I thought I might as well follow the example of the wall digger, though I didn't expect I could escape from my prison cell. But how could I excavate a well? Chinese legend has it that Panku, the creator of heaven and earth, had a divine axe. I wished I had a divine axe, too, instead of merely two bare hands, so that I could create a world of my own!

I started with my bare hands. If I could not escape by this means, I thought, I could at least kill time. Night and day I dug on and on, training my hands to become picks and shovels. As I dug, sand and pieces of clay showered my face, body, and legs. Occasionally stones and broken pieces of rock would fall down as well; I could use them to dig with, and though I had no water to wash myself, I frequently bathed in sand and stone. After a month, I had dug a hole in the well as big as the basket used to send down my meals. Then it occurred to me that I might well use the hole as a pit for the ever-increasing excrement. I dumped all the collected filth into my new excavation. And from then on, the hole was my commode.

One day I had a whim. Now that I had dug a commode, why shouldn't I dig a much bigger hole and make it a room? Suppose they should send down another prisoner; wouldn't I therefore save myself from fighting with him for the already limited space? I immediately put my whim into practice. I knew the soil in the bottom of the well was strong enough to stand my digging.

Usually I began digging soon after breakfast. I dug with my bare hands first and then used large stones to break the rocks; I used splinters of rock, or pointer stones, to dig further into the hardest part of the soil. I took my time; I was in no hurry. I had no watch, deep down there, and I knew the time only by the coming and going of the meal-basket.

Engaged in my "big construction," I found I could pass the days more easily. Many times I felt as zealous in doing my work as a religious man practicing rites. The work became the center of my life. Through it I forgot I was in the bottom of a well-cell completely in darkness. Sometimes I fancied I was a secret agent working on a strategic tunnel.

I planned to dig a narrow corridor first, two meters in height, one meter in width, and eight meters in length. That corridor would serve a great purpose. I would be able to turn myself from a crawler into an upright ape. As soon as I could walk upright in the well, I would consider myself already half liberated. As I had stayed without light for a long time, my eyes had become used to the darkness. I found I was beginning to be able to see things in the cell. As I dug on, I was able to tell sand from stones by eyesight only, without the aid of my hands. This facilitated my work. About a month later, the corridor was finished. Thenceforth I could enjoy taking a walk in the bottom of the well. Then I went on to dig a cave to serve as my room. A year later, the "room," a space four times as big as the bottom of the well, was also finished.

I did not know for sure whether or not the Communists knew I had been digging. Perhaps they knew it but did not care. Maybe they just took my excavation below as a sort of harmless exercise. Anyway, since I received meals every day, they knew I was still there. And they seemed not to bother about what I did as long as I remained in confinement.

When I had finished constructing my cave, I imagined it was not just an ordinary room, but a palace for my life and a sepulchre for my death. The day I completed it, I was happy beyond description. I felt I was as great as a pyramid builder. And I began to believe that the Foolish Old Man from Chinese legend was truly never foolish at all; a determined effort can indeed move a mountain; where there is a will there is a way indeed. In the "palace," I moved freely and joyously in all directions, forgetting I was a prisoner. Sometimes I ran, sometimes I leapt, and sometimes I stretched my hands and legs as if I were taking my morning exercise. The first night I moved into the "palace," I rolled myself back and forth on the floor, imagining the sandy ground was a soft carpet. I pictured myself as a newlywed spending the first night of my honeymoon in a luxurious suite. I even saw myself as a great mother or a helpful midwife who had been responsible for the birth of a child which turned out to be a room.

My imagined happiness lasted quite a few days. Then sorrow began to set in on me like a dark cloud. I realized that I had spent a year and a half in the well-cell. Such a long stay in the dark had gradually destroyed my eyesight, though I had been happy for a time about getting used to life without light. When I had "work" to do, I never noticed the condition of my health. Now that I had nothing to do, I suddenly realized that I was blind not only to my surroundings but also to my health problems. I started to ponder the problem of my eyesight; it was not the lack of light alone that caused the weakening of my eyesight, it was also my lack of nourishment. While I was busy working with a purpose, I was miraculously full of vigor. Now that I had ceased to be occupied by anything, I found I had lost not only my eyesight but my strength as well. I examined my body. I was indeed skinny. All my bones were giving me pain because, I thought, I didn't have the flesh to protect them from being hurt.

I had been of the opinion that I was a strong man because for the sixteen years since 1951 I had been able to overcome a great variety of difficulties. Now after fewer than two years' imprisonment in the well, I knew I was no longer able to stand further torture. There were things that those outside couldn't understand, because they hadn't experienced them personally. If I was like something which had sunk into the bottom of the waters, the outsiders were like duckweeds floating on the surface. I couldn't expect them to have sympathy with me. Most people know what hunger is, but to miss merely one or two meals results in a sort of hunger quite different from fasting for three or four days. In the well I was given three meals each day, but each meal was insufficient. I was hungry every day for almost two years. This long-term hunger is yet another sort of hunger, which, thankfully, few people come to understand.

It's the same with darkness. Few people spend as much as a day in full darkness. Can anyone understand how it felt to be lost in darkness for over a year and a half? While I was digging the cave that was to be my "room," I was concentrating too hard on my work to let my thoughts wander to daylight. But during the night I often ran after the sun in my dreams. It was hard on me to remember the bright outside world while I was prevented from any contact with light. When I did nothing but think, I felt the lack of light made time pass much more slowly. Darkness was like a huge mountain falling in on me to squeeze the breath out of me. I became afraid to think, or to remember the sun of past. In fact, I tried to direct my thoughts toward the things near at hand. As I touched the sand and stone, I often imagined with pleasure that I was a grain of sand or small stone myself. Perhaps I really belonged to the world of dust. I came from dust and I should be glad to return to dust. With this idea, I went on to fancy that every grain of sand was like a ray of light. Thus I was temporarily released from melancholy. For a time, I could continue to live what was for me a normal life.

Strange to say, except for the loss of my eyesight, I never fell seriously ill while in the well. In the days of "labor corrections," I had high blood pressure and heart disease. But I never suffered from heart trouble in the well. In the past I had had problems with my digestive system, but even this seemed to lessen now. I thought I was able to remain so healthy because, first, I did not labor under pressure in the well; second, my poor meals were in a way merely the equivalent of a strict diet; third, I was not exposed to extremes of climate in the well; fourth, I was blessed with an unusually hardy constitution; and last, I still had a strong will to live.

When I now consider my health at that time, I think the last reason was perhaps the true one. I could not claim to be healthy solely on the grounds that I had no serious disease. Though I hadn't fallen prey to consumption, my strength and vigor were dwindling as I was gradually reduced to a framework of bones covered with a threadbare garment of flesh.

One day toward the end of my second year in the well, I suddenly felt I could see nothing at all. At noon when the meal basket was lowered down to me, I saw only a dark shadow. After a minute, even the shadow disappeared. I was so panic-stricken then that for the first time in a year and a half I used my voice. "I'm blind! I can't see! Wait!" I croaked out. My voice was hoarse, but I thought the meal senders above heard me. They waited patiently until I got the basket, took the mug of gruel out of it, and put back the finished mug from the last meal. I've heard that in northern Norway people see the sun twenty-four hours a day for half a year and dwell in darkness for the other half. That may be true, but I don't think the Norwegians really have no light at all during the dark half-year. Besides the starlight and moonlight, they must have candle light, electric light, and much more. In my cell, however, darkness was nearly constant. And it was destructive. It had, at the very least, deprived me of my eyesight.

It was chiefly through my strong will that I was able to live two years in the well. But the exercise of one's will-power is not unlimited. One's physical condition can often restrict the free play of one's will. When I became blind toward the end of my second year in the well, my will to live on began to crumble. I became desperate or, to put it more precisely, resigned to fate. And with this change in my will, my health changed as well. Every part of my body seemed to itch. And where I scratched became immediately afflicted with some sort of rot. I grew weaker and weaker each day. I lay on the floor for the greater part of each day. I didn't even have the strength to crawl to my commode—though, thankfully, since I ate less and less, I seldom felt the need to use it. I was like a poor swimmer who had fallen into the sea. After struggling for a while, I soon became exhausted, choked on the water, and lost consciousness.

When I awoke, I was no longer at the bottom of the well. I was on an earthen bed. But when I opened my eyes, I couldn't see anything except some dark shadows moving against a brighter background. At that time, I was too weak to sense anything except that I was still alive. Some time later I began to hear people talking around me. Then I was aware that some of them were speaking to me and that somebody was pulling my hand. And then I clearly heard this somebody's voice.

"Old Han, it's me, Liang Chih-shen. How are you feeling now?" I wished to answer, but I hadn't the strength to utter a single word. I remember I only groaned. Liang took that as a good sign and went on:

"You've lain here two days and two nights without opening your eyes. They've been giving you injections. The doctor says you'll be all right. Don't worry, Brother Han. You're on the way to recovery."

These were indeed consoling words from a good friend. Liang was a Cantonese. I'd known him when he and I were both imprisoned at Tilan Bridge Jail in Shanghai. We used to meet each other every day in the prison yard when we were let out for exercise or other activities. He was lean and wore spectacles. He had graduated from Nankai University in Tientsin and had once been principal of Jinjen Middle School in Shanghai. He was arrested and sentenced to imprisonment because they said he had something to do with the CC Group.* Later he was, like me, sent to Chinghai for "labor corrections." He was working on Gobi Farm when I was sent down into the well.

After I regained consciousness and was able to understand him well, Liang told me what had happened since I passed out at the bottom of the well-cell. He said the meal senders found that I had left

---

*A political group associated with the Kuomintang.

the mug of gruel untouched when the basket was drawn back up, so they reported it to their superiors. The superiors thought something must have happened to me. (I might have been dead or seriously ill or I might have run away or been trying to starve myself.) To get the truth, they sent three men down the well to bring me up. Finding me not quite dead, they sent me to the hospital.

"But why didn't they let me die?" I would have asked if I had been able to speak. Even if I had been able to ask the question, however, I do not think Liang would have been able to answer it. Was it because they still wanted to learn something from me? Because they wanted to torture me even further? Because they wanted to prove that they could make men live or die as they liked? I think no reasonable answer can fully justify the Communists' treatment of their fellow men. As they are malicious, so are they capricious.

Anyway, I came to life again, although at the time I felt that to be alive was not necessarily better than to pass away unnoticed. I still couldn't see anything, though I could by other means sense the existence of many other patients in the room. I lay motionless on the earthen bed for five days. They gave me several injections a day. Later, they began to feed me liquid meals. After the sixth day, I was able to move. Sometimes I turned on my side, and sometimes I raised my hands. Once I even had the strength to croak a few words. Ten days later, I was able to sit up. Twenty days later, I could get down from the bed by myself. And three months later, I began to eat normal meals. My improvement was steady.

While I was still recovering, Liang came to see me once again. He told me that when he saw me the day I was sent to the hospital, I looked just how he imagined a ghost would look: a lean pale face covered with disheveled locks, emaciated limbs as stiff as tree branches, and a scrawny body spotted with rashes and sores. I was barely recognizable; on first seeing me in the hospital, he really could not believe it was Old Han lying there.

Liang's mention of my appearance made me remember that I had not cut my hair, nor shaved my face, nor cleaned my teeth or any other part of my body while in the well-cell. I must have been frighteningly ugly and dirty. If I had been able to see myself, I might have shocked myself to death, as had some other feeble souls I'd known. In the hospital they had cleaned me up somewhat, though I still never got the chance to brush my teeth. The nurses gave me wet towels occasionally, with which I hurriedly wiped myself off. But since I could not see, I could only suppose that some places were cleaned while others were left dirty.

I stayed in the hospital for six months. When I'd entered, I'd weighed only forty kilograms. By the time I left, my weight had increased to forty-six, still far less than the normal weight for a man 182 centimeters tall; in my carefree days I had weighed eighty-six kilograms. Yet my biggest problem was not my weight but my eyesight. In the hospital Dr. Oaliu had tried to cure my blindness, but when I left the hospital, I could still see nothing more than dark shadows. Later, Dr. Oaliu prescribed some Chinese herbal medicine, which had some effect. A year later, images of big objects began to be clear to my eyes. But I still could not read newspapers; it would be five more years before I was able to read, and even then I'd have to wear spectacles and use a magnifying glass. Reading for ten minutes without rest was enough to cause pain in my eyes.

After I left the hospital, I was returned to my original "labor correction team." And when I had somewhat recovered my eyesight, they made me labor again with the others. The rashes on my skin continued to annoy me. Whenever I exposed myself to the sunshine, I would itch all the more; where I scratched continued to ooze yellowish liquid and pus. I applied various kinds of balms and oils to my skin, but none had any effect. It was not until I poured a certain strong medicinal liquid on my skin and almost burned it off that my itches were cured at last.

Although I had cured my diseases and survived the well imprisonment, I couldn't get over the terrible feeling that I have come to connect always with the well-cell. Later, when friends came to see me and congratulate me on my good fortune (that is, that the Communists did not kill me), I always wondered if it was better for me to live on than to have been shot dead.

But now I am sure that it is good that I survived. If I had passed away, who would remain to tell of the Communists' brutal treatment of the people they governed in the secretly blockaded area of Ching-hai? Who would know that they could turn a well into a cell and confine a "stubborn anti-revolutionary" like me? The following is my story, my testament, and perhaps my revenge.

The third time they questioned me, I still would not confess. The questioners (four leaders and three guards) then beat me savagely. I was so brutally kicked and knocked around that I pissed my trousers involuntarily. I even fainted away two times before they finally sent me back to the bottom of the well.

Back in the well-cell, I no longer felt like I was in a secluded hermitage; instead I felt like I was in hell. Now I lived in great fear. Every three or four days, they would lift me out and question me again. Each time I denied having anything to do with the arson, they would beat me again. After having been thus persecuted some ten times, I refused to get in the basket to be lifted up. Still, they wouldn't give up, and sent down two big men who tied me and forced me into the basket. I still pleaded not guilty. Eventually, they had to cease interrogating me.

About three months later, violence again broke out on the farm. A "positive member" and a "leader" were killed, and some barns were burned. Although during those months I had been in the well-cell and had had no chance whatsoever to communicate with outsiders, I was, strange to say, again suspected. The Communist leaders seemed to have decided that I was the "plotter" of any "anti-revolutionary action." Since I was suspected again and again, I was put to the rack again and again. Each time their violence failed to make me confess, they would return me to the well bottom by dropping me from the midway point, thus giving vent to their anger. I was ill-treated that way for half a year before they left me alone in the well-cell.

After that "eventful" half-year, I lived comparatively undisturbed in the well-cell for about a year and a half (530 to 540 days, I think). During those long grim days, I rarely saw the sun, the moon, stars, flowers, grass, trees. I never saw a single friendly face, nor even a worm. In those two years I never brushed my teeth, washed my face, changed my clothes. Morning to morning, no matter what season it was, sitting or sleeping, I wore the same thing. I saw no change of seasons or of day and night in my cell. There were many times when I lost my sense of time. I was never given any water to drink. The only liquid I drank came from the gruel at mealtimes. Naturally, I had no toilet paper. Each time I finished using my toilet

Tilan's Rage

In 1950, when the Korean War broke out, the Communists were busy fighting, too, suppressing rebellious peasants, or "anti-revolutionaries." The Red leaders' frenzy seemed to have become the whole world's madness. An earthquake seemed to be occurring, shaking the three hundred million hearts of the Chinese peasants. Later estimates indicate that during that time of the Korean War, an average of one Chinese every three seconds was "put down" by guns or other means. The Dragon's Land was red, too.

Meanwhile, tidal waves of people were trying to escape. Those who failed were arrested and immediately sent to jail or put to death. Those who got away all thronged toward Kowloon.* The railroad station in Kuangchou† soon became a great life buoy that everybody was desperate to reach. In less than a month, from December 1950 to January 1951, the only outlet to freedom was choked with a furious deluge of landowners, rich farmers, town mayors, county executives, merchants, Nationalist Party members, and soldiers, all fleeing the provinces of China to swell the "sea of refugees."

Suddenly, but not unexpectedly, on January 15, 1951, the authorities in Peking declared that Luohu Bridge, the place where Yin and Yang met,‡ would be closed immediately, and only those who

---

*Kowloon is a peninsula opposite Hong Kong island: it is part of the British colony of Hong Kong.
†There is a railroad leading from Kuangchou to Kowloon.
‡"Yin," denoting the realm of ghosts and the afterlife and "Yang," denoting

held passes given by the Ministry of Foreign Affairs would be allowed to cross. This new measure naturally increased the desperation of the refugees and led to the execution of many more who tried to contravene the new regulation.

It was at this time of frantic flight that I came to Hong Kong secretly, for a second time, in order to hear the secret directive from the Republic of China on Taiwan. During the Korean War, the Chinese Communists in Peking had secretly ordered their high-ranking officials and military officers in eastern China to prepare to move their families to the Northwest: they were afraid the Nationalist army from Taiwan might attack eastern China suddenly. General Yu, who was in charge of the North China Area, instructed me from Taiwan: "Return to Shanghai at once. Make quick preparations for attack." And Mr. Li, the Taiwan commander in charge of the South China Area, told me to get control of the railroad lines in Shanghai, Nanking, and Hangchou. When the time came, we would cut off the enemy supply lines so that their retreat westward would not succeed.

We were at that time convinced that General MacArthur fully supported Taiwan's plan to attack the Chinese Communists as soon as the U.N. forces crossed the Yalu River, and that his plan was waiting only for approval from President Truman.

After receiving our orders, our "news reporter" (i.e., our intelligence agent in charge of sending news to Taiwan), Wang Yolung, and I had returned to Shanghai secretly. We planned to establish three intelligence stations: Shanghai (for the eastern China area), Chingtao (for northern China), and Ninghsia (for northwestern China) within the shortest time possible.

But luck was against us! Only twenty days after we left Shanghai our first and second defense lines* were already broken. The "Red

the realm of the living; Luohu Bridge was considered "the place where Yin and Yang met," because it connected the dark Communist world of Canton and the bright free world of Hong Kong.

*The "defense lines" actually refer to those people who helped to defend the intelligence stations. The first defense line was composed of people who had sympathy with the Nationalist Party and were willing to collect intelligence hounds" were snarling and sniffing and chasing us everywhere, threatening to catch us all, dead or alive. During this unfortunate time, two of us were captured at home and another leaped from the third floor of a building and killed himself. Soon, our third defending line was cut off. Those of us who hid behind the line were the object of an intense search, since the Communists wanted to get to our directing center. Fortunately, my secret refuge was not known to many even among our companions. Wang Yolung had "turned himself into a rodent," hiding in my father-in-law's food store in the daytime and going out to "work" only at night.

Though the situation was desperate, I received no new directions for further action. Therefore, on my own I ordered some of my closest comrades to go to Ninghsia (where the Communist control was much tighter than in Shanghai) to conceal themselves in Yinchan with the aid of my mother. I told the others who remained to proceed with our present task in Shanghai, but I thought we should not all be captured in Shanghai.

The time of blood was approaching. I knew we would lose everything if we allowed even one minor mistake. To guarantee success, "Mr. Tseng" (Fung Hsiung-fu, a division leader of Shanghai Station) and I called together some eighty Nationalists and had them swear to remain loyal to our Party and country (the Nationalist Party and the Republic of China) at all times. The vow was made just after dinnertime at my hiding place in my father-in-law's store. Four or more of us at a time pledged ourselves in the presence of a simple national flag, made for the occasion, and a portrait of Dr. Sun Yat-sen, father of our country and founder of our Party. As each of us took the vow, we were moved to tears. We felt that in these dark times, when no Chinese were spared the calamity brought about by the Communists, we had no better occasion to let every drop of our blood be shed to help save the nation. When the handsome Wang Yolung (who, as the last two characters of his Chinese name suggest,

---

for the stations. The second defense line included those who were strongly anti-Communist and had intimate relations with the stations.

was like a young dragon) took his vow, he was as awe-inspiring as a stroke of lightning. To show his bravery and determination, he decided to dispense, from then on, with any special protection we wished to give him.

"Live and all live! Die and all die! We'll share hardships! And we'll struggle together to the end!" These were the words held in all our hearts.

Now the Communist net had been spread and was being drawn tighter and tighter. Like birds and beasts of prey they were searching every corner, ready to seize with claws or paws any unfortunate creature who smelled of flesh.

At about 1:00 P.M. on March 23, 1951, I returned to my dwelling place on Haige Road to have lunch. At my house I pressed the door bell, but it didn't ring. Curious, I went to the back of the house and unlocked the back door. As I entered, two big men grabbed me by the arm and around the waist. Two more hurried to close the door and block the way out. Then nine plainclothes men surrounded me. One of them handcuffed me while another searched me for weapons.

I was soon brought upstairs to the drawing room. "What are you doing?" I asked, coldly.

One of the plainclothes men showed me a warrant but he only let me see it from a distance, fearing perhaps that I might destroy it.

"You are Mr. Han, an enemy agent, aren't you?" he asked in a chilly voice.

"Agent? What kind of agent?" I pretended not to understand his question.

He wasn't going to believe I was innocent. "The secret sort, aren't you?"

"No. I was just looking for somebody." I saw that they were all covering me with guns.

"Looking for somebody? Yes! That's what you agents have been doing." One of them seemed amused by my answer, but another said, "Come on, just tell the truth and we'll let you go. We're Communists. We never lie."

"I'm only a teacher!" I protested.

They would not believe me. A tall man took a photo from his

pocket and showed it to me. "What's this?" he demanded. In the photo, I was wearing a military uniform. In fact, the photo was taken when I was vice dean of the United Military Training Office, at Shanghai High School.

I continued to deny that I was a secret agent. That afternoon, thirteen interrogators and I had a marathon court session. They accused me and I defended myself until nine o'clock that evening. They missed their dinner and I missed both dinner and lunch. The saliva we spit at each other during the session could have filled a soup bowl. When they took me to the toilet, I saw my wife and our nurse imprisoned in a room and guarded by two female plainclothes agents.

A black police car brought Liu, leader of the interrogation division. He was a short man but very animated. He soon made me feel the threat of impending death. He ordered the thirteen cops to train their guns on me and take me to the Shanghai Bureau of Public Security. There I was put in a cell and further interrogated.

Five men prowled in like hungry tigers and pushed me down on the floor. Around my ankles they riveted a pair of heavy shackles, which clanked like a blacksmith's hammer on an anvil. After fettering my feet, they put an old pair of manacles around my wrists, so that all my movements were completely impeded.

I was put on "trial" for four days and four nights. The trial was an exhausting bombardment of questions intended to shatter my personality and "individualism," and to prepare me to accept their collective consciousness and radical socialism. When I made no answer at all to their questions, six or seven of them, who had originally been very civil to me, instantly dropped this mask and became grim and threatening. Their faces seemed to turn from white to green.

"We will not permit stubborn idiots to be stubborn for long, understand?!" hissed an inquisitor, slapping the table violently. But I remained stubborn. Three days later, at about eleven o'clock at night, I was moved to a dank, dark dungeon. There, more than ten inquisitors continued to howl at me.

"Confess! . . . Admit! . . . Tell the truth, and we'll be lenient. Resist and you'll only meet death!" This tactic, of constant yelling and overbearing noise, was commonly used to break a prisoner's will.

It was also of no avail. They then bound my arms with a thick cord and hung me from an overhead beam. "Pull!" one commanded, and I was hauled up in the air, twisting this way and that. Thirty or forty minutes later, my whole body was shaken by fits of agony. I felt dizzy, and started to black out. Then I began to gasp for breath. Finally I felt as if all my bones were going to be dislocated.

"He's passing out," I heard them say. Suddenly they let me drop heavily to the floor. That brought forth a gush of blood from my nose and mouth, which gave me the privilege of sleeping for three days, during which time my arms were in such pain that I couldn't raise them, even for a moment.

I remember that they said something especially agonizing at the fourth night's trial. They said, "Han, you're really cruel. How can you disregard even your mother? We grieve for your father-in-law, too. How unfortunate to have a son-in-law like you! Really, your doings can exterminate your folks. How can you keep talking the way you do? Forever anti-revolutionary and forever stubborn. And who in Taiwan will be the wiser for that? You just choose the path leading to death. Is it really loyalty to choose not to live?"

A fortnight later, I heard the terrible "red voices" again. Only this time the voices sounded especially severe, like a solemn judgment.

"Don't think you're the only one we've arrested. Hear me. All your men are in our hands. Do you want to see Fung Hsiung-fu? Wang Yolung? How about your father-in-law, Lu Jen-chow? And Tseng Ping-hsiung, the man you dispatched to Ninghsia? Don't you see? You have brought disaster to them all, not just to your mother."

"Now," the voices went on, "you are our prisoner. You have to realize that your life no longer belongs to you. If you try to stay tough, you'll taste something even more bitter. So be frank. Accept each trial. This is your only way out. . . . I shall decide your fate according to your reactions. I'll now remind you once more: We shall allow no lying, no arguing, no resistance! . . . If you persist in being our enemy, then you give us the right to end your life our way. Now, do you have anything to say?"

I did not.

Then came time for the last "grand trial." I was brought to a large courtroom with a large desk; sitting behind it was a big middle-aged man with a long face and glittering eyes. He spoke very good Mandarin, but his voice was always edged with malice. He wore a dark gray, brand-new woolen uniform. A man and a woman sat beside him to record the proceedings. Behind him stood five guards. As soon as I entered the room, he politely told me to sit in a chair in front of the desk. He even poured a cup of tea for me and asked me, courteously, "Are you eating and sleeping well?"

From his manner I concluded that he must be a senior leader, a man of high position; so he could be terribly severe in spite of his gentle tone. I soon learned that he was the notorious Ma Nai-sung, head of the Criminal Department of the Shanghai Bureau of Common Security and a leader of the Long March. He had so much power that all lists of people to be arrested in Shanghai had to be approved by him, and in essence he issued all warrants for arrest. It was said that hundreds of thousands of men and women had been shot in the head after he had reviewed their cases, and millions of other victims had been imprisoned or sent to places like icy Chinghai. They had a saying then in Shanghai: "The Communists call the roll with machine guns." He was one of those in charge of the roll calling. After his initial show of politeness, his true nature emerged in a speech he directed at me. In fact, it was hardly a speech, nor a court investigation, but rather a "sermon," if communism could be compared to a religion. He preached for a long time, emphasizing the words "you," "I," and "we" whenever they occurred by drawing them out, giving them a sustained rising pitch, and pronouncing them heavily. I could not help but respect him for his ability to communicate, just through such simple pronouns, the gist of Marx and Engels' theory of class struggle. But what he said, I knew, was meant to be a sort of "ultimatum" for me.

This final judgment did not move me. I was then in the prime of my life. My education had etched in my youthful blood only one word: "Revolt!" So I got angry and rebellious. With a rumbling growl I kicked the desk over, and the tea cups shattered on the floor. My fury brought a storm of accusations, and Ma Nai-sung quickly left.

The faces of the remaining judges turned iron gray and then fire red. They raged like King Kongs, ordering the five guards to drag me against a wall and beat me soundly. As I lay on the floor, their boots kicked at me, then stomped on every part of my body. Before I passed out, my face was streaming with blood and my body was bruised everywhere.

I came to lying on a bed. For twenty days I stayed there, not bothered by any interrogations. I was sure they were about to shoot me. I kept a clean suit of clothes (which I had been allowed to bring with me) at hand, ready to wear it when I was called to meet my fate. One afternoon, the door opened and two officers came in along with two soldiers. They pulled me up by the arms. "Have you had your meal?" one officer asked. I thought it really a fox's kind of mercy to ask me that question when he knew I was on the verge of death. Wrath seized me. "Are you asking me whether or not I've had my sacrificial meal? My children have not yet come to make the offerings. Do you mean to take their place and give me the head-down meal?"*

This fox of an officer stared at me for a moment with wide-open eyes. Then he remarked, "All right. I hope you've vented your anger now. But this is your last time."

"Wait!" I pleaded. "Please unshackle me and let me change clothes. I haven't changed clothes for fifty days. Can't you let me die a clean death wearing a clean suit of clothes?" They agreed. I was unfettered. "Behave yourself—this is a special treat for you," they added. I knew it was special indeed.

A big red van containing ten soldiers backed up to the door. The two standing in front held in their hands ropes as thick as their

---

*A last meal; food offered to the dying. In China, before a criminal is executed, he or she is often allowed to eat a substantial meal (the "sacrificial meal"), which is usually provided by the criminal's closest relatives (children in most cases). Since the meal is offered before the criminal's head is laid low, it is sometimes called the "head-down meal."

fingers. The rest all trained their guns on me. Two soldiers seized me from behind and dragged me through the iron door. One of the two soldiers with the rope put a loop around my neck and pulled it so tight that I had difficulty breathing. The two of them began to bind my arms with two lengths of rope, while another bound more rope around my chest. This was called "grand variety" binding, the most effective at preventing a prisoner from struggling.

Now that I was helpless, three soldiers had no difficulty pulling me into the van, where I saw eight more soldiers, two of them holding pistols ("ten-bullet guns," named for their loading capacity), and the rest carrying rifles. In the van, also, were two other captives condemned to death, and four inquisitors who had questioned me before.

"Put your head down!" two soldiers shouted.

I paid no heed.

The two soldiers came over and one of them pushed down my head. In my anger I gave him a mighty kick, which sent him sprawling on the floor. He jumped up and sprang at me like a wild beast. But again I gave him a surprise kick, and this time he backed some distance away. At the sight of my fierce resistance, the other soldier rounded off the event by saying, "All right, since you are going to be shot anyway, we may as well pardon you."

Half an hour later, we arrived at the execution ground. "Get them down," a soldier on the ground shouted, and he opened the back door of the wagon.

I leaped down, knowing I had come to the execution ground, and turned my back to my executioners. At this, three inquisitors stared into my eyes and grinned like monkeys.

Waiting for us were seven or eight men in military uniforms and four or five in plainclothes. There were also two long tables; at one sat the chief executioner, and at the other a "clerk of court."

The chief executioner was of medium build but tall. I guessed he was originally a peasant. He had a broad face, a large wide chin, a flat nose, and two triangular eyes, which were fixed on me. He had blackish yellow teeth, too, which looked stained from constant smoking, and as though he seldom brushed them.

The other two condemned prisoners were brought to the tables first. The triangular-eyed man asked them their names, ages, birth places, military experience, and "crimes." They answered all these questions.

But when I was questioned, I kept saying "I don't know." That enraged the officer in charge.

"Damn you! You don't know this, and you don't know that. Do you know you are dying? I suppose you don't know that either."

"I don't."

"You damned bastard. Stubborn till death! You're still pretending you don't know anything."

I thought that since I was to see King Yenlo* soon anyway, I might as well have a last bit of fun. I asked the officer, "Do you yourself know when you are going to die?"

This question enraged him even more, and he rushed toward me with his fist raised. But Triangular Eyes stopped him, and my case was put aside for a while.

They then returned to the other two condemned men. At this time the nooses around our necks were loosened so that we could answer questions.

"Wang Kuo-hsi!" Triangular Eyes called loudly.

"Here!" a soldier answered, loudly, indicating the person to be shot.

"Kneel down!" The soldier kicked Wang on the foot and Wang dropped down on his knees as commanded.

"All right, do it!" Triangular Eyes ordered and opened his eyes as wide as the copper bells of children's games.

A uniformed soldier walked two steps forward, raised his gun, put the muzzle against the back of Wang's head, half closed his eyes, and fingered the trigger.

BANG!

In the quiet night, the shot sounded startlingly clear.

Wang dropped instantly, flopping on his belly and stretch-

---

*King Yenlo of the Underworld.

ing out his limbs like a big African turtle. Yet he still twitched convulsively.

The soldier raised his gun again, aimed at Wang's back, and fired a second time. The bang ended the counter-revolutionary's life; more than forty years' struggle finished with a sudden end to his convulsions.

"Li Hsi-yuen!" Triangular Eyes loudly called again.

"Here!" another soldier answered for him.

Li was a young man. He saw his own fate in Wang's, and it made him cry like a child. I was afraid myself, but I pretended to be calm. I even tried to console Li when he burst out in tears.

"Little Li," I said, "don't give yourself up to crying. Let's face it to the end. Be a man! Don't die a big lump of bean curd! Twenty years from now we may be reborn tough men again—"

Before I could finish, an officer got behind me and stuffed my mouth with a handkerchief. Gagged, I could not even protest against the soldier's turning my head.

Then the second execution continued. After Li knelt down, Triangular Eyes again commanded, "Do it!"

BANG!

Li fell with the sound, his skull blown apart. The white liquid substance of his brain spilled out with the blood and made a pattern on the ground not unlike white blossoms on a red carpet of silk. His legs were still kicking, however, as chickens or ducks do when their throats are cut but they are not quite dead. The soldier had to shoot him a second time.

But Wang's and Li's deaths and my impending execution no longer filled me with fear. Instead, I felt only an intense hatred, a hatred increasing every minute toward those I called my enemy. I stared fiercely at the soldiers, grieving that I had no weapon now other than my will.

"Kneel down!" another soldier shouted at me. I ignored him.

"Kneel down!" he commanded again.

I still ignored him.

"You kneel down! Are you deaf?" He took the handkerchief out of my mouth and stood face-to-face with me.

"Pih!" I took the opportunity to spit a mouthful of saliva in his face. "It's you who is deaf!" I shouted back. "Why don't you kneel down yourself? What kind of bastard are you to tell me to bend my knees?"

"Beat him!" he roared. "Go ahead—shoot him!"

He wiped the spit off his face, kicked my leg twice and was ready to rain blows on me. But Triangular Eyes abruptly ordered him to stop.

"It's no use," he said. "He's still stubborn as a mule! We'll use another way to teach him to bend his knees. Beating him and shooting him is just to neglect his education. Come on, men, take him back. We have plenty of time to make him learn, and ways enough to make him kneel."

Hence two soldiers came, dragged me away and pushed me into the red van again.

When the van stopped, I was led to a big house, in which I saw various instruments of torture.

The house was as solemn as the palace of the Judge of Hell. The electric lights were as dim as will-o'-the-wisps, and cast ghost-like shadows. Eight soldiers stood stock-still like dead tree trunks. Two cadres and an officer sat behind three office tables. Their faces resembled those of wax figures.

It suddenly occurred to me that just now when they sent me to the execution ground and threatened to shoot me, they were playing a trick. They had tried to terrify me first by putting to death two other men, and now they meant to torture me. When they had taught me to bend my knees, they would coax or trick me to acknowledge the "crimes" and betray the secrets of my organization and mission.

This sudden realization made me feel very sad for the two put to death just now. Maybe they were not guilty of any "crime" punishable with death at all. They might just have been tools used to terrify me, or to "educate" me, as my captors preferred to call it. That is why the Communists did not bother to give them any "public prosecutions." What a shame it was that they should be executed without being sentenced in a court, and judged without any defense from a lawyer or even from themselves!

"Tell him to sit there!" one leader said to a soldier, and pointed.

They forced me into a big chair, circled my waist with an iron chain, barred my front with an iron plate, locked the chain and the plate, and told me to sit there "securely." I could not even move.

"Now you have your last quarter of an hour. To live or to die, it's entirely up to you. But there's one thing you must understand. We are not patient enough to wait any longer." One cadre said this and then again asked me my name, age, birth place, educational background, profession, position, family condition, and so on, as if he had never heard of me before.

But I still kept silent.

"You goddamned son-of-a-whore, are you deaf and dumb?!" the officer yelled, thumping the table with his palm.

He then pointed to another desk. The female clerk there picked up one object after another from the table, holding up each in turn to show me. I saw three pistols, several boxes of rifle bullets, some commissions, and a few letters from Ma Hung-kei, the Nationalist Governor of Ninghsia Province, and Jen Chung-chie, president of the Ninghsia Provincial Assembly. I also saw a lot of my photos: one taken with Ma and Jen; another with Chien Ta-jun, mayor of Shanghai, Li Chi-lan, commander-in-chief of the Shanghai Security Forces, and other political and military figures; in addition to my personal and family photos there were photos of Yu Yo-jen, and President Chiang Kai-shek. All these things had been packed in a box by my wife and buried somewhere in our garden. I had never thought they could be found and dug up.

"With all this evidence, don't you deserve a death penalty?" the officer asked.

The woman clerk gave me two blank sheets of paper and told me to write my confession. I refused. She consulted with other leaders and then asked some soldiers to remove the rope from my neck but shackle my hands. "Won't you write?" she asked again.

"You write first," I replied. "You were all members of the Eighteenth Corps of the Nationalist army. You had better confess first

and earn your own death sentences." Thus we began the argument;
it was a hard combat of the tongue. That time I was determined to
fight them all to the end.

"To hell with you, you son of a bitch! How dare you talk like
that? Don't you know you're a dead man! We'd kill a thousand, ten
thousand, stinking and hard-skinned bastards like you before we'd
say sorry."

The officer came over and boxed my ears and face repeatedly
and savagely. My nose and my mouth both began to bleed. When he
stopped hitting me and began to curse again, I spat in his face twice.
The spittle was part saliva, part blood.

The officer exploded and cried out, "Beat him! Go on, beat
him—teach the son-of-a-bitch a lesson!"

Soldiers rushed up and rained blows on me. When they tired of
that, they dragged me to a wooden post, pulled my arms behind it
and handcuffed my wrists, forced me to sit on a narrow board, then
bound me tight to the post. They placed my feet on a wooden stool,
laid some long wooden sticks across my knees, and started to play
their game. Four hands rammed my head to the post while two big
men pressed heavily on both ends of the sticks to "squeeze juice" out
of my knees.

"How does it feel? Do you like it? Even if this doesn't kill you,
your legs won't able to carry you far, I'm afraid." Cruel laughter
sounded in the solemn house.

"To tell you the truth, if we wanted to, we could add some
bricks to the sticks and that would guarantee you broken knees. Get
smart, man. Grasp the opportunity—this is your last chance."

I mustered up my strength. "Is this what you Communists call
'good will to captives'? Is this how your 'no beating, no blaming'
treatment works?" I demanded.

"So you still want to be stubborn? All right, let's see whether
you'll bow your head or not, you stubborn lump of dirt."

"What are you going to do to me now? If I'm going to die, tell
me how!"

"Want to know? Good, an eager student. Then listen, student.

This is called 'Tiger Stool.' Some people used to call it 'The Sinews-Plucking Bed.' Now, what else do you want to learn, you dying student?''

Two soldiers used a strap to bind my head to the post so tight I could not shake it. Then other soldiers jammed some wooden bricks one after another beneath my heels. That was meant to press my legs and feet from two opposite directions. As they increased pressure, I heard popping sounds, and it felt like my sinews really were being "plucked." All my muscles began to contract as if afflicted by a wave of cramps. I felt I was shaking myself to pieces; it was worse than ague. Meanwhile, drops of sweat as big as peas began to pop out on my face, my neck, my limbs, every part of my body. I bit my lip with all my strength to endure this "plucking." But I only bit my lip open; I could feel it bleeding. Then I began to gasp for breath and everything went dark before my eyes. In a moment I could not feel anything at all.

When I came to, I found myself lying on a bed with two nurses standing by my side. I saw one of them still holding a syringe and thought they must have given me an injection of some sort, a heart stimulant perhaps. But to regain consciousness was the cruelest torture of all. I shut my eyes, but my legs ached so fiercely they felt like they were being sawed off. I realized I was as wet as if I had been out in the rain, but I hadn't even the strength to move. That was the first time I knew the real horror of my punishment. Triangular Eyes was right in saying that they could "pick me up" very soundly and make me learn.

Two hours later, two husky men came in to me. They did not say a word, just pulled me up by the arms and hauled me up from the bed. They "walked" me out of the door, and they kept "walking" me. That torture was indeed agonizing. I felt as if every cell within me were a bomb exploding. My muscles trembled violently, and every pore in my skin again rained beads of sweat. In this extreme state of pain, I longed to smash my head hard against a post so that I could die and escape. I had been unable to lie on the bed without feeling great pain penetrating my legs and feet—how could they now make me "walk"? If one really can go mad, I was mad then. No Hollywood actor playing my role could adequately express my anguish.

They dragged me on and on, never uttering a word. Sometimes they dragged me quickly, and sometimes they dragged me slowly. They did not know that every breath I breathed was likely to be my last. But, strange to say, after about three hours' walking like that, my blood was circulating better, and I began to breathe more easily. They then walked me at a very slow pace, but the walking continued for the whole night.

The next morning after breakfast, four other men came to walk me again. They divided into two pairs and walked me by turns. After I finished the day's walking and returned to the cell, I felt every part of me was sore, and every bone seemed to have been dislocated, ready to drop off. I lay on the bed, confused about everything. Then I managed to fall into sleep. But before long two men came again and took me out for another walk, which lasted the whole night until daybreak. The third day, I was walked in the same manner. So, for three days and three nights I was trained to be a great "walker," not knowing that the brutal treatment was in effect the Communists' way of showing mercy. For without being "trained" like this, anyone who had undergone the punishment of the Tiger's Stool would be crippled forever.

Still, the "curing penalty" was a bit too brutal for me. After three days, I found I could no longer take off my trousers, for my entire legs, from sole to thigh, were like two big tree trunks swollen and stiff and stuck to my pants.

Every day a nurse came to give me injections. After some days my legs began to return to their normal size.

One afternoon, I was hustled through three iron doors into a big building. There I was asked to leave fingerprints and change my prison number. My original number was 3015. Now they changed it to 30362. I realized, at this point, that a four-digit number was given to a prisoner under investigation, while a five-digit number was given to a criminal whose case was already decided.

Some forty or fifty people were imprisoned in the building.

Some of them were familiar to me while others were not. To my great astonishment, I caught sight of an old couple who stood in a corner among other captives, with tangled hair and dirty faces, cheeks that seemed to be made of yellow wax, protruding cheekbones and sunken eyes. This couple was no other than my father and mother-in-law!

So I was not surprised to find that my wife was imprisoned there, also. She, too, had disheveled hair and a face sharpened by hunger. She sat on the ground holding our eight-month-old baby, looking at two old men, her face reflecting a deep sadness. But I must say I was surprised to find my second elder sister's husband, Liu Chun-ting, there. He had served two terms as a county executive in Hunan Province. He was known as Liu Ching-tien ("Justice Liu") in his county but was reported to have escaped to Hong Kong. His unexpected appearance in the place made me wonder if I would see Fung Hsiung-fu and Wang Yolung and other men under my direction. And I did eventually find them there, too.

At the sight of these relatives and friends, I suddenly felt that my heart was really breaking with anguish. I passed out again, and again I recovered, perhaps with the injection of another dose of some heart stimulant. But in my mind one word echoed all the time: "Ruined! Ruined!"

Not long after, at the end of June, I was transferred to Tilan Bridge Jail.

Shanghai's Tilan Bridge Jail was the biggest jail in Asia. After 1949, when the Communists had taken China, the jail became a monster's den full of skeletons, and a magician's cage for turning human beings into wild animals. Its concrete buildings, as formidable as citadels, were built in the twenties by a construction bureau of the British Concession. Until 1949, its eight prison houses were named Chung, Hsiao, Jen, Ai, Hsin, Yi, Ho, and Ping. (After that year, the eight houses were numbered from 1 to 8 instead.) Each house had five stories, and each story had eighty-eight cells. An entire house could accommodate 2,200 prisoners. So the eight houses together could take in 17,600 prisoners. Later, an all-female prison house capable of holding 7,200 women was added. Still later, another prison house with a capacity of 6,000 was incorporated into the complex. Ultimately, Tilan Bridge Jail became a leviathan able to devour a total of 30,800 criminal minnows, so to speak. Besides the ten main prison houses, the jail complex boasted a hospital, a factory, and a large cooking works.

As you walked down any floor of the prison houses, you saw on both sides of the corridor a long succession of cells, the design of which was much like that of an American chicken farm. Each side of the corridor had forty-four cells, each of which was three meters long and one and a half meters wide. Such a small cell was often crowded with three to six prisoners. To get to the cell, you stepped into an aisle that led to all the other cells that were on the same side. The aisle looked very long, but it was so narrow that it barely allowed two people to pass each other. On the other side of the aisle, there was a horizontal iron pipe more than one meter above the floor. The pipe extended to all the other cells on the same side. Below the pipe were many horizontal iron plates constructed a few inches apart. Behind the iron plates was barbed-wire, through which you could see another iron pipe and many more iron plates. After you crossed all the iron barriers, you came to another aisle. Only after you crossed the second aisle did you at last reach the "cage" for the "birds."

In the center of each prison house, from the top floor to the ground, there was a large circular opening ten meters in diameter. Looking down from the top floor from the edge of the opening, the guards could see clearly what was happening on each level below. Should there be any need, they could speak to everyone from this point. Beyond this was a thick concrete wall over three meters high. Beyond the wall there were eight towers where guards watched the surroundings day and night. Not even a bee, they said, could escape without being seen.

The immensity of the jail can be inferred from the fact that meals were sent to prisoners by a small train. It took eighty criminals to wash the tin boxes used to serve meals at the jail every day. These criminals washed the boxes at a long sink only one meter high, which forced the washers to bend down to work. After two hours' in such a position, almost all the washers were doubled over, not unlike dead lobsters.

A jail often brews the thick and unpleasant atmosphere of a grave or a funeral parlor. The Tilan Bridge Jail was like that but it had also something special, something uniquely its own. Unlike most other jails, the Shanghai jail was very quiet. It was so quiet that you would be terrified by the silence as soon as you entered. Sometimes you might even be led to doubt that your ears were still working. For how could a gargantuan jail jammed with more than thirty thousand prisoners maintain such an unearthly hush? Its perfect silence made one think of the dead stillness at the bottom of the sea. The horror produced by the ruling Communists, I think, was best suggested by the jail's lack of noise. Once you were behind the bars of Tilan Bridge, you would never forget its atmosphere. It made you feel as if you were pickled in a mysterious element, mundane yet unbearable. The taste and the smell of imprisonment kept surging in your senses. There were times when you felt that all the walls had feet and were walking steadily and dismally toward you and that once they reached you they would hug you, pressing on your chest, your back, and your head, hugging you and pressing on you again and again until you thought your bones would break and your flesh would burst.

The overactive imagination was never entirely without material. For one thing, you no sooner entered your cell than you found twelve regulations written on the wall. Instantly, the twelve regulations were like twelve eyes watching over you, and your senses were immediately strained. These twelve rules were:

1. Sit still and behave well.
2. Resistance to repentance will bring ruthless reprisal. Criminal leaders will never be excused, though forced followers may be condoned.
3. Merits will always be rewarded. Great merits may result in release.
4. Stick to the regulations. No discussing them and no acting against them.

5. Obediently observe one another and quickly report anything suspicious to the managers.
6. Discuss no cases and exchange no addresses. Never call one another brothers. Do not attempt to build up affection.
7. Make no noise. Do not shout "Report!"*
8. Never shelter anyone, nor conceal anything.
9. Do not try to cultivate any feelings of unity. Do not send gifts nor share food among yourselves.
10. No tête-à-têtes and no gestures of any sort.
11. Live regularly. Never stay up too late and never rise too early.
12. When meeting visitors, no private conversations and no shaking of hands are allowed.

Such rules are like so many cords or ropes constricting you. But what constricted us even more tightly was the space. A prison cell in Tilan Bridge measured 2.5 meters in length and 1.3 meters in width. When the British ruled here, such a cell held at most three prisoners. But when the new management took over, the same space was often crowded with six men, sometimes seven. It was also occupied by a stool, a stand, and a shelf. The space left for the poor jailbirds, if you can believe it, was so limited that six occupants were invariably forced to sleep all on one side, keeping their legs and bodies straight. They were so tightly packed together that to turn over was always a collective action; no individual could hope to roll over in his sleep without the others' cooperation. Even at midnight, supposedly the quietest hour of all, the terrifying silence of the jail would be broken by sounds of swearing and cursing—because some troubled sleepers were struggling for sleeping space. But the biggest problem was if you woke up and had to relieve yourself: You didn't dare to just get up

---

*In the event of prisoner quarrels, fights, injuries, deaths, or other serious events, the inmates of Tilan Bridge were required to shout "Report!" to summon someone of authority to the scene. Generally, at the jail, a prisoner would have to say "report" before addressing anyone of authority. What the prisoner had to say was required to be of some importance. Hence the rule against careless use of the word.

and go. Once you left your place, it would immediately be occupied by the ones sleeping beside you. And once your sleeping space was occupied by the others, the only way to regain it was to wake everybody up and ask for a total rearrangement of the shared space. In fact, those who could not refrain from getting up during the night often roused their fellow sleepers, causing arguments. The wardens never seriously punished such arguments, although they broke the jail's silence and were obviously against the rules. Actually, the "managers" of the jail were only too happy to have some quarrels among the jailbirds. They thought quarrels prevented the prisoners from uniting and made them eager to spy on each other.

Crammed into such small cells, the inmates naturally had no room to exercise. During the day, we just sat and ate and excreted. We were asked to sit all day long. Worse still, we were told to sit cross-legged with our hands on our knees and our heads bent down in a manner of meditation. This position was held from early morning till nine o'clock in the evening, when whistles were blown to signal bedtime.

One summer, it was said, the weather was very hot. There were bedbugs in the cells. One hungry bug crawled onto a sitter's foot and bit him. The sitter could not bear to be so ill-used by such a tiny creature and slapped at it. Just as the prisoner struck at the insect, a prison guard was going by. He singled out the offender at once.

"What do you mean by doing things like that, you bastard?" the guard shouted.

"The bug was biting me, you know. I had to—"

"You had to revolt?"

"It really hurt."

"You bastard, what an aristocratic thinker you pretend to be! Not yet corrected? We proletariat have been bitten by all sorts of bugs the year round, and we think nothing of it. How can you make such a fuss when these little things are kissing you? Are you still an elitist? Are you still particular about your hygiene? It seems you're as anti-revolutionary as ever. Don't you know your crimes? Write, write down your self-criticism quickly! Otherwise, I'll make you eat those manacles!"

This anecdote illustrates the true nature of the first regulation, "Sit still and behave well." But the poor guy in the story was lucky; the guard was obviously in a good humor. It if had been otherwise, even as a minor offender of Regulation One the prisoner would have had his hands fettered at once. He would have been forced to "keep digging out the roots of his anti-revolutionary ideas" and condemned for "revolting against prison regulations, agitating malcontents for an uprising, and attempting to annihilate communism."

Those who were asked to write down their self-criticism were already in a sort of danger. Later on, their self-criticism might become evidence of their crimes. And in most cases such "evidence" could bring about severer penalties, even capital punishment.

Even if the inmates had not violated any regulations, they were often called individually to the police office and were pressured into disclosing their fellow inmates' "unlawful" words or actions. For the Communists such disclosures were grounds for a "suspect" being shackled, confined in a "rubber cell," or even put to death.

Every day the prisoners had only half an hour to "fang fang," that is, to take a breath outside the cells. Prisoners were given just two meals a day, one in the morning and the other in the afternoon. The morning meal was a small amount of a very thin porridge made from a little rice in a lot of water. Two hours after you ate, or rather drank, that gruel, the gnawing feeling in your stomach would return. The afternoon meal was always boiled rice with a little vegetable, never with any meat. Cooked with neither oil nor salt nor any other seasonings, the meal really had no flavor at all.

Every prisoner was allotted a ration of rice each month. There were three different allotments based on the prisoners' ages and statures. The big allotment was twenty-two jin of rice per month; the medium, twenty jin; and the small, eighteen jin. The rations were barely enough to keep the prisoners from starving. But if a prisoner could survive his first five years in the jail, he would be considered fit to live on. He would then be entitled to such meager amounts of food three times a day, and he would be given more rations and even be allowed to eat enjoyable food (one jin of dry meat and ten apples per month), legally sent to him by his family or friends.

No inmate at Tilan Bridge Jail ever stopped feeling hungry. And each "hungry ghost" there had a sentence of at least ten years' imprisonment. Fortunately, one might say, few really lasted their terms. Many died an early death from all sorts of causes. Many others were sent for "labor corrections." The most usual places for such "great deeds" were North Chiangsu Province, Anhui Province, Kansu, Ninghsia, Chinghai, Hsinkiang, Mongolia, Tibet, and other frontier provinces. Those who went to the provinces, however, had an advantage: their entire families, male and female, young and old, could "emigrate" with them and "work" together with them there.

There was a popular "tongue slipper"* among the Tilan Bridge Dwellers. It went something like this:

Once you enter the gate, two by two you walk to your fate. For three meals you eat but rice, yet four words ["Strictly follow the regulations"] you've got to memorize. Five hours before dawn you'd be called [they called the roll at midnight], to see if in bed are six of you all. Seven times the word "kill" is said every day, while eight iron bars hold you at bay! Nine cases are never properly judged, out of ten that should not be so gingerly smudged. The remaining one, alas, is properly judged so as to send you to the Severer Judge† below to be more gingerly re-judged!

Tilan Bridge had eight factories attached to it with about three thousand prisoner workers. Once, in a carpentry works, a worker named Tsai Ching-chih had a terrible accident. He had been sentenced to death but was on two years' reprieve in the factory. Unfortunately, on a particularly busy day, he was not paying attention to his own safety, and to everybody's horror, the five fingers of his right hand were cut off in an instant by an electric saw. He fainted and was sent to the hospital. Twenty days later, however, he was imprisoned

*Verse-like talk that slips off the tongue, supposedly without much thought.
†King Yenlo of the Underworld.

again, and on the day before Labor Day the next year he was shot dead for "resisting labor corrections by means of cutting off his fingers deliberately."

Almost the same thing happened to another prisoner working in the same factory. Cheng Ping-hsiung, one of my acquaintances, was originally sentenced to life imprisonment but then sent to the works for "labor corrections." There he worked very hard in the Big Tool Section (the above-mentioned Tsai was in the Small Tool Section). He shared his work with a fellow prisoner; their duty was to push timber onto a big electric saw so as to make planks. One day, after several days' hard work without enough rest, he and his co-worker were asked to push an especially large piece of timber. His co-worker, for some reason, suddenly slipped as they pushed the timber onto the saw, instantly cutting off one of his legs and somewhat damaging the saw. Not long after that, the poor cripple was shot for "hindering production."

It cannot be denied that among the Tilan Bridge jailers were some kind-hearted ones, who would have been willing to save the prisoners from abuse had they had the power to do so. Under the strict control of the system, however, discipline was valued well above compassion. No one could act kindly toward others without risking his own safety. Rampant abuse, on the other hand, usually went unnoticed.

July, the month of "flowing fire melting stones and metals," paid its annual visit to Tilan Bridge Jail with culinary intentions. In July, we became the ingredients in the sun's frying pan. During the cooler months we might welcome, in a way, the constant embrace of the prison walls, but not in the hot months, and never in the hottest month. An overcrowded jail can indeed become a kitchen in July. It seemed that we were being made into such dishes as "Red-Roasted Shanghai Man" and "Stewed Man Fresh" to entertain this annual visitor. But for most of us Tilan Bridge Dwellers, the sun's heat was not the most terrible of things in a hot month. The Communists' "fiery deeds" were.

One morning at dawn, a succession of explosions tore us from our sleep. BANG! BANG! BANG! BANG! BANG! Some ten or twenty small explosions went off in succession. I could not believe children were playing with firecrackers at that time of the year. Such sounds were, for us, often associated with the bursting of our blood vessels. So I asked Chen Wei-ta, who was sleeping beside me, "What is it?"

This former boss of Wei Ta Hotel on Hsia Fei Road, Shanghai, replied sadly in a low tone, "At the execution grounds, they're shooting again. . . . These Reds! Sons of bitches! Bad! Too bad!"

Shanghai had been an international metropolis, where someone like Chen could hardly have seen people executed. Those sounds made him especially irritated. I tried to get up, but Chen pulled at me with his hand and said in a soft voice, "Be careful. Someone's coming." The creaking of leather shoes came nearer and nearer. We were all familiar with such sounds and we all took them for a warning. Chen and Chu Cheng-wen, who lay on my other side, instantly started to snore while I closed my eyes, not daring to make any noise.

Wherever the creaks went, there ensued a docility about the Tilan Bridge Dwellers. There were times when I thought thirty thousand men had been miraculously transformed into lambs by the fearful sounds. But if we were docile lambs, what were they? Shepherds? Surely not. They were worse than wolves. We lay still like terrified lambs, not daring to move, not even to stretch hands or legs. Then the metamorphosing sounds gradually passed away and we became ourselves again.

Once my soul came back to me, I would venture to accomplish some feat. This time I chose to see what had happened outside. So I got up stealthily, tiptoed out of an iron door, went to a window, and looked down from it to the little execution ground, which was about a hundred meters away.

What did I see there? A lake of blood, it seemed. Or rather, a red carpet, worn out and torn to pieces. Such a sight seemed ironic at the time when dawn was just about to spread her rosy mantle over us. I counted. Seventeen corpses littered the small ground, among them a female body. The dead, like us living, were wearing only short white underclothes. One could clearly see the white was stained with red. In fact, the black was also tinged with the awful color, as the b llets had pierced the prisoners' heads and made the blood flow over their black hair. The black and white in red; what a colorful world! In that colorful world the dead did seem to be asleep. But their manner of sleep was far from beautiful. While I was still gazing at the scene, someone came and grabbed my hand. It was Chen. He saw the tears on my face. I told him that, soldier though I was, I had never seen so many people shot dead at once.

"I can't blame you," he said. "You've not been here long and haven't got used it. But by and by you'll take everything as a matter of course. Do you know something? Since April twenty-seventh, no week has passed without a collective shooting at the grounds. Each time more than twenty or even thirty died. This is the smallest number executed to date, I guess."

Back at our place, I heard Chu confess his greatest fear to me in a very low tone: "I myself am sentenced to death with two years' reprieve. The day you came, Chen was given the same sentence. We are both waiting for the bullets. And we know they can come any minute!"

Then I learned that the executed had never been tried openly; they had had no lawyers to speak a word for them; they were all secretly judged, secretly sentenced, and secretly executed. Such information matched exactly with my own experience. I was aware that many who had suffered cruel penalties with me had suddenly disappeared at the Station Road or Tilan Bridge without any of their relatives knowing it.

The jail was always as silent as the depths of the sea. There, only the persecutors had freedom of speech. The persecuted had nothing free except Death, the silence-maker. Fear was at every corner, imposed on the prisoners' souls to make silence.

September 30, 1951. At about two o'clock, deep in the night, we were all asleep. Dead silence drowned the whole Tilan Bridge Jail, so that you could have heard a pin drop. Occasionally some patrolling guards broke the dead silence with their footfalls. The rows of lights were but dumb mourners.

"Report!" A shrill cry suddenly broke the dead silence. It also brought with it the feeling of an impending massacre. It was as if a big bomb had fallen on Death's silent graveyard. All at once a rapid chain reaction was set off in our five-story building. One shrill cry begot another until the whole building was reverberating with thundering echoes of the initial sound.

"Report!"

"Report!"

"Report!"

"Report!"

On each floor, on every side, there were at least ten prisoners shrieking that shrill cry. The mad cries seemed to have turned the jail into a battlefield, on which soldiers were dashing, attacking, yelling, and shouting. It was like the sudden eruption of a big volcano accompanied by incessant rumbles. Later it was estimated that, at the time, there were at least five thousand prisoners yelling "Report!"

This sudden occurrence surprised many and dismayed others. Many thought a great disaster was occurring. Many rushed to the iron bars and shook them violently, crying, "Open! Open the door!"

"What is it?"

"What is it?"

"What are they up to?"

All the jail guards were wakened from their sleep, all were in dismay, and all got up and began to gallop to us. Their dwelling was in fact some distance from the prison houses. So none of them knew where the first shout of "Report!" had come from. When they got to the site, they could only revile and curse without any specific target, just as they had often done. But the guards' reaction brought on an even stronger reaction from the inmates, more yelling and shouting, forceful enough to move the mountains to the seas.

"Down with communism!"

"Down with Mao Tse-tung!"

More than thirty thousand jailbirds began to bring up their deep-buried lava. The whole jail became a madhouse. Those who did not know what was happening also became active volcanoes, erupting ashes and flames of hatred. Never before had the jail witnessed such an act of revolution. The thundering sound scared the jailers and made them flee with the guards to open ground. There they fired some warning shots into the air, hoping to threaten the mob into silence again. But that failed. It didn't even help them regain a bit of their lost courage. The Communists' ropes had at last bound the enslaved multitude of Chinese into one people with one soul, a freedom-loving people struggling with a free soul. In the thirty-year history of Tilan Bridge Jail, no night was ever like that night in its frenzy. It seemed that all the insults, persecutions, penalties, abuse, threats, tortures, fears, and despair that had ever made the inmates suffer had been joined into a raging flood. As the crowd roared in anger, every iron bar seemed to roar, too. The crowd spit anger like fire, and every piece of barbed wire seemed to flame. Everybody and everything was as mad as mad can be.

To tell the truth, I was one of the plotters of that scene. But for my own safety, I did not join the outcry until it echoed from every cell of the prison houses. When most of the inmates seemed to be shouting, four of my roommates began to shout with me.

"Down with Mao Tse-tung!"

"Down with communism!"

The "shouting carousel" lasted only about ten minutes. Yet it seemed to the Communists to be ten years long and as devastating as an earthquake.

The shouting stopped abruptly, as planned, and the jail resumed its dead silence. The former vitality seemed to have sunk into the bottom of an abyss. The active volcanoes seemed suddenly to halt their eruptions. The night was so very dark, so deeply silent.

Then all of a sudden, the jail wardens hurled their own retaliatory thunderbolts. They seemed to resent the dead silence too, and wished to continue the "carousel." The loudspeakers in the thirteen big buildings of Tilan Bridge formed a network to broadcast angry curses, vituperation, and outrageous speeches, at which the Reds were especially good when they felt impotent. The loud broadcast seemed to be a cataract, a huge torrent striving to outdo the volcanoes in their thundering.

"You fucking anti-revolutionary devils!"

"Damn their anti-revolutionary attitudes, shoot them, get them all out and shoot them!"

"Don't bluff, you scoundrels. We Communists aren't afraid of any riots. You'll be paid back for this, don't worry!"

"Chiang* is the people's common enemy! You are society's detrimental members! We'll shoot you one by one! None will receive mercy!"

"Look how you're mistaken! Are you expecting a change of regimes? Yes, America is the world's anti-revolutionary policeman. But you're beyond help."

"We have got sufficient information concerning this riot of yours. But you need to confess first, for mercy's sake. We allow no resistance. We will reward every merit. Be frank! Repent!"

To the Communists, such "torrents of abuse" were a necessary means for regaining lost confidence. But they so often lost their confidence that they were all too often adopting that measure. After an hour of "blackguarding," the loudspeakers stopped. After breakfast the next morning, however, every inmate in turn was called to an office for further inquiry.

One of my cellmates had contracted a disease. He frequently sneezed during the day. When the investigation began, he was one of the first to be called to the office.

"Why are you sneezing? And why so loudly? It's a signal or something, isn't it?!"

"I didn't sneeze then."

"The other four said you did."

"You call them here and let them speak face-to-face with me."

The four of us naturally denied having said anything. Nevertheless, the jailers still hoped to use any craft at their disposal to discover the plotters and the leader of the tumult. So their investigation continued day after day, though without any success.

Toward the end of October, the jail had two more tumults. (We called it a "prison tumult," but the Communists preferred to call it a "riot" or "sedition.") The two successive disturbances were con-

---

*Chiang Kai-shek was a conservative Nationalist and militarist, close to the Confucian tradition and supported by an alliance of the old Confucian gentry and the newer merchant middle class.

ducted more or less like the first one. But the third one lasted fifteen minutes and was the longest and most destructive.

When the third tumult occurred, the Communists changed their tactics. They gathered tens of thousands of police officers and soldiers from the city government of Shanghai and had them surround the jail, block all the nearby roadways, and put the region north of Suchow River under martial law. They even stationed police soldiers with machine guns on the walls surrounding the jail. Terror was everywhere, inside and outside the prison houses. Meanwhile, the hounds howled through the loudspeakers again and again. No midnight was ever so tumultuous. The next day a more vigorous investigation began. But still no degree of severity could extract any useful messages from the jailbirds' mouths.

The three "prison tumults" shook the whole city of Shanghai, and shook the Communists' hearts. Yet not even one citizen of Shanghai, it seemed, knew the true facts behind the tumult, not to mention the free world far from the city; news was blockaded. Notwithstanding these extreme measures, no secret in the world can withstand the attack of time. I am now here to reveal the truth.

The most pitiable fact is this: Our secret was also made known to the Communists as time went on. (The Bolsheviks really had the ability to "squeeze water from a stone." That is how they were able to seize all of China.) Our secret organization was called "The April 27 Sufferers' Anti-Communist League." The leader of this organization was Yu Hung. A doctor who had graduated with honors from Tung Te Medical College, Yu Hung first taught at his alma mater but later served as a prison doctor after he was arrested and sentenced for some reason I never learned. He was of medium height and sturdy build. His face was round, and he looked amiable. He had treated my illness several times when I was in Prison House No. 8. From my conversations with him, I sensed his extreme hatred of the Communists. I found out later that he was leading an underground anti-Communist organization.

He had two assistants, both prison doctors, too. Chou Fro-shan was slender and handsome, with thick brows and large eyes. The other was Yuen Jei-san, a short man with a round smooth face that went with his scholarly manner. Chou was a chief physician of Kuang

Tsu Hospital before he was captured. Yuen also had originally served in Kuang Tsu Hospital before he and Chou were sent away to be prison doctors.

Prison House No. 8 was a medical prison house; it took in sick prisoners only and had eight prison doctors. Unlike other prison houses, this one kept at most three prisoners in a cell instead of six; like the other prison houses, it had two nurses who were also prisoners and whose duty it was to give prescription medicine to the prisoner patients.

The jail had another medical building, an eight-story hospital. The prison doctors saw their patients from 9:00 to 11:00 A.M. and from 2:00 to 5:00 P.M. in their consulting rooms. They returned to their cells after lunch every day and stayed there for about an hour before they went to see the afternoon patients. Every afternoon they returned to their cells at half past five. Every morning, starting at seven o'clock, the nurses of each prison house would pass by each cell asking, "Any patients?" Any prospective patients were registered. Then by nine o'clock a "manager" would appear at the patient's cell and take him and the other patients (usually 20 to 30 people at a time), to the hospital. During each morning or afternoon, the doctors treated all the patients; any who were seriously ill would be allowed to stay in the hospital. Those who were not seriously ill but needed further treatment might be sent to Prison House No. 8. Patients who could easily be cured were sent back to their original prison houses.

There were several rows of wooden stools in the hospital's waiting-room. Normally the sick prisoners were accompanied by a "manager" to the waiting-room, where the "managers" became guards against escape or disallowed behavior. The "managers" were often impatient, however. When they got to the waiting-room, they often left the patients there alone while they ran off to talk to the nurses or attend to their own private business. So the sick prisoners often had chances to exchange messages with each other.

"Well, what ails you?" one might ask.

"Consumption," the other might reply.

To say consumption indicated that the person belonged to the same "organization," and so a secret conversation could begin.

"Your name, please?" the first one might ask.

If the other caressed his own hair as an answer, that was a special message for "you know I am your comrade."

If the first man pinched his own nose and made a gesture with his thumb and index finger, that could be another message for "the eighth prison house is the place for getting news." The patients showing the Chinese character of "eight" could always convey messages by their gestures and know what the "organization" would have them do next.

The three prison doctors could exchange messages with their patients while in the consulting rooms, and they were permitted to arrange cells for their patients. Thus, it was comparatively easy for them to organize the "Anti-Communist League" within the jail. In fact, for those prisoners who wanted to join the League, there were always ways. The meal distributors on the Labor Team and the porters on the Conveying Team were ideal errand runners and message carriers for the League. Dr. Chan Wen-hu, who acted as a nurse in Prison House No. 8, helped greatly with the spread of "sensitive" information. Through the special relationship between physician and patient, and the help of some energetic helpers, Yu Hung was able to organize his league successfully without initially being detected by the Communists.

The "tumults" were the result of Yu Hung's plotting with some of the staff of the league (including myself). We were all proud of our achievement in those tumults, especially of uniting thirty thousand people into one. In my opinion, Yu's knowledge of psychology was very good. He was using the "camp-disturbing device"* to cause prison riots when he planned the tumults. I thought that this brave man deserved a place in the anti-Communist history of the world and that his actions ought to be remembered by future historians.

*   *   *

*The "camp-disturbing device" is a surprise attack made on an enemy while they are resting in their camps. It is intended to send the camps into confusion and dismay so that the army's morale may be shaken.

The tragic part is that Fate did not grant Yu Hung success. Some time after the "tumults," we knew we were doomed, and we felt that even the air was quivering with this understanding. On October 9, the day before the National Day of the Republic of China, at about five o'clock in the afternoon, we were preparing for dinner when we suddenly heard the prison police give orders: "Labor convicts, get into your cells quickly!" Then we heard iron doors being closed. Two thousand inmates in the same building at once became very quiet, waiting for something to happen. Chiang Kang-hu, an old man in my cell, sighed a long sigh, and his big body started to shake. He then said in a low tone, with his eyes looking down, "Many will be shot again! . . . My god, what kind of world is this?"

Before he finished his lament, we heard a series of gunshots. BANG! BANG! BANG! BANG! BANG! BANG! BANG! BANG!

The sound shook everything. I felt as if it had gone through my heart. Terror, strain, dismay. For an hour Chiang's words described every prisoner's state of mind. For an hour everybody felt as if a pistol were being placed against the back of his head. I felt that my heart was sinking into darkness.

Then we heard a series of different sounds. Many "labor convicts" were being let out of the iron doors. They were "innocent" for the time being. And they were allowed to continue their labor by distributing meals, sending water, and carrying tin cans.

While everybody else was busy eating dinner, I took the opportunity to go to a window to look down at the small execution ground. Chu Cheng-wen, Chen Wei-ta, Tsai Lo-fu, and Huang Jueiyu saw me and followed after. I hadn't looked for long before it seemed like something heavy had struck my head, leaving me completely dazed. I could not stand any longer, so I sat down on the floor. Meanwhile, I experienced a fit of literally, heartache. It was as if my heart were pierced by several daggers at the same time. I began to feel short of breath, too. I strained to close my eyes, but that did not prevent them from shedding tears.

What scene had such an impact on me? The lake of blood on the execution ground had grown. The corpses littering the ground were more mangled than usual. Broken heads, distorted faces, penetrated chests, red blood, white cerebrum, stained clothes, and stained ground—all so horrible! I really could not believe those bodies and those lives should have come to this. But I knew what had caused this and it made the pain strike home.

"Did you see any relatives or friends among them?" Chu asked sadly.

I wished to answer his question. But my throat could not draw any breath from my lungs. I just answered with tears.

"Spare your sorrow, Brother Han," Chu said chokingly. "On the same ground many good colleagues of mine have been shot . . ." His eyes reddened. He had meant to console me, but now also felt it difficult to utter any words. After a good while, he finally managed to add mournfully, "My sister's husband died there, too. Skull broken. Brains out. Lying on his back. Not a bit like him. This, Old Chiang over there knows. . . . For three days and three nights, I could neither sleep, nor eat . . ." As Chu began to shed tears, too, I recalled that he was formerly a member of the Nationalist Party's Shanghai Commission of Laborers' Affairs.

The penalties continued. The Communists had decided to react strongly to the thirty thousand inmates' riots, but they had to find out all the suspects first. They investigated thoroughly for a good while; then, on April 28 the next year, at about ten o'clock in the morning, the jail's "management" suddenly ordered about one tenth of the inmates from each prison house to gather immediately on an open area of ground, located between Prison Houses No. 3 and No. 4. More than two thousand in all were asked to sit on the ground. From this area one could see the high walls as well as the long iron bars of the two prisons. But what particularly drew one's notice were the fifty police guards surrounding the gathered crowd and fixing their attentive eyes on them.

There was a wooden platform temporarily set up for the occasion. It was about ten meters away from us. On the ends of the platform were two machine guns aimed at the crowd, ready to shoot, we thought, at those who dared to approach the iron palisade that separated us from the platform. Behind and on both sides of the platform were twenty more guards, each well-armed and ready for action.

Liang Tung-fang, a tall man with one arm who was vice-director of the Labor Correction Bureau, began to announce four rules for the "meeting" in a voice as harsh as a broken gong. (His harshness could be connected with the loss of his arm when he was bombing a Shanghai depot during a riot.)

"First, no shouting of any slogans and no raising of any hands!

"Second, no whispering and no gestures of any kind!

"Third, no standing up or squatting without permission!

"Fourth, no turning heads from side to side and no eye-and-brow signals of any sort!

"Those who act against the four commandments will immediately be shot dead!"

With this proclamation, the "meeting" began. At that time, a Mr. Chen, a department chair of the Shanghai People's High Court, stood up on the platform. Another cadre came forth, an important Communist commissioned to preside over the "meeting." He put a briefcase on a table, pulled out some papers, and handed them to Chen. Chen, a fat pig looking like a butcher, then began his own announcements.

"Yu Hung, prison physician of House Number Eight!"

"Here!" answered the soldier who was escorting Yu.

Then the chairman loudly proclaimed Yu's crime: "Organizing in the houses an illegal group called the April Twenty-seventh Sufferers' Anti-Communist League. Sponsoring three riots within the houses. Repeatedly instigating malcontents to sedition." And then he gave a sentence: "Originally sentenced to fifteen years' imprisonment. Now re-sentenced to a death penalty. To be executed immediately."

After the sentence had been proclaimed, footfalls were soon heard from behind the platform. I could not see clearly what was happening there. But I guessed some soldiers were taking Yu away to put him on a red wagon waiting somewhere. Then abruptly some words were shouted.

"Down with communism!"

"Down with Mao Tse-tung!"

I had not expected that Yu would continue to rebel that way. The dignity underlying his shouting was perhaps beyond the grasp of people in the Free World. But the dignity expressed in that way under those circumstances was touching to us. I believe many of us felt the pain of one bayonet after another being thrust into our breasts when we heard him shouting those words. His bravery and consistent rebellion against the Communists made him comparable to the ancient martyrs who adhered to their principles and sacrificed their lives. I think his dignity represents all mankind's dignity in confronting evil, and is thus able to move all deities in heaven or on earth.

We believe Yu had intended to shout more words, but he was soon gagged and taken away. That was why we heard only some more unclear burrs and whirs from him. Yet, those sounds were strong protest, too, against the horror-makers.

Thereafter, not even a burr or whir was to be heard, for the Communists had learned to gag all those who were to be resentenced. As to those of us who were assembled only to listen to the resentencing proclamations, who dared to invite death by uttering a sound?

I myself was only a suffering coward, so to speak. Knowing that our beloved Yu was going to be shot, I could only let my heart break in pain and let my eyes lose their sight in darkness. Even today I cannot forgive myself for not taking any heroic action in the wake of Yu's brave shoutings.

We were all silent, breathless and motionless. But our inactivity was also a sort of protest, which might become an activity in time. This the Communists knew only too well. Therefore, sensing our emotional instability, a "leader" leapt up and checked any straying thoughts.

"Bow your heads! Don't move! One move, and you die!"

Then some of the leaders whispered among themselves for some minutes, before the "meeting" was carried on. When the resentencing was resumed, the Chairman no longer harangued about the victims' "crimes." He only made brief announcements of the new sentences.

"Prison physician Chou Fro-shan. Originally eight years' imprisonment. Now imprisonment for life."

We understood they meant to finish it hastily.

"Prison physician Yuen Jei-san. Originally five years. Now twenty years."

Following this were six names: Chang Kuo-liang, Chou Chimin, Kuan Hsin-liang, Chang Ming, Chu Chih, Chu Chih-hsin. These six were originally sentenced to death on reprieve. Now they were to be executed immediately. In addition to the six, there were six others whose cases were changed from life imprisonment to the death penalty, and nineteen others who would die, too, instead of spending fifteen to twenty years in jail. Fifty-eight men were spared their lives, but their terms of imprisonment were all greatly lengthened: a term of five or eight years often became life, and a term of ten years became death penalty on reprieve. Altogether thirty-four deaths plus fifty-eight longer imprisonments resulted from the "tumults" following that fateful September 30.

Such a heavy consequence naturally made us very anxious to know who was the Judas who had betrayed our Yu. Later it became clear that the renegade was no other than Shao Fa-ming, a graduate of Ta Tung Medical College serving as a group leader of the prison doctors. I remember he was then about thirty, with a big mustache. He ratted on the league and therefore was considered a hero on the Communist side. Later, he was set free before time for his "merit." I thought his soles and heels must have been stained with blood when he stepped out of the gate of Tilan Bridge.

Not long afterwards, Chu Cheng-wen was shot dead too. In the fall, under the direction of the Shanghai Commission of Military Control, I was re-sentenced to life imprisonment. All my property, including my house, was confiscated. My wife, Lu Su-chen, with our eight-month-old baby, was sentenced to a two-year jail term. Later, the Communists forced my wife to divorce me and move with the baby to her native town in Shantung Province, to become a peasant attending "labor corrections."

My father-in-law, Lu Chen-chou, was sentenced to fifteen years' imprisonment. As he was over sixty and could not bear any long-term torture, he died at a labor-correction farm in Pinhai County, Chiangsu Province. His food store and estate were also confiscated. My mother-in-law received a two-year sentence and died in jail before the term ended. My brother-in-law, Lu Yun-hai, was sentenced to two years, but thirty years later he was still a "controlled member." He had been working at a power plant in Teng County, Lingsha Province, as a cleaner of toilets. I did not know at that time what had happened to my mother. But some years later, my second elder sister told me that our mother was beaten to death in Yin Tsuan, Ningshia Province, during a "public prosecution." My sister also told me that our eldest brother was given a sentence of fifteen years' imprisonment and sent to Hunan Province for "labor corrections," and that she herself was also beaten savagely in a "public prosecution." Such things amount to the total ruination of a family.

Why did I deserve all this? In the verdict for my sentence, the Communists accused me of "refusing to be frank, bearing grudges without repentance, and choosing to be stubborn to the last." In the Communist world, no one with such crimes could hope to live even if he had three skulls to be broken. Yet they let me live.

When I analyze the matter now, I can find four reasons. First, because I would not "frankly" tell them everything related to me, they decided that I must be keeping many important secrets. So they delayed my sentence in the hope that I might eventually confess.

Second, the high tide of the Chinese Communists' suppression of the anti-revolutionaries was 1951, especially in the spring and summer of that year. Any case that could make it through that year would be tried with more leniency. My case was delayed until 1952, which helped save my life.

Third, there might have been some Communists who wished to make use of my kept secrets to earn merits, and they were still waiting for me to reveal some of these secrets to them.

Fourth, believe it or not, I think it was due to my ancestors' good conduct in the past. My great-grandfather was a governor in the Ching Dynasty as was my father in the time of the Republic of China. They were both honest, upright, and kind to their people. I think their goodness prompted Heaven to spare my life so that I would have this opportunity to disclose the evils of my oppressors.

* * *

Prison House No. 7 of Tilan Bridge Jail was a special prison for those convicts considered particularly dangerous. Before I was sentenced I had been in House No. 1. I had once pretended to commit suicide there, though, so I was considered dangerous and moved to No. 7. There I thought I would suffer more severely. But some ten days after I came to No. 7 (toward the end of August that year), we heard, quite unexpectedly, a loud and clear broadcast from the building's loudspeakers.

"Listen, men. You are soon to go to a new environment. There, everything is better. There, you can have meat for meals, and you can eat your fill. There, you will all get fat because you will be well fed. There, you will have fresher air and can have enough exercise. In a word, you had better go there rather than stay here for good."

The words were obviously from a "leader," who purposely softened his usually rough tones. The broadcast was repeated twice, and the next day a female voice repeated the same message. The third day it was a man's voice again. For three days the broadcast penetrated our ears like bullets, although it had been so toned down as to make it sound like music or even like a nightingale's song.

We knew we were about to be sent somewhere for "labor correction," but we did not know where. Finally, the day came when each of us was given a suit of thick black cotton clothes along with a cotton cap. They also promised to give us each a leather suit later. These signs showed that we were to be sent to the Northwest or the Northeast.

The next day we started. After a long year's life enclosed in concrete, iron bars, and barbed wires, we were on our way to a "freer place." But for the trip we were put in a tighter enclosure, this time of iron—a train. We started from the Jen-zu Station at Shanghai, buried within layers of iron—the train was like a big coffin for us. The compartments of the train could hardly be called "cars." They were actually "tie mentz che."* Usually these were used to convey horses, cattle, hogs, and sheep. The Communists obviously regarded us as

---

*Literally, "iron pen-you-up vehicles."

animals. What was worse, the compartments had not been cleaned for us. When we crowded into them, we found all sorts of dung. We had to remove it with old clothes or any paper we happened to have before we could place our straw mats on the floor. The air was still very unpleasant.

The first day on the train, we were each given a loaf of black bread, which we found too dry to chew. We had little water to drink and were often very thirsty. At midnight we stopped at a station where we found well-armed guards standing on the platform. We were told to carry our common commodes out of the train, clean them, and carry them back with two big barrels of water for each compartment. After a long day's thirst, we all drank the water and filled our canteens with it as happily as one who sees rain after a long drought. But by the next day we suffered from thirst again, as each of us had to make do with only one mouthful of water for the day.

There were four small windows on the ceiling of each compartment. The windows were blocked with fine iron bars to prevent escape, so the circulation of air was hindered. Day and night, watching from our crowded compartment through the four small squares of barred windows, we saw only three kinds of skies: bright sky, cloudy sky, and dark sky. As to the passing landscape, we could see nothing except when the train stopped and the iron doors were opened for a moment. We were often allowed to stay on the platform for a while if the train stopped at night, though there was nothing to see but a few lights glowing in the dark. Soon we were sent to the train again and buried in the iron coffins, which offered no egress.

Each cattle car was about ten pings and held about seventy or eighty of us packed as tightly as sardines. Day and night, whether we were sitting, standing or lying, we could never straighten our legs and were always in close contact with one another. Flesh stuck to flesh. In such an overcrowded space, the air was always dirty, and we never had enough oxygen. What came into our mouths and noses was mostly carbon dioxide. Ammonia emanated from the commodes and our sweating bodies twenty-four hours a day. There were times, indeed, when we felt we could no longer breathe.

Some of us began to get sick. Fever, headache, dizziness, diarrhea, and stomachache were the most common symptoms. Those who started vomiting were left vomiting until they dirtied themselves, their nearby fellow sufferers, and the already filthy compartment. Those who suffered from diarrhea had to crawl or run over the others' bodies and rush to the commodes. If they were too slow, they just ended up emptying their bowels into their shorts or pants and polluting our small living area. As for those with fever, we could not help them in any way; there wasn't space enough for them to lie down for a good rest.

The train ran ten days and ten nights from Jen-zu to Hekou in Kansu Province. We took turns reclining, sitting, and standing. In any position, we jostled, squeezed, and stuck to each other. When we stood or sat, we were like so many candles on a candelabra. Only we did not burn with light. We just consumed our energy and got sore legs, which gradually grew worse until we lay down and had them massaged for a while.

I believe horses, cattle, hogs, and sheep were better treated on the train than we were. For they were treasures alive. And they were more used to being penned up and conveyed by such vehicles. When we arrived at Hekou, more than half of us packed in the iron cans had fallen ill. Fortunately, however, the sick were all sent off to a hospital there. The ten days' journey was for us only a prelude to our new nightmarish life. I had a presentiment that even though I had been lucky enough to escape the diseases, I would not be so lucky with the nightmares to come.

We gradually became aware of where we were: the Tarim Basin, or more precisely, the Telingha Labor Corrections Farm which was located in the basin's notorious Gobi Desert. The farm belonged to the Labor Corrections Bureau of Chinghai Province. When we arrived there, the farm was still a no-man's-land, nothing but a large expanse of sandy desert. No road led to it. It was just waiting for us to turn it into something, and everything that came there later, every stone, every piece of timber, would be the result of our hands, which never stopped picking, cutting, lifting, and carrying.

Pu Ning

We realized eventually that this region of Chinghai Province was a secretly blockaded area of Red China. No outsiders were ever allowed to enter this zone. Relatives could not visit their families there, even if they had come from overseas. Usually the Communists would send the family to Lanchow for the visit. As far as the outside world was concerned, here was a place truly behind "the bamboo curtain."

Some years later I learned that our place was not the most secretly blockaded area. Somewhere in the Pamirs, in the most western part of Hsinchiang Province, was a region even more forbidden. No one in China, except perhaps some "leaders" of the Communist regime and a few secret agents in the Department of Common Security knew where the place was. In order to reach it, you had to take a train to a small town called Huching, get on a bus, travel two days, and walk another day or so. It was known as the "unwalled jail." Regular workers there enjoyed double wages but had to stay three years at a time before others could replace them. All daily necessities—food, clothing, even tissue paper and soap—were imported from the outside by air. On this "Roof of the World," all "labor redresses" could not but feel they had reached their "Eternal Home."

When we got off the train at Hekou in Kansu Province, we found more than a hundred trucks already waiting for us. They took us to Hsining in Chinghai Province in the Nantan Labor Corrections Area. The trucks drove one after another in a line, looking from afar like a long serpent. Again we suffered from overcrowding. Each day we saw ourselves as groups of kung-fu practitioners devoted to the training of Marx-Lenin-Stalin-and-Maoism. But the strenuous exercise on the trucks never improved our health. It only made us sick.

The area finally reached was originally a burying ground. When it became a labor corrections camp, untold numbers of graves were dug up and removed, without any agreement from descendants. South was a series of high mountain ranges, and to the north were the winding headwaters of the Yellow River. The area covered an open plain of about ten thousand pings—an ideal place for labor. In addition to the forbidding mountains and rivers, there were also circles of guards surrounding us. Escape was beyond everybody's hope. More than ten processing factories had been built to accommodate the tens of thousands of laborer-prisoners, but no "criminal worker" was ever paid, except with threats, punishments, and death. What a profitable business the Communists had there!

It was not until now that I began to realize the true meaning of the Communists' "leniency," a word they had used constantly in 1949, when they had just taken over the Chinese mainland. Later, the word was used only in some limited areas of the coastal and central provinces. It was less present in the big cities because the urban intellectuals were harder to deceive, and less isolated from the outside world. In the frontier areas and the countryside, leniency meant, ironically, merciless arrest and imprisonment. Hundreds of thousands of Chinese living outside of the cities were arrested and sent to the Northwest for "labor corrections" as a result of this leniency.

Eighty percent of us were long-term prisoners. For the first eight or nine days after our arrival, we had no place to live. So, in imitation of the area's indigenous people, we built ourselves a "yurt," a tent with a conic top and a central supporting post, covered on all sides by a single layer of canvas. It was a strong structure, and it served as good temporary shelter from the elements. During these initial days, we were led by previous convicts to where we were to build roads.

While we followed them, we could not help but think how cruel it was for the tortured to be forced to teach others to be tortured. They showed us how to dig the soil with a shovel, how to loosen the ground with a pickax, how to crack rocks with a hammer, how to use a drill, and how to shoulder a pole with loaded baskets. In fact, they were showing us how to repeat their tortured lives. I looked at their faces. They were all lean and dry. Many had been unshaven for a long time. Their hair was too long and looked as unkempt as loose bits of straw. They were a bit frightening, at first sight. Some resembled old stumps of trees, branchless and leafless. But the most miserable sight was their eyes, hollows holding waterless orbs. We could see our future in our predecessors. But our most immediate concern was hunger.

Our meals were only steamed bread and some vegetable leaves

in boiled water, no oil and no meat of any sort. Worse still, everybody was allowed only one jin of food per day. The poor quality and small quantity reduced us each, in less than a week, to real weaklings, dizzy and feeble all the time. In despair, two fellows tried to escape but failed. They were captured and shot dead. Another was imprisoned in a special cell. There he became even more desperate and in a fit of frenzy hit his head against the wall and died. Another took his life with a loop of rope.

No matter how hungry we the living were, we always had to finish our task. And our present task was to start working on a road leading from Chinghai directly to Tibet. First we had to go to Huang Yuen, about 200 li from Nantan.* We were ordered to carry our own baggage, walk the whole distance, and arrive within two days. Even if you had been trained for a long march, you still could not possibly cover 100 li in a day. None of us had ever been trained for a long-distance walk, and we were hungry and dizzy. Still, we had to walk. We carried our baggage, ate two meals a day, and walked. We walked while munching cold hard bread. We walked with little water to drink. We walked thinking of the next black loaf made from wheat chaff mixed with flour and carrots. And, of course, we thought of death.

As we stumbled along in what resembled a column, the well-fed soldiers and "leaders" guarded us by our sides, two by two at intervals of twenty to fifty meters. They were better walkers. They scolded us, kicked us, struck us with rifle butts, and whipped us when we slowed down. As a result, some prisoners fainted away on the road, and others lay down exhausted by the roadside, caring nothing. Almost all of us developed blisters; some of us had bleeding feet. The sighs and groans formed a dirge for our pathetic march.

The Communists reviled and cursed us instead of pitying us. "Exploiting class! Parasites! You can't even walk this far? You damned good-for-nothings!" Before we had enough rest, the "leaders" ordered the young ones to lift the older ones and resume walking. We did, but some fellows still simply refused to get up, despite

*One li is about a third of a mile.

the guards' kicks and whips. Those "stubborn ones" were left behind as we moved on, but before we had traveled far, there were shots, and we knew what must have happened.

A man named Ling Hsien-yang was one of my group. He had been a university president and was used to traveling only by car. He had never walked farther than five miles, nor ever carried a burden of more than five pounds during such a walk. It was indeed hard for him to walk such a long distance, with baggage that weighed more than ten jin. I saw him often lagging behind during the long walk, and therefore being whipped by the guards. When he fell down on the road, I knew I had to help him or he'd be doomed. I carried baggage as heavy as his, but I was much stronger than he. I rushed over and offered to carry his baggage along with mine. I also called over two strong men—Chu Dan, formerly a lieutenant general, and another to aid him. We held his arms and half pulled him along with the rest of us. There were people like Ling among us, most of them scholars and professors. The first day we managed to cover only about 90 li (30 miles), somewhat short of our goal. But we were already exhausted. The next day we walked much more slowly, so it took us a third day to complete the journey that had been "planned" for two days.

It was not a walk, nor a march, but a torture. As we moved on, our legs became heavier and heavier. The ground was sandy, but it felt as if we were trudging through a marsh. When we arrived at Huang Yuen, our destination, we didn't feel relieved. Instead, we kept thinking of our past sufferings. We remembered the three men who were shot the second night just because they had no more strength to move on. We imagined we were still being driven on like cattle and that finally the whole herd's blood was shed by night. There were times, of course, when we marveled at ourselves for having been able to survive the journey. They said Huang Yuen would become the juncture city of the Ching-Hsin and Ching-Tsang (Chinghai-Hsin-chiang and Chinghai-Tibet) highway systems. They also said the city would become the common market for Han Chinese, Mongols, Uighurs, and Tibetans. I knew nothing of the city's future. I only knew of its present state. It was at that time a "slough of despond," a cursed land, and a display of Communist vanity.

The day after we arrived at Huang Yuen, the Communists held

Scarlet Predators

In 1952, not far from the borders of the Tsaidamu Basin, a blizzard had been raging for two days and two nights. The outside world was blockaded by its rage. It was only October, not yet deep autumn. Nevertheless, this was the longest blizzard I had ever experienced. Now I knew what I heard was true—in the Tsaidamu Basin it can snow up to June, and the whole year has only a hundred days or so without frost. Nor were these downy flakes dancing in the wind. Hardly snow flakes at all, but shafts of ice, each shaft thrown at you, trying to pierce your clothes and skin. We felt as if we were naked there, fallen into a sea of icy needles.

I was wielding a pickax, tightly, trying to crack the ice. I had repeatedly lifted it and brought it violently down on the ice for almost an hour, but was still making no progress. I found, instead, that I had hurt the inside of my hand, and my palm was full of blisters that dripped blood and water. The pain kept me from sleeping that night. A pity I hadn't learned not to hold the pickax too tightly when using it.

What was happening to my fellow men? They were looking so odd and queer that they might easily be taken for figures coming from the List of Apotheosis.* Hoo, hoo, hoo! Everybody was whooping out spurts of steamy breath, which whitened even their brows. Tears and mucus constantly trickled down faces that would soon look like red

---

*A famous Chinese story of superhuman achievements, in which many mortals are apotheosized.

walls hung with small icicles if the tears and mucus were not wiped off in time, before turning as blue as Yang Chih, the "Blue-faced Beast" from the Legends of the Water Margin.

All of us were freezing. Our hands were so stiffened that we were not able to hold the pickaxes or shovels any longer. The legs of the older ones were so stiff that they could no longer stand on their feet. Some forty of them fell down pitiably like scarecrows swept down by a strong wind. Among them were Ling Hsien-yang, president of Shanghai University; Chan Wen-hu, vice-president and editor in chief of *Shanghai News Report;* Chen Meng-yu, president of Liangkiang Junior College of Physical Education; Teng Chung-ho, a Shanghai banking tycoon and president of the board of Hui Chung Hotel, and other big enterprises. These men, along with other officials, celebrities, and professors of former times, were now sentenced to "reform by labor" for fifteen years, or for life.

Guards were rushing here and there, cursing and chiding us with white leather lashes. They plied the meter-long weapons against the raw flesh of those who had passed out and dared to "lie down and rest." Some guards even drew out thick sticks and used them indiscriminately on the prisoners' heads. Blood dripped down to redden the white snow. This treatment, however, did not make the fallen ones rise to their feet. I saw them lying still on the ice, not uttering a cry under the sting of the lash. Their nerves, central and peripheral, felt nothing. They seemed purposely to refuse to revive, after they had been so "unnerved." The younger ones' teeth chattered with the cold and their bodies shuddered with fear. Some simply could not help groaning or even crying out loud. Seeing all this, the guards knew that they had done enough for that day. Feeling the chill themselves, and tired of their labor with the whips, they blew a whistle to call it a day. Each fallen older prisoner was held up by two young ones and dragged back to the camp. In the tent each was covered with a thick cotton quilt to warm his blood and prevent him from being crippled by numbness.

These events had continued for a month now. I was at that time comparatively young, just over thirty. I considered myself very strong, too, as I had a big body. I often boasted that I was vigorous enough to work two or three nights in a row without sleep. In reality, however, every night when I came back from my toil, I felt like someone just getting over a long illness. I couldn't even walk steadily. Sometimes I doubted that I had legs. Pain pervaded my whole body and built to a peak in the soles of my feet. My hands hurt so much that I could not hold a basin of water, nor did I have the strength to make my bed. My bruised fingers had shed so much blood that my cotton gloves were pasted to my skin and could be removed only when I had warmed my hands after the evening meal. When I lay down to rest, the pain coverged in my head and face. It was then that I began to realize the effects of bursting ice under my pickax—it had cut my face and had swollen parts of my head.

In those days, the universe seemed to be nothing but snow. In my mind or in my memory, the ice was forever there. I kept picturing the next snowy scene and dreaming of the icy ground ahead. It seemed every place was an expanse of whiteness, a whiteness so ghastly and horrific that one imagined heaven and earth were a featureless blank immersed in it.

Occasionally it did stop snowing for a while. Only then was my mind brought back to reality, to the four small flags of red cloth, each hung on a two-and-a-half-meter bamboo pole emerging from one corner of the snow-covered ground. The four flags marked off a rectangular enclosure about 100 meters long and 14 or 15 meters wide. As they fluttered in the wind, their redness in the great expanse of white was grisly, like the red on the face of an angry monster with its jaws wide open ready to bite you in two.

On two sides of the enclosure, some 30 meters from the central area, fourteen guards stood deployed. They moved here and there, fixing wolfish eyes on us. Their leader was an obese devil with a pistol at his side; his eyes were the fiercest of all. Of the other guards, four had machine guns, and the rest, a variety of rifles.

Seven inches, and then another seven inches. We found we could move only seven inches forward at each step with the guns aimed at us, and each step took us at least twelve minutes. This pace, we believed, was the slowest of all human paces.

We were working with pickaxes. Each of them had a wooden

handle of about two and a half feet and an iron head nineteen and a half inches wide. Every time we lifted the tool up and smashed it down on the ice, we had to exert almost all of our strength. When it struck the ice, the collision was so violent that it hurt our hands. Yet, each violent collision only created a small concavity about one centimeter deep. The more visible results of our hewing were the bursts of "popcorn ice" which flew up to cut our faces.

After a whole day and a whole night's blizzard at a temperature continuously under five degrees, the ground was covered with a frozen plate as hard as iron. We found we had to hack with our axes at least ten times to penetrate an ice plate ten centimeters thick, and twenty or thirty times to dig a hole through the ice plate big enough for a person's foot to fit into. Toiling like this, we were like ants gnawing on bones.

Our toil did not end with digging holes. After we dug through the ice plate, we had to crack and remove it. Then we had to fetch broken pieces of rock and mix them with clay and sand. We dumped the mixture into the holes we had gouged out of the ice. Finally we had to fetch water, sprinkle it on the mixture and tamp down the surface. For we were paving a road! And it is no exaggeration to say that during the entire process—digging the hole, cracking the ice, fetching the stones and water, sprinkling and pressing—we took more than twelve minutes to move forward seven inches.

Each morning at six, we were roused by shrill whistles. We climbed out of our beds and got ready immediately. In the past two months we had forgotten what it was like to wash our faces. We finished our small bowls of soup with bread as fast as we could. Then our team, more than four hundred people, wormed its way to the Chinghai Plateau amidst a bleak world of white skeletons. Countless people had perished there, their bodies reduced to bones. At break of day, we were fully exposed to the intense light reflected from the ice and snow. All of us wore black caps, black jackets, and black trousers. On the sleeves and the backs of our jackets, as well as on the legs of our trousers, however, were painted two white words: LAO KAI, or "Labor Correction." The two white characters were set against our black clothing, which was in turn set against the white outside world.

Any stranger, not familiar with our status might easily be frightened at the sight of so many ghostlike figures appearing in the broad daylight.

We were divided into twenty gangs, each group guarded by fourteen armed men. We labored for six hours at a stretch after we arrived at the work site. For lunch we were each given two rolls of bread, a bit of pickle, and some water. We had twenty minutes to eat our lunch. Every night at eight o'clock the whistles blew at last to signal the end of the day. We estimated that we were forced to endure an average of fourteen hours every day, and in weather always 60° to 70°F below freezing.

I cannot tell exactly how many times I must have wielded my pickax during those months. But at least a thousand times a day, I guess. That makes more than thirty thousand times a month.

A consolation for me was the fact that I was not the only ax-wielding machine on the Chinghai Plateau, over two thousand meters above sea level. Twenty thousand other people shared my fate. We were fighting the storm and ice to build a road from Huang Yuen (a place near Hsining, the capital of Tsinghai Province) to Lhasa (the capital of Tibet). I belonged to one of the first two big "pioneer teams," which had four thousand men divided into ten smaller teams; we were the first to come and feel the difficulty of "reform through labor" there. You can imagine what a sight it was to have such a great host of laborers all being "reformed" at the same time on the bleak plateau. Reportedly, four hundred thousand unfortunates had been delivered to Chinghai for "labor reform" in twenty years, though most of the late-comers were not assigned the task of building roads.

We had no holidays, no vacations, no free days of any sort. When all Chinese were enjoying feasts on the Lunar New Year's Eve,* we were wielding our pickaxes, shouldering baskets of sand and stone, pulling carts, and battling against hunger and ice to reach the

---

*It is a Chinese custom that all family members gather together for a feast on the eve of the Lunar New Year.

goal, which our keepers called "Man-tang hung."* On New Year's Day, when Chinese elsewhere were entertaining themselves with traditional festivities, we were doing what we did every day, exerting ourselves to complete our fourteen-hour labor. This particular work day they labeled "Kai-men hung," which means "open-door red." As the New Year signifies "the opening of a new door," this means to start the New Year off right, or "red." To the Chinese Communists, this expression came to be associated primarily with what was "good" in their eyes—starting the year with a new, more intensified labor effort. We really could not figure out the import of all those reds. We only knew we had lost our years, our months, and our days. In fact the "red deeds" had deprived us of our sense of time, and our sense of space as well.

There were times we felt our bodies did not belong to us. The extreme cold and the threat of the keepers' guns, clubs, and whips, which backed up their curses, contributed to nothing but our loss of physical feeling. We knew flesh and blood were there, however, we felt it was not our own flesh and blood, but the flesh of strange animals which could feel no pain because they had neither soul nor consciousness. It seemed that these animals were merely engaged in strenuous exercise to speed the flow of their blood and warm their bodies. It was only after we had suspended our labor at night that we began to identify these animals with ourselves and have feelings, allowing the realization that every part of our bodies was dissolving in pain.

Then the time came when we felt like old trees shedding their

---

*"Man-tang," meaning "full inside," and "hung," meaning "red," the color traditionally used in China to denote happiness, luck, and plenty; the term was originally used to signify a "full house" at the Chinese Opera and, in later years, at a movie theater. The expression is also used to describe the reunion of a family under one roof, another "full house," certainly worthy of the happy color "red." In Communist China, however, the same expression took on a more utilitarian meaning. The "full house" became "a maximum amount of incessant laboring," and the "red" denoted plenty, this time in terms of production.

leaves in autumn. When pain gradually surrendered to fatigue and our "leaves" had all fallen, we knew we had only a trunk left, a sleeping trunk waiting to die a final death.

Each of us was allotted a ration of twenty-six jin* of flour per month. But part of this ration was kept by the superintendents, and the rest was often stolen by the kitchen workers. So what we put into our mouths was in fact less than three fourths of the allotment. Such a little quantity of flour, with no additional meat or oil, naturally did not provide us with enough calories to resist the cold, especially when we were short of clothing, too. Faced with such a reality I gradually developed a peculiar sense of life. I began to feel that all the novels I had read were not really fictitious; they were only blank pages detached from real life.

Could you believe it? One of us was holding up his pickax, intending to bring it down on the ice. But as it fell, he fell with it, never to rise again. The motor in this human machine had stopped suddenly and forever. Could you believe it? One of us was gasping for breath while trying to raise a basket of stone. But before he lifted it all the way up, the basket fell to the snow and he with it, never to get up. Could you believe it? We had finished the day's work and were carrying our tools back to our camp when all of a sudden, one of us dropped. Soon it was apparent that he had not stumbled, but had gone to join the ranks of our dead. Could you believe it? A fellow was carrying water, coming to sprinkle it on a section of newly paved road. But before he could reach the spot, he tumbled to his last resting place on the cold ground.

You must believe my eyes. We had returned to the camp, and one of us had just received two brown loaves of bread. He put the loaves to his nose, smelled them, and began to laugh. And while he was still laughing, he suddenly fell sprawling. We rushed to his rescue, but he soon stopped breathing while his hands still grasped the loaves. Carrying a bamboo basket full of loaves, one of us had scarcely walked ten steps before he plunged headlong into the basket,

*About 15.6 kilograms.

leaving the loaves scattered and his body lying on the ground. There were others who went to bed at night and simply refused to wake up the next morning despite the shrill whistles. If you went over to shake them, their stiff bodies would tell you that theirs was an eternal sleep.

After winter had fully set in, in the two or three months of repeated blizzards, no day would pass without a report of eight or ten deaths among the two thousand wretches that made up our "great team." I witnessed more than twenty deaths in my own group during this season. Those who died from cold and hunger usually passed quietly away, without disturbing others with groans or cries. They didn't even show any signs of pain. They just burned up their calories, became scrawny, and then yielded up body and mind. They were like big candles burning hour after hour; by the last hour everything combustible had disappeared, so they died very naturally. Comparatively fewer of us died while working on the roads. Perhaps working under the threat of death, we really became strange animals that had time only for fear and effort, or machines with motors running at full tilt. It was not until we ceased to work that we began to damp our fires and, thus, our lives. At first, it was sad to see or to hear of deaths. But after a while we saw so many die that death became a matter for indifference. After seeing so many disappear from our ranks, I found I could look at a new body just as if I were looking at a blank page in a book.

Did this indifference in my mind echo the numbness in my body? According to the regulations, each group of four of us had to pave a stretch of road five meters long and three meters wide every day. If any of us were unable to finish his assigned task for the day, he would be punished that evening after returning to the camp, no matter what excuse he had. The usual punishment was to let the guilty one stand outside the tent to be "publicly prosecuted" by words or actions. This prosecution proceeded under the direction of the guards and was always carried out by some "positive members" of the teams. Normally, the one to be prosecuted had a placard reading "anti-correction" hung from his neck. The placard would not be removed at any time for two months, except at bedtime when it was hung in front of his bed instead. After he stood outside the tent for a while, all the "prosecutors," that is, the whole team, would a big meeting of ten thousand men, including all the survivors of the "long march." The vice-chairman of the Chinghai Bureau of Common Security, a man called Hao Teng-ge, began to harangue us with advice, threats, and commands. He imposed on us a "holy task." He wanted us each to become "the Foolish Senior"* who succeeded in moving mountains. To be precise, he wanted us to construct a new Shanghai in the Gobi Desert!

We rested just two days; then we got started. We were to begin our magical work in a wilderness of mountains, snow, and ice. We went across Hsining to the western part of the Chinghai Plateau.† It was only autumn then, but it was already very chilly. Snow began to fall frequently. The landscape from Huang-Yuen to the Tarim Desert was all silvery white. We seldom had sunny days. The occasional appearances of the sun never altered the white scenery of that world.

---

*According to Chinese legend, the Foolish Senior tried to move a mountain by hoeing; through his perseverance in carrying away its earth every day he did finally succeed.

†The Plateau is located in Chinghai Province, bordering Tibet and Hsinchiang.

come to carry on the prosecution, which often began with the "positive members" severely reviling the malcontent. Once I saw a Mr. Wu from Shantung thus prosecuted.

Mr. Wu was a middle-sized man, about forty. He had to stand there without speaking while the "positive members" reviled him for being dishonest and "anti-movement," and for an hour urged him to tell them why he was so obstinate. He remained silent. This "civil disobedience" made the keepers so angry that they gave orders to take further actions. The "positive members" then stripped him, leaving his bare body at the mercy of the weather. But this Mr. Wu was indeed very "stubborn," for he still refused to say a word. Finally, the −15°C temperature made his whole body shake violently and his face turn blue. Then he collapsed. Seeing his fall down on the ground, some "positive members" shouted all at once: "You're faking!" And others added, "Come on! Be honest, tell the truth!"

But for a good while the naked body, now blue as well, lay on the icy ground motionless. Some of us went over to check if he were breathing . . . he wasn't. But did this trouble anyone? I don't know. I only heard a superintendent curse: "Stubborn bastard! Let a hundred of them die at once! I won't say it's too many."

This, of course, was not the outcome of every "public prosecution." In some milder cases, the prosecuted were lucky enough to stay alive, but to survive the ordeal never meant that a prisoner had been pardoned. After the prosecution, the prosecuted would still be kept outside the tent while the others went in for dinner. He was normally asked to stand there reflecting on all his offenses until he realized the origin of the sin of his radical nature. And when everybody went to bed, he would be asked to write a self-criticism before he was allowed to eat his two cold brown loaves with some pickles and salty water, and finally get into his quilt, which was as cold as an icebox.

I often felt as if we were not on this earth. It seemed to me that we were in another world surrounded by mythical figures, for reality always seemed so far from real. One afternoon, when I was using my pick as usual to crack the ice, I heard a shot. The terrifying noise made my muscles cling even more tightly to my bones. I glanced toward it. To my horror I saw a man on the snowy ground lying perfectly still. We all watched, but none of us dared to go over. We knew the convict had "gone back to his Old Home," and more than ten guns were now aimed at us.

It was the tall Chen Wei-ta from our group. He had been carrying a large basket of stones with another man. This other man told us later on the sly that Old Chen had been walking so carelessly that he had passed over the limits marked by the red warning flags, and a single bullet had ended his fifty-year life.

Old Chen, in fact, had been with me in a prison in Shanghai. I remembered him as an amiable man with peaceful eyes. His kind enthusiasm toward others had given warmth to all of us behind the bars of the Tilan Bridge Jail. So after the day he ceased to be, I kept thinking of him and could not believe that such a man should have met his end that way. The incongruity between the man and his death was just like the incongruity between the red warm blood coming from his bullet-pierced brain and the white cold snow that sucked it in.

Some days later I was again struggling with my pickax in the blank world of ice and snow when I heard another bang. This time the noise did not stir my curiosity. I knew only too well what it meant. I did, however, take a quick glance at the scene of the incident. This time it was Tsai Lo-fu lying there. He had been the owner of Lan Chiao Funeral Parlor in Shanghai and had also been my fellow prisoner at Tilan Bridge. He was stout and had a glass eye. When he looked at you, his fake eye shed no light. Like Chen Wei-ta before him, he had transgressed the warning flags when carrying stones and so had to be shot. But unlike Chen, he did not die immediately; the bullet went through his abdomen, but he was already beyond hope when sent back by stretcher.

From incidents like these, one can conclude that the four red flags were flags of Death, and the lines demarcated by them were the boundaries between this and the other world. Yet, Death did not come only to those who were "disciplined." It came also to those who rebelled, and even to the purely innocent. But whatever the case, it was always tragic in the deepest sense; it was so tragic that any heroic act or word would impress you everlastingly.

Tai Lung-de was an intellectual, a graduate of Southwestern United University. He was originally a clerk in an institute in Shanghai. But he was arrested for being "anti-movement," as he had spoken against the Communist Party and its regime, and sentenced to fifteen years imprisonment. When jailed at Tilan Bridge, he could not stand the prison regulations. Once he complained and was called to an office where two jailers beat him soundly, and his nose and mouth bled. But Tai was not cowed. In his anger, he struggled loose, picked up a small stool nearby, and smashed the two jailers with it. Later they found one of the two jailers had lost seven teeth in the scuffle.

Tai was given a death sentence on reprieve, and sent to the Chinghai Plateau for "reform through labor," where he joined our road construction team. But he still had his fiery temper. One day he was called away from work to have a "talk" with the superintendents. It was later revealed that at the talk, the guards accused him of evading labor, scolded him, and then beat him with clubs. This drove him into a rage again. Some of us saw him back up a few steps when the guards started to beat him. But suddenly he rushed forward and launched himself at a club-carrier. We heard a rifle shot, and poor Tai fell dead. Later the jailers explained that they had no choice but to "put him down" since he meant to snatch a gun for further rebellion.

Another rebel was Teng Ching-chih, an obstinate young man. He seldom yielded to beating and scolding. One evening, a "public prosecution" was arranged for him. After all of us had arrived at the scene of the performance (the last place, in our fatigue, we wished to be), orders were given that Teng should be stripped of his clothes right at the start and have his arms bound with cords. This was, they said, because he was seriously guilty of "agitating the group, leading astray, and resisting reform through labor—in sum, totally anti-movement."

The orders were quickly carried out. The superintendents sat down behind a wooden table. But before they could make themselves comfortable to force a confession out of him, Young Teng dashed toward them and, with a kick, turned the table upside down. The superintendents leaped up in dismay and retreated a few steps. Then, seeing that Teng did not continue his attack, they halted, and the one in charge screwed up his face and declared coldly: "The meeting is dismissed! The rest of you get ready for dinner!"

We were all surprised to see the prosecution come to an end so abruptly. Afterwards, we learned that it actually did not end so simply. Later the same evening some "positive members" were instructed to bind Teng's legs and take him to a roadside. There, he was stripped, and his arms and legs bound fast to a withered tree. After two hours or so, he was found frozen to death. He had turned into a withered tree himself.

We really pitied such heroes as this. But who dared express it? We could only add silent sympathy for any of the newly fallen to our sympathy for the past dead.

Chen Ching-ju, the Old Convict, as they called him, was a Cantonese. He had long suffered from asthma and often had difficulty breathing, like an exhausted racer who has run too fast for too long. He often coughed violently. We all pitied him and hoped our keepers would send him to the hospital. But they took no notice of him. They gave him neither medication nor rest. Once, after a long day's hard labor, he fainted on the snow just before the whistle was blown to finish work. The superintendents only accused him of "faking sickness." After he regained consciousness, some of us offered to take him back. But the guards would not allow us to help him. They said he could walk home alone. On our way back, we heard a gunshot. The next morning before we started out for work again, the guards told us that the Old Convict had tried to grab a gun and they had to shoot him. We knew this was a lie. But we realized too that henceforth we would have to take some sort of action; otherwise each of us would die a premature and shameful death.

We knew now that what they called "reform through labor" was just a means to squeeze every bit of labor out of political dissenters. So any "old convict" who lost his value as a laborer was to be "disposed of." So we decided to take good care of the old ones. Every day now, when we walked back from work, we would let the old and weak ones walk ahead of us. Sometimes we let them support themselves by leaning on our shoulders. We would rather walk back slower than let them risk their lives by falling behind.

There were people who, like Ling Hsien-yang, Chan Wen-hu, Teng Chung, and others, were so exhausted when they came back from work that they simply had no more strength to move. Lying on their beds, they seemed paralyzed. It was only the fits of pain eating into their bones that made them occasionally roll over and move their limbs, showing that they were not yet dead but only under the shadow of death. When eating, they couldn't sit up, they just bent over their beds and licked up their food like dogs. To give some relief to our miserable fellow inmates, young ones often secretly did their assigned chores. Within the boundary of the four red flags, we also managed to help them finish their daily tasks.

We had a "labor song." We were made to sing it as loud as we could three times a day before meals. The song was a good description of our fate:

Seize cloudy days, grasp sunny days;
Good days are windy and rainy days.
Snowfall makes but redeeming days;
Let one day equal twenty days.

Each time we finished singing the song, the guards would ask us, "Isn't it a good song?"

"Yah! Geh, geh, geh, geh!" Five or six Tibetan fellows in our group used to answer the question with their native version of "Good." That language sounded queer and ghostly to us. It was ironic that we should shout "Good!" when we stood there shuddering and hungry, bending our heads against the driving snow. Our singing and shouting were swallowed by the raging of the blizzards.

Nevertheless, in these ironic moments we did seem in good condition to struggle for life. The more terrifying the weather became, and the more the knives of ice and snow attacked us, the hotter our hearts seemed to grow. We glowed and burned simply to withstand cold, to meet snow and ice, and to dissolve night and death if possible. When a man is afflicted with news of death every day, when he feels death is ubiquitous, surrounding him, wrapping him, or is just a millimeter above his nose, he will then take it for granted, and breathe it as naturally as he will the air. What is unbearable is the waiting, and the knowledge that you are waiting for it. To wait is to expect with a certain purpose. But we could not very well say that we were waiting for Death with any specific purpose.

I will never forget Hsiao Pao. My memory of him haunts me like an unending nightmare. This Cantonese was first assigned the task of carrying stone and dirt because he looked tall and strong. He did it by shouldering a pole with baskets dangling by strong cords from its two ends. As time went on, the heavy loads caused the pole to bruise his shoulders. At first his shoulders just swelled and discolored. Later he began to shed layers of skin from the bruised areas. Then pustules began to develop. He was given no medical treatment of any kind, and the inflammation soon caused his shoulders to trickle pus and blood. By now Hsiao could no longer keep from groaning with pain. At night we would hear him crying out "Pa!" and "Ma!" His groans made us all want to find a cure for him. But we could only pity him and suffer along with him.

No longer able to shoulder anything, Hsiao still had to work during the day. His next task was to pull a cart, which they said required him to move only his legs, not a bit of shoulder work at all. He was certainly still able to walk, but could he pull an overloaded cart of straw, a weight of seven or eight hundred kilograms? The first day he had to perform this feat, he managed to go just a short distance before he came to uneven ground. The cart overturned, throwing Hsiao down into a nearby pit. His legs were broken. So for a time he was permitted to stay in the tent without having to go out to work. However, an injured laborer received only two thirds of his rations.

Poorly attended, Hsiao became permanently crippled. Did he then no longer have to work? Far from it. Some years later he was sent to Telingha Farm to continue his "reform through labor." His hands were still capable of work, as they said, and during the harvest season he was taken to a field to help reap the wheat. He would sit and mow the grain with a scythe. After he finished mowing the grain within reach, he would move himself a little farther forward with his hands. His effort was really worthy of praise. But when famine came during the winter, he was among the first to starve.

In the Communist world everybody knows the "Internationale." It begins with "Arise, ye prisoners of starvation!" This phrase could indeed have been used to address the four or five hundred thousand people stationed in Chinghai for "reform through labor." They were really "prisoners of starvation" of the ruling party. But when thousands of guns were aimed at them, how could they rise up? When hunger and cold pressed them down, could they get up again for anything? As far as I know, in the first year when I was sent to Chinghai, at least four thousand men died from cold and hunger. And for some years that followed, deaths from that sort of privation were about the same each year. In the years, 1959–61 (the so-called "three years of natural disasters"), when I was moved to Telingha Farm, the number must have increased threefold. I cannot give an exact figure, of course. But in those years, an average of twenty to thirty thousand additional men were sent to the plateau each year in the spring and fall.

The great number of deaths meant nothing to the officials in charge. When six or seven hundred men out of a team of two thousand starved or froze to death in winter, the ruling party seemed to regard it as a matter of course. In our rulers' eyes, our lives were worth no more than those of ants. Whatever the real reason, the doctor's report for a new death always read: "Relapse of his old disease, beyond cure this time. . . . Let him be claimed and well buried."

One needs some imagination to call hunger and cold an "old disease" that can "relapse." In fact, the doctor never saw his patient. How could he know what disease the hungry and cold laborer had? And who would thank him for his kind suggestion when the dead man's relatives were hundreds or thousands of miles away and perhaps as cold and poor as the dead man? Even if the relatives had the money, time, and will to go and claim their dead, there was still the question of whether they could really get him back. Besides, who would risk being known to be connected with an anti-revolutionary criminal? Anyone who died of his "old disease" on the plateau would most probably be claimed and buried by two appointed fellow "criminals." They would put him in a cart, convey him to nearby hillside, dig a hollow, dump him in, cover him with some handfuls of sand and rocks, and that would be the end of it. A burial good enough, they would hope, to guarantee the complete dissolution of the dead man's body, if no hungry wild beast came by and felt interested in it.

Those who could survive hunger and cold had to suffer more. Malnutrition made many feel so dizzy that they could not even recognize their own limbs, but no one dared to say the word "hungry" in the presence of a superintendent. If anyone should be so audacious, we would have another performance to watch that evening, where the offender would stand outside the tent, scoffed at and reviled by "positive members," who, by that time, had become used to the ritual of "public prosecutions," and who did not dare to present the show poorly. "By uttering that indecent word," they might say, "you were obviously spreading a rumor in order to bring about anarchy." And if the prosecuted should defend himself by denying that accusation, they would proclaim that he was "rotten to the core" and a "criminal who will never repent until death." Then the prosecution would change its tactics, and action would be taken to ensure that the "rumor-spreader" should acknowledge at last that he did speak with the intention of destroying "our basic idea of productivity."

Is it not an unimaginable thing that thousands of people were starving, yet none of them dared to tell the simple truth, that they were hungry? "Hungry" was an indigestible word forever lodged in our stomachs.

The night was deepening. The birds had come back to their nests. The beasts had returned to their caves. Every living animal had settled into its own corner for rest, leaving the white icy world devoid of any life except when we, the "labor reformees" and some accompanying gunholders, were still struggling with the icy ground into our fourteenth hour of work for the day.

At last, we were also allowed to return to our tents. No nests, nor caves, but ice-vaults. When we returned from the outdoors to our tents, it seemed like we had returned from a big icehouse to a smaller ice-vault.

About a mile away, the "leaders" and their soldiers were very warm. They were in tents with rectangular tops and double-layered canvas, with a third layer of cotton for insulation. Inside each tent was a burning coal fire for warmth. Their faces were red with warmth. They drank hot tea, prepared snacks, and cooked with oil, flour, meat, and vegetables that they took from us. It was spring inside those tents. Soon it would be summer there, too.

Meanwhile, we had only a single layer of canvas and no fire. We hugged one another for warmth. We slept in our cotton clothes. We covered ourselves with the few quilts they gave us and anything else that we thought could produce warmth. The tents were far from being shelters; they were our enemies. When we got familiar with them, they just attempted to kill us with cold.

We often could not get to sleep. Cold winds invaded our tents. We were nervous about whether the guards would pay us unannounced visits. They always came two by two, maintaining a space of about twenty meters between them for fear that we might pay them unexpected "visits," too. Their night visits were indeed very courteous. They carried no guns, only whips, cudgels, and flashlights. They were prepared to meet us "with courtesy" in case one of us suddenly emerged from the dark.

The leaders' tents were strategically located to allow ours to be besieged, but not near enough to allow us to make a surprise attack. On cold nights when even our bones were chilled, the rancor and suspicion between us and our guards deepened. The hostility seemed ready to burst into war at any minute.

In fact, even in the daytime, we were always conscious of the layer of hatred between them and us. There was the danger of death on both sides. Just as wild beasts are often ready to bite and eat one another, so they and we were always ready to hurt and kill each

loaded baskets, the situation was even worse. They often found their garments would last only twenty days. Furthermore, any wear and tear on our clothes was beyond repair, for we simply had no patches. A year later, when we had finished the road and were beginning to work at Telingha Farm, we found we were allowed some patching material to mend our worn-out clothes. The farm imported fertilizers from Japan, Holland, and other foreign countries, and the fertilizers were often packed in sacks that, to our great joy, were made of a plastic-like cloth capable of serving as patching material.

With or without mending material, none of us ever dared to make full use of our clothes. The most economic wearers of clothes left their upper bodies bare all summer and during much of the warmer seasons. By doing so, they could save their shirts for winter to use as underwear beneath their jackets. Some cut their long trousers into two pairs of shorts. Some thought they could dispense with any underclothes, but without any underwear one's cotton clothes would often be soaked with sweat and would wear more rapidly. To prevent erosion from sweat, we thought of washing our clothes, but we really feared to do so. More often than not, washing was equal to tearing, and we did not have much clothing to abuse. We learned to be careful with what we had.

Another example of our misery touches upon an inelegant topic. We were not provided with any toilet paper. Every time we relieved ourselves, many of us just drew up our drawers and rushed back to work. Some cleaner persons could not bear doing this, but since they had no paper of any sort, they had to make do with a bunch of straw, some dry leaves, or even a clod of earth. Dirty! Yes, we were all dirty. We could not but be dirty. We perspired too much and we washed too little to get rid of the smell. In such unhygienic conditions, the smell just got worse.

What most annoyed us about our clothes was not the bad smell, but their failure to function well as clothes. As we labored, the cotton filling often sank into the hems of our shirts or our pants and formed a thick cotton padding. When we wore clothes in this state, it was as if both summer and winter had come upon us at the same time, with summer on top of winter. But our bodies were never combinations of seasons; when winter came, we were all winter; when summer came, we were all summer. To wear such "summer-and-winter garments" at any time was to suffer simultaneously from fever and cold.

When our clothes became "summer-and-winter garments," it was time for us to operate on them. We cut them open, we searched for thread (Dear God! Where could we get cotton thread? We could only use the coarse hemp thread taken from the sacks), we searched for needles, we took the cotton "sediment" out of the clothes, we divided the cotton equally, we restored every section of it to its original place, and then we sewed the openings back together. We were never good "clothes-surgeons," but to help ourselves survive, we had to try to be experts.

We were each given a pair of cotton-filled shoes and a pair of plain shoes every year, but we were given no socks or stockings. When we dug the ground, we had to put one foot upon the upper head of the shovel and stamp heavily to get the tool into the soil. This hurt our shoes tragically. In a month or so, their soles would break and fall away. When the tragedy ended, the comedy began. This time we used our God-given soles instead. We stamped our bare feet on the tools. To everybody's surprise, our soles never fell away, but they tended to crack open. As time went on, our broken soles ceased to bleed and began to harden with layers of tough skin—no, cast iron.

After clothing comes eating. For our three meals the Communists gave us six black "woh-woh toes,"* each bigger than a toe, about the size of a fist. For each meal we usually had two such "toes" plus a bit of pickle, a bit of rape-turnip soup, and some salt water. Three such meals were naturally not enough for fourteen hours' labor on the snowy and icy ground. Therefore, we needed additional food.

For breakfast, we had a sort of gruel as our additional food. It was produced by boiling rice bran, pea husks, and coarse wheat flour together in a large pot of water. This gruel, called "thin boiled rice," was so thin that we drank it; we never ate it. Worse still, we each

---

*Steamed loaves of bread made with wheat bran, pea husks, and oat or millet flour.

could only drink a double-size mug of it. Quarrels often arose because of unfair distribution, or because of greedy people who attempted to have a bigger share. For lunch, sometimes our meal was supplemented with a bowl of boiled cabbage or turnip. On a festival day, we might occasionally have some fried food, but it was cooked with a bitter local vegetable oil. Our dinner was often the same as our lunch.

On the cold plateau of Chinghai, people grew only wheat, barley, and peas as staples. The vegetables they ate were mostly from Russia; the onions, garlic, rape-turnips, cabbage, leeks, and potatoes were all imported. Onion, garlic, and leeks were regarded as high-class food there; only the "leaders" were entitled to enjoy them. If we were lucky, we might sometimes be granted the peels of such vegetables, along with some potatoes as small as doves' eggs.

During all four seasons, we ate mainly three vegetables: small cabbage in spring and summer, and large cabbage and rape-turnips in fall and winter. To add variety, we sometimes ate a native herb called "Hui Hui Tsai."* There are two kinds of Hui Hui Tsai. One has leaves that are green on the upper side and red on the back side. This kind is poisonous. After eating it for two or three days, every part of your body swells, and then you die. The other kind is edible. It is not difficult to recognize because, unlike the poisonous kind, the back side of its leaf is gray or white with lush hair. However, this edible vegetable is anything but tasty. It has a bad smell and tastes bitter. Sometimes, to make up for our inadequate nourishment, the Communists had the herb dried, ground into powder, and mixed into our loaves of bread. Another herb we ate on the plateau was called "Ku Ku Tsai."† It is indeed bitter, as its name suggests. In order to encourage us to eat it, the Communists told us that it was what Wang Pao-chuan, the "Chinese Penelope," had eaten for years while she was awaiting the return of her husband.

In fact, we had enough bitters. We would rather have had some

*Literally, "gray gray vegetable."
†Literally, "bitter bitter vegetable."

sweets. The only sweet thing we ate on the plateau was the rape-turnip. It is often as heavy as seven or eight jin and can be cooked or eaten raw. It is rather sweet, but in Russia, its native land, it is grown as a forage crop for sheep and hogs, never for human beings. Undoubtedly we were treated as livestock rather than as people. Rape-turnip is really not suitable for human eating, as it is hard to digest. Those of us who welcomed this "sweet" ended up, nine cases out of ten, with ulcers or other stomach diseases.

But bitter or sweet, we consumed all edibles, for we were really hungry. We used to say, jokingly, that we ate three "chis" a day. (The word "chicken" and the word "hunger" are pronounced the same, "chi," in Chinese.) If you had happened to have seen us eating our "chis," you would have thought that our performances, if filmed, would have been able to win us Academy Awards, they were so dramatic. Once a black "woh-woh toe" got into our hands, it instantly turned into an enemy we hated so bitterly that we wished we could gorge him down with one bite. He was often so tough, though, that we had to bite three or five times, chew many more times, and take in many mouthfuls of water, before we could make him perish to save our own lives.

Our meals never changed, whether we were building roads or farming at Telingha. Once a fellow laborer, who was originally a Communist "leader" but was sent to labor with us for some error or another, said to me: "For each mouthful of food from the Communists, you always have to pay a drop of blood." I knew what he meant. But if drops of blood could really have been used to buy food, I believe many of us would have taken pleasure in the business.

No dictionary in the world contains a correct definition of the word "hunger," if you're looking for one truly in accordance with our situation. When we felt hungry and had no food to eat, we often drank water or ate snow. When our stomachs were filled with water, we could stop feeling hungry for a time, but then our stomachs swelled and started to ache. When we had stomachaches, we could neither stand, nor sit, nor walk, nor sleep: every position was wrong. If our stomachs did not ache, when we had gorged them with so much water, they were like big, overinflated balloons: ready to blow up any minute. In that condition we felt dizzy and hated ourselves for not really being balloons. For if we had been, we would have all flown away in a moment.

To cure the "disease of hunger," some would save a "woh-woh toe" from dinner for later on. The spared loaf was often torn into pieces and then squeezed into balls as big—or, rather, as small—as peas. When night deepened and the devilish disease came again, the victim would then throw a ball or two continually into his stomach to "scare it away." Some said this tactic was very effective. Others said otherwise. I am not sure who was right; I never tried it myself.

The plateau in the west of Chinghai Province (about two hundred li from Huang-yuen) has an average height of two thousand meters above sea level. It is a composite of high mountain ranges. When you looked up at the mountain tops or down into the valleys, you could really feel the sublimity of nature and see its beauty. But we were not sightseers. We were road-builders. For us, those sublime and beautiful hills and vales were obstacles we had to overcome. According to the lunar calendar, the three months from the middle of the Tenth Month to the middle of the next year's First Month are the coldest months of Chinghai. After the Eleventh Month, the skies never clear. Blizzards are frequent. Snow covers the lowlands as well as the uplands, the grass as well as the trees. Before the snow comes, you can see a little winding path leading to Hsining, the capital of Chinghai. It was an important route for the Mongolian and Tibetan hordes of the old days, and is still an important passage for the wandering nomads there. On a good day, you can see camels, yaks, or sheep driven along the path and appearing between the peaks. When we arrived there, part of the path was only one or two feet in width, and the whole path was thickly covered with snow. We were asked to widen the path so that two trucks could pass each other on the road. You can imagine how tremendous a task it was.

And you can imagine how the task was made more gargantuan by the fact that we had no modern machines of any sort. To build the road, we had only pickaxes, shovels, hammers, baskets, and carts.

We dug through layers of ice, shovel by shovel. We cracked the ice plates with pickaxes and cleared the ground with spades. We ate away huge rocks bit by bit with hammers and chisels. We tied baskets with ropes to poles and loaded the baskets with earth or ice, rocks or gravel. We shouldered the poles with loaded baskets. We removed all the bumps in the road and used these to fill in the holes, all with our hands. We occasionally used carts to carry sand, soil, and gravel for the same purpose. We also carried buckets of water to sprinkle on the pavement before we smoothed it with whatever heavy object (not necessarily rollers!) we had on hand. All this was manual labor indeed.

But this was not all you would see while we were at work. There were also some unexpected scenes.

"Thud!"

A poor fellow fell to the bottom of a deep valley. Some said he plunged in on purpose.

"Whoosh! Crack! Crash!"

By a precipice, a man in black clothes and a black cap was said to have fallen, carelessly. It was getting dark. In the dark places "careless" laborers kept falling from crags or cliffs. And nobody seemed to care. Then there was a miracle. With a series of rumbling sounds, rocks big and small, earth high and low, trees, moss, and men, all moved and rolled and glided and slid. Some minutes later, on a hillside, corpses loomed pitiably. We could not tell exactly when the earthquake occurred. We had lost our sense of time. In our world we had only two colors other than red—black and white. We also had only two sorts of time, daytime and nighttime. We thought the "miracle" happened during the dark time, for we did not see it very clearly.

But we knew why men continually fell. There were those who fell to kill themselves. Such were people in despair. They often fell at a good site, on the brink of a steep face of rock, perhaps. From there they needed only one jump to fall straight to the bottom without having to be bothered by ivy leaves or branches. From there they could imagine themselves as eagles descending down and down and down on their prey.

There were also those who fell because the "leaders" forced them. These were often "stubborn" prisoners, whom the "leaders" were not satisfied merely to blame, curse, and threaten. Hence, when the time came, they were forced to fall (probably with guns). Such men never fell at good sites. When they fell, the nearby trees and rocks rushed in to mangle them.

The third class of people who fell were those who had a poor sense of balance. They did not know they would fall. They just worked and walked until suddenly, one slip, and they had lost their chance to complain that it was too dark to see anything.

The fourth group fell, of course, because of a natural disaster, a disaster that probably happened because Heaven and Earth were not happy about being constantly annoyed by us: "How could you dig, strike, and crack all the time?" they might ask. If you want to be exact about the total number of casualties, I can tell you only this: Each group had at least several dozen and at most several hundred. Not too heavy a number, was it?

If you construct a road on a plain, you can at least stand securely, but on the plateau, the ground rises and falls abruptly. The slopes are often difficult to climb, not to mention to walk or stand on. When the snowy season comes, the slopes become so slippery that even to climb them is dangerous. We were asked to build a road on such slopes.

It is superfluous to emphasize how difficult it was for us to crack ice, shoulder baskets, carry stones, etc., on such uneven ground. It is not superfluous, I believe, for me to repeat that we were asked to build a road there by hand, without any modern machines. I believe twenty thousand bees can build a big hive very easily in a tree. But I do not believe the same bees can build the same hive easily in the water. We were like so many bees there. We were also asked to build, in an alien environment, what was beyond our ability to build. So we were not sensibly exploited at all. If you want to squeeze any meaning out of that fanatic enterprise, you ought to view it from a different angle. You must know that we were not only being exploited, we were also being punished and tortured.

Later, they sent rollers to us. These were not machine-operated rollers, but rollers to be pulled by horses or donkeys, each weighing over a thousand kilograms. But instead of letting beasts do the work, the Communists ordered us to pull the rollers back and forth over the uneven ground. In doing this work, we were not just tortured, we were humiliated too. For we were treated no better than beasts.

Once, in the course of constructing the road, we came to a hillside, where a big hole, some twenty meters deep and over twenty meters wide, lay ahead obstructing our work. On the left-hand side of the hole was a deep ravine, while on the right was a steep mountain wall. Seeing this, some "leaders" suggested that a declivity be made over the pit instead of digging a new hole through the mountain wall. To fulfill this whim, they ordered some of us to climb up to the top of the mountain wall and strike down rocks to fill the cavity. "In the 'Great War of Delivery' millions of us Communists were killed by the Nationalists. Now, even if thousands of you anti-revolutionaries are killed, you should call it fair." This was the Communists' usual excuse when they bid us to do anything fatal.

A strong young man among us was commanded to climb first. He didn't dare resist. He started to climb up the steep and icy cliff by holding onto the withered branches of small trees while placing his feet on the protruding rocks. We all held our breath watching him perform this feat.

After he had climbed up ten meters or so, he stopped, unable to go any farther. Then under the "leaders" instruction, he took out his hammer and chisel, and began to cut the rocks beside him. It was obvious that if he wanted to be safe, he ought not to use too much force, for that would shake his own body as well as the rocks he was chiseling. But the young man was not cautious enough. He knew only that the "leaders" below were looking at him, perhaps even aiming guns at him. He thought he'd die if he didn't exert himself to finish the task. So he held the hammer high up over his head and struck down on the rock violently and repeatedly. The rocks did start to break, and some broken pieces did begin to fall into the pit below. But—

"Thud!"

Something much bigger than the small falling rocks suddenly hit other. But we were the weaker animals. We seldom took the initiative. It was they who often threatened to devour us, and that threat put us on the defensive. But any behavior on our part, defensive or offensive, was enough cause for their caution and further threats. Every hour of every day we were pressed by a sense of fear. We often thought of our plight, but thinking only caused insomnia. We could never understand why we came to this ice-vault to be made helpless. We could never understand, either, why we were waiting obediently for bullets, whips, ice blocks, and death. Were there any others who had suffered like us? This was a question we often asked ourselves.

The colder the night, the harder it was for us to get to sleep, and the more questions we asked. We hated the weather and hated the plateau. We could not bear to think of living in a place where there are only one hundred days a year without frost. Facing the wintry weather all the time, I had no tears to shed. I only felt blank.

In the first year, when we were constructing roads, we had no permanent dwellings. We just built tents where we worked. We had no long-term addresses, and the Communists used this as an excuse to refuse to forward any mail to us. Thus, for that long year we received no "alms" of any sort from outside. This, in fact, was the Communists' strategy to break us and make us as obedient as horses. For the Communists always hold this philosophy: that a man is most easily managed when he has nothing and is still struggling to have something.

We did have nothing then. And we were forever struggling to have daily necessities. For one thing, we had a serious clothing problem. Every one of us was given a cloth ticket every year, which we could exchange for a piece of cloth, or for clothing equivalent to that quantity of material. Under this system of clothing allowances, we could have one suit of clothes without linings a year, or a suit of cotton filling of double-thickness. If we saved, we could have a full suit of cotton clothes in two years, or a bed quilt in five years. As we were in such unimaginable want of clothing, we normally wore no undergarments in the spring and summer. Whether we were working or sleeping, we wore the same outer garments. Consequently, our clothes wore out quickly. For those who had to shoulder poles with the bottom of the pit. Some of us cried out. We looked into the pit. We saw there a body, with a hammer and a chisel nearby. Liu Hsiang-tung, a leader who had a pockmarked face and often bullied and browbeat us laborers with threats and cudgels, came forward to deal with the situation, not knowing that we hated him most.

"Bastard! Good-for-nothing! Just a bit of climbing. And he failed!" the leader said, full of anger. "You, up again, you!" he pointed to another young fellow. "Hurry up, mind the task, no failure this time, get up and get it done!" His language allowed no hesitation.

The second unlucky young man climbed warily.

"Hurry up, can't you hear? Keep climbing. Don't bow down to hardship. Never fear danger. Task first!" The pockmarked man held a whip in one hand and a cudgel in the other, and waved now this hand, now that hand. While he was still waving and shouting, the second victim fell likewise into the pit before any rocks were broken. Another dead.

Liu was really seething. He refused to suspend the work. He became even more eager to send others up the cliff. Meanwhile, the cloudy sky was becoming stormy. Chilly winds began to blow. It threatened to snow again, but for two or three hours that afternoon pockmarked face kept sending people to death or injury. I remember there were four dead and seventeen injured. Those who were only injured were mostly incompetent climbers. They often climbed up just a few steps and then rolled down to the hillside without falling into the pit. When the last one was sent up the cliff, Liu still shouted threateningly.

"Up! Up! Farther up! Or—"

Before he finished his command, a hammer was brought down on his back from behind. He staggered and fell. The same hammer was brought forcefully into contact with his skull, breaking it instantly. The hammer was held by Ho Hai-tsing, a native of Shan-hsi Province, who was indignant over the "leader's" behavior. He was so indignant that after killing Liu, he kicked him into the pit as well. This indignant brave man was, of course, sentenced to death and executed soon after. But the Communists did not let him die easily. Instead of shooting him, they first had his eyes dug out, then had his nose removed. Then they beat him until he died.

After this terrible incident, the chief leader came and asked the laborers' opinion regarding the task at hand. He then decided that we should forsake our present strategy of filling the hole by striking down rocks. He suggested, instead, that we move earth to fill the cavity. His suggestion was more feasible but demanded much more labor from us. We naturally accepted his advice. We knew we could never avoid laboring, though we could avoid instant death.

The north wind blew constantly over the plateau. Our clothes were useless against it. It chilled our hands, our legs, our souls. We wielded the pickaxes, the shovels, all the tools in our hands, up and down, back and forth, high and low; we exercised ourselves in every possible way, every possible direction, hoping that we could thus keep warm and hold back the chill of the north wind. But we failed. We had no more strength. As we stopped plying our tools vigorously, the wind began again to bite into our flesh and bones. We were exhausted. We were numbed. The weak ones, aged or sick, suddenly fainted away. Some of us dropped, never to rise again, and falling snow began to cover the bodies with white shrouds.

By the time we reached the site for work early each morning, we had already begun to shudder from the cold. We stretched out our hands to pick up the tools we had left on the ground the previous night. (The Communists dared not let us take the tools back to the tents at night for fear that we might use them for rebellion.) But our hands were so stiff that they didn't even take our own orders. Besides, the tools were already buried deep beneath the previous night's snowfall. We strove to remove the ice. Then we held our tools tightly. Much too tightly, in fact. For we suddenly realized that our palms and the tools had been glued together. I did not know what to do next. I simply shook and pulled my hand off the tool with brute force. A layer of skin from my palm was pulled off too. My palm began to bleed. I wiped the blood with my coat sleeve. I also wiped the tool. Then I started to work.

My case was not the worst. Many others' hands were chapped from the cold, many had slits on their hands as long as babies' mouths, and the raw flesh there, they said, was deadly quick to pain. After eighty or ninety percent of us had got frostbite or chillblains on our hands, the Communists reported the situation to the higher officials, and we were each given a pair of cotton gloves.

The time we suffered most during the day was toward noon. By then we were already too hungry to do anything. But we dared not stop toiling, especially when a leader passed by. There were times when we were able to see our lunch boxes which had been sent to our working place, but the leaders refused to allow us to rest and eat immediately. On the contrary, they bade us work harder and try to finish the job at hand. Actually, they wanted us to wait until the meal was freezing cold so that we might suffer even in eating. We knew their maliciousness. But what could we do? We could only go on toiling until they blew the whistles.

Eating lunch was indeed a painful thing for us. The loaves of "woh-woh toes" had by then frozen as hard as stone. And we were so hungry. How we wanted to get them down into our stomachs immediately. But we couldn't. Besides some vegetable leaves, we had only some pickle and a little cold water for soup. We had nothing tasty or warm enough to help us chew the tough bread. Therefore, by the time each of us had finished getting down the "two hard stones," it was already time for the leaders to blow the whistles again, signaling us to resume our drudgery.

"Cold comes before frost, and chill comes after snow." This saying applies to our experience on the plateau. During the cold seasons on the plateau, we occasionally had one or two sunny days. But to see the sun did not necessarily mean that we felt warmer. A sunny sky after a heavy snowfall was often accompanied by a strong northwest wind. That wind was the coldest of all, sharper than a razor. Once our faces were exposed to it, they would soon start to shed layers of skin. So, during the cold periods, we were really afraid to see the sun and hear the wind.

It was often difficult for us to say how or why our fellows died. Many starved to death. But many froze to death, I believe. In fact, all sorts of deaths could be reduced to two primary reasons: hunger and cold. Some died exhausted. Others died spitting blood. Some killed themselves by jumping into the valley. If such people had been sufficiently fed and adequately sheltered, they would not have come to such ends. To die from hunger or cold is of course not to die a "natural" death. But after we had seen so many deaths in the cold time and in the cold place, we gradually became accustomed to seeing people dying or dead. We developed "cold eyes." We even developed a philosophy toward death. We thought all deaths were natural deaths. We were like flowers. Flowers can wither, be blown away, be stamped on, be nipped, or be scorched. All ways that lead them to death are natural in the world of nature. The same with us human beings. To be tortured to death has been natural in human history, too.

Even with this knowledge, we shuddered in the shadow of death. After all, we were no real philosophers. We still hated the Communists for their whipping, cudgeling, and shooting. We regarded them as cruel death dealers. In the eyes of the Reds, our lives were insignificant substitutes for things insubstantial. For them our lives were no longer lives, but opportunities for torture, means of creating climaxes for tragedies.

I looked up ahead and saw the Sun Moon Mountain Range with its crags, cliffs, peaks, and precipices all steep and all covered with snow. As I looked farther, I saw the Mo-tien Ling, even loftier and more precipitous than the Sun Moon Mountains, with a summit capped with a thicker layer of ice. Then I looked at the rugged ground I was standing on and thought: "How can we ever build a road over this?" With this thought I looked at the mountains again; I suddenly felt that the mountain peaks were all devils' or monsters' heads gazing at me. I looked at myself and my fellow laborers. Our flesh was too thin and our bones too weak, and every pore of my skin felt the chill.

We had cherished a ray of hope during the Korean War. We fancied that the U.S. armies might cooperate with the Chinese Nationalist armies to counterattack the Communists and deliver us, including us laboring "redressees," from the Communists' tyrannical regime. But soon our hopes perished. We heard the war was drawing to an end and no army was to come to our rescue. The news broke many of our hearts. Some hanged themselves in despair, among them Li Chin-ho, a tall handsome man from Chekiang Province, who was sentenced to death on reprieve for having been an official in the Ministry of Justice of the Nationalist Government. Li hanged himself by tying a long piece of cloth to the highest branch of a withered tree. Others chose to die in different ways. Sung Tse, formerly a vice-commander of a division of the Nationalist army, chose to jump off a cliff. He was short, with a round face. He seldom talked but he was very tough. Once he was accused by the leaders of "negative resistance to labor." The fact was he didn't have enough strength to move the big stones and carry the heavy baskets. One day, as a leader whipped him and accused him again of refusing to admit that he was plotting a riot, he got very angry. He picked up some nearby stones and threw them at the leader. Then, failing to win the fight (for the leader was much stronger than he), he shouted: "Down with communism! Long live the Republic of China!" Then he jumped off a cliff into the valley.

Any struggle against the coldblooded leaders was turned into memories. We only regretted that we had died too "cheaply," without succeeding in any disruption of the Communists. As you know, we suffered from long-term malnutrition. As a result, many of us became night-blind. When we returned from labor at dusk, many could barely see. They just walked behind the others. When they came to a pit, a slippery slope, or a sharp turn of the path, they barely knew it. People often fell or slipped down into valleys and pits, killing themselves. If such people got up and went outside to relieve themselves, the same thing often happened. "One slip, then a regret at midnight for all time." This saying held a special significance for us.

The regrettable slip was experienced by many who explored and surveyed ground ahead, before the construction plans were made. They went to places where cliffs loomed on one side of the path and crevasses opened on the other. They walked around abrupt turns and navigated up and down steep ascents and descents. The ground along the path was often covered with slippery ice or heavy snow, which made it difficult to distinguish the passable areas from the impassable. So, scores of them slipped quite unexpectedly down into crevices deep below the ledge they stood on. Such accidents were often fatal, of course.

Most of our accidental deaths stemmed from the leaders' unwise leading, or rather, from the Communists' mistreatment of us prisoners. On the brink of a precipice around a sharp corner of the path in the Sun Moon Mountains, for instance, we were made to dig a tunnel into a mountainside. (They would rather have a thousand of us pass away than admit that the spot was impassable.) As we dug and dug and dug with our inefficient implements, we were as slow as sculptors carving masterpieces, and as careful. We were divided into small groups, each group provided with two big chisels and four big hammers. Every chisel, as thick as one's wrist and about 1.7 meters long, was held by two men while it was punched into the rock. Each hammer weighed about eight kilograms, and five men took turns using the four hammers. After we dug to a certain depth, we used shorter chisels and other implements. We toiled as always, fourteen hours a day. We often thought we were like a handful of termites nibbling at a sequoia tree. Yet we were much slower and did not enjoy our work at all.

When we were about to finish digging the tunnel (it seemed as though we had only one more meter to go), we suddenly heard a big "bang," followed by a series of rumbles. We saw all sizes of rocks and clumps of earth cascade down like a dry deluge. We fled immediately, but more than seventy of the tunnel-diggers were buried alive. And more than fifty were injured by the rolling rocks or the falls precipitated by them. Most of the injured died later. We just had no way to stop their bleeding. Similar accidents occurred twice after that, though on a smaller scale, each time causing only about ten deaths.

It might have been much easier and safer for us to use dynamite to dig the tunnel, but the Communists were afraid that we might use the dynamite as a weapon for revenge. So we had to go on with our inefficient way of digging holes. As we tried to bore through the rocks, we could never be careless. Any careless moment might bring injury or even death. Sometimes a big rock would fall and crush one of us. Often the chisel caused small splinters of rock to fly into our heads, faces and limbs, while the hammer caused larger splinters to hit our bodies and break our bones. We frequently became "Red-faced Kuan Kungs"* when splinters cut our faces and made them bleed, and our hands were constantly damaged from holding the tools too long and too tightly. When our hands bled, the hammers and chisels became red with blood. That was what the Communists liked best to see, I presume; our red hands holding the red tools and gradually constructing a road on the rugged plateau.

Red, in fact, was for us a symptom of approaching death. Many spat blood, passed blood in their urine, or shed blood from their old bruises or new cuts. Others had bleeding stomachs, bleeding bowels, or bleeding lungs. Many died of heart diseases. Blood was something none of us could spare, though we shed a lot. And anything wrong with this precious fluid was a sign that we were soon leaving for our last, eternal home. Those who were lucky enough to die of diseases usually got little sympathy from us. We thought them very lucky, compared with those who were starved, frozen, shot, or beaten to death. Nevertheless, their "natural deaths" did leave us a chance to say a few words to the "management" about our medical conditions on the plateau. (Though we did not dare to "complain".)

In a sense, we had almost no medical care at all. We had only a few "barefoot mountebanks"† for doctors. They carried some wooden boxes with them in which were stored a little counterfeit tiger balm, some dubious pills, and some scarlet liquid that looked like tincture of iodine. They didn't ever have aspirin tablets. Whenever they applied anything to our bodies, we were sure to feel worse later. Therefore we always avoided seeing our "doctors."

The best way to save our own lives was to feign work (as they

---

*Kuan Kung was a Chinese hero of the "Three Kingdoms Period" (circa 200-240), who was famous for his loyalty and his red face. He is now worshipped throughout China in the form of a red-faced general.
†In China fraudulent doctors often went about barefoot, soliciting patients. They hoped that this quirk would enhance their already mysterious reputations.

feigned medical care). Whenever the leaders came by, we would pretend that we were working very hard. But after they went past, we would work as slowly as possible, hoping thereby to save our energy. The Communists perhaps knew our strategy, but they had no way to prevent it with efficiency. On an open plain, they could easily use fourteen guards to encircle a whole company of laborers and see clearly which laborer was taking it easy. But on the plateau, while we were working along a long, narrow, winding path, the leaders could only station one or two men at several points along the way and ask the others to patrol intensively. This was not completely effective. In fact, we occasionally had good opportunities to slack off.

There was an extent beyond which our idleness could not go; every day we were expected to accomplish a goal. If we fell too far short of the goal, we would be punished. So we just managed to relax for a moment when the guards were not watching. We never really stopped working. In fact, our strategy could only save the strong ones who did not need to rest long. The weak and sick simply did not have a chance to rest long enough to recover their strength. Even if they had been allowed to stand there without having to work, they would have perished soon, due to their poor health, just as poor swimmers would drown in a flood.

After three months' hard and dangerous work, we finally finished the road through the Sun Moon Mountains. Then we continued to extend the road into Touch Heaven Ridge, which we felt, in effect, was like inviting Hell to crash down on us. Fortunately, however, spring was approaching. The snow storms became scarce, finally the ice began to melt. When the bitter cold departed, our labor didn't seem as fatal as before. The mortality rate among us lowered a little bit. Three months later, we opened the road through Touch Heaven Ridge. We then went on toward Black Horse Lake, which was in a wide area of dense forest. Working in the forest, we seemed to be imprisoned in a dark cellar, and seldom saw the sky. In those "dark days" we continued to risk our lives, but, compared with building the sections of road through the Sun Moon Mountains and the Touch Heaven Ridge, this section was easier for us.

Looking back upon the days when we left White Skeleton Beach and came to work among the seven ridges, eight valleys, twelve ledges, and other countless crags and cliffs and valleys in these two big mountain ranges, we really could not believe what we had accomplished. Were we men of miraculous power? we wondered. No, the places we left behind us had been given such nicknames as "Soul-Perishing Vale," "Corpse-Accumulating Dale," "the Slope of Sweat," all suggesting our feelings and the hardship of building the Chinghai Highway. Some years later when the road was finished, sightseers began to travel the path of our misery. They took pictures of camel caravans and scenic vistas, not knowing that these scenes hid our tortured bodies and souls, figures clothed in black and white toiling in red.

It was later revealed by the leaders themselves that in constructing the road through the two big mountain ranges, about 1,720 of us had died. In those months we were really like beasts of the underworld trapped in an endless life-in-death. We believed that in the whole history of mankind no one had ever been made to labor as brutally as ourselves. On one hand we were proud of our achievement. We thought we outdid the tightrope dancers and acrobats in creating breathtaking moments and miracles. We risked our lives everyday for at least ten hours and for over two hundred days on end, whereas they only risked their lives for a few minutes every day when performing. On the other hand, we could not forget the inhumanity with which we had been treated. Corpses shedding blood and littering the frozen ground painted forever a heartbreaking scene in our minds, in contrast to what is our legacy: a scenic road reddened with the beauty of peach blossoms for sightseers.

After finishing the sections through the Sun Moon Mountains, Touch Heaven Ridge, and Black Horse Lake, our new ordeal in constructing the road was to build a bridge across the Pa Yin River.

We began early in the spring of 1954. At that time snow fell almost every day, and the river's surface remained frozen. We found the Pa Yin was different from other rivers in that the water at the surface and bottom remained frozen in early spring; the water at the bottom of other rivers was rather warm at that time. The river was normally five hundred meters wide. The more rapidly flowing water of its middle usually occupied an area three or four hundred meters across. In days of heavy rainfall or quick thawing snow, the river could become as wide as six hundred meters and as deep as three hundred meters in some places.

When we tried to build the bridge, we were performing a burlesque with our legs in the cold weather. Legs! Legs! Legs! Yes, nothing but legs and legs and legs! It was a big forest of legs—thirty pairs, fifty pairs, one hundred pairs, two hundred pairs, or a thousand pairs of legs at a time! As snow kept descending from the sky, the countless legs formed ten concentric circles in the river. Ten or more people standing arm in arm in the river with their bodies close together formed the innermost circle. Their legs were covered only with thin trousers and their feet were bare. The next circle was about one meter away and was composed of about fifty pairs of legs. The circles grew in size, and the legs grew in number until, at the outermost circle, they totaled over two hundred. But what were those circles of legs for? Believe it or not, they were planted in the river to form a dam so that the construction of the bridge could begin!

Those legs were all "select" ones. They belonged to people the Reds considered "criminals." And none of them were too short. Long legs, the Communists thought, were best for obstructing the flow of the Pa Yin River. If you counted them all, you would find about twelve hundred pairs of legs, all standing with their owners in the water. And with what effect? After being planted in the river for three or four hours, they seemed to cause the water to flow a bit more slowly. And that was enough for the laborers to dig a channel in time to drain the water. It might seem incredible, but the draining channel was fifteen meters deep, thirty meters wide, and about six li long—a tremendous handiwork completed in less than half a month by the tens of thousands who were undergoing "labor corrections" under fear of death.

With little flowing water to obstruct the work, we started to lay a foundation for the bridge within the innermost circle of legs. We laid the foundation by driving wooden stakes (sheet piles) into the ground and filling the staked-off areas with huge rocks and stones, so that these areas would eventually look like round terraces, each having a diameter of one meter and rising two meters above the riverbed. While we built the terraces, we were asked to sing: "Yi Yo Hai Heh, Yi Yo Hai Heh! Are we providing for our country or is our country providing for us? . . . We'd better get it through our heads!" With the terraces as foundation, we built the abutments of the bridge. When finished, the abutments were as high as three- or four-story buildings. The Pa Yin River Bridge was built entirely by hand, without the aid of modern technology. And the manual work proceeded in the cold season when snow was frequent.

On the first day, some six hundred young "criminals" were selected to stand in the shallow part of the river. As they stood there, the water lapped at their thighs or their bellies. Each of those chosen suffered from two sources of cold: his upper body, which was above the water, had to withstand the frequent snow while the lower part of him, which was beneath the water, was chilled by the icy current. Most people could not bear standing there for long. After three hours, their legs would lose all feeling. Some people would faint away and drop into the water.

Those who collapsed were quickly carried back. They were then put in front of a fire made from heaps of recently reaped dry weeds. It was hoped that the warmth would help the men to regain consciousness and thaw their frozen legs. They were no sooner treated that way, however, than an astounding thing happened. One of those being thawed by the fire dropped to the ground as his lower legs suddenly dislocated from his knees, like two living branches snapped on a young tree. This astonishing thing happened not just to one victim, but to many who were being "cured" with fire. All of us were appalled to see one lower leg after another dislocate from the upper leg as the fire hastily warmed the frozen people. We later learned that the lower leg is attached to the knee by bands of tissue, the ligaments, which, frozen through, will break easily if heated suddenly and quickly. We made this discovery too late. Within the first two days of the "fire treatment," no fewer than a hundred pairs of legs were dislocated, and some three or four hundred men had contracted arthritis, though they had been spared dislocated legs.

"A sacrifice of ten thousand, fifty thousand, or even one hundred thousand people cannot be too dear a cost in the building of our bridge!" shouted Hao Teng-ke at a rally of ten thousand people involved with the construction. The "leader" was plainly adopting the traditional communist tactic of the willing sacrifice of a great multitude of people in return for victory, when he was commissioned to conquer the Pa Yin River with a bridge.

It was only natural that the leader should force the "criminals" to battle the river with their legs when he could think of no other means. Even the leader was not without some reservations, however. He was concerned about the possibility of the failure of his mission, as too many people were losing their legs or lives in following his plan. In order to save his own skin, he called a meeting to discuss how the sacrifice could be reduced to a minimum. Some of the more daring prisoners suggested that they should thenceforth be allowed to take turns standing in the water for only half an hour at a time. The suggestion was followed, but it was soon clear that half an hour was still too long a time for the all-too-human legs. Finally, the time was cut to twenty minutes. Thus, the poor men could save their legs from being dislocated though they could not prevent themselves from getting arthritis.

Fortunately for me, I was assigned the task of boiling water for the bridge builders. I did this along with Ling Hsien-yang and Chan Wen-hu. We were only occasionally asked to take a twenty-minute dip in the river, so I was able to spare my legs any serious damage.

The Communists planned to establish "the State Government of West Chinghai" on the bank of the Pa Yin River. They made the plan because the site was in the center of a great basin (covering an area of about one hundred square kilometers), surrounded by the Chilian Mountains, and their extended ranges in the West and North, and by other mountains and hills in the East and South. The site was also at a strategic place on the Chinghai-Tibet Road. They planned to establish a government there with a view to making it an important military bastion so that the four provinces of Kansu, Chinghai, Sinkiang, and Tibet could be well prepared for war against Russia or India. But the establishment of the state government depended on the building of the Pa Yin Bridge. So at the Rally of Ten Thousand Men, we all heard Hso Teng-ke speak emphatically: "This bridge construction allows for no sabotage, strike, feigned sickness, idleness, or resistance of any sort. I will allow your overseers to execute anyone who acts against my prohibitions." The construction was in effect the destruction of the poor "criminals," who had only their arms and legs to sacrifice for the work. It was indeed perverse to attempt to finish the bridge within so short a time without the use of any modern machines. But the Communists were so used to being perverse that to try to stop their perversity would be like trying to get tigers to become vegetarians. Their perversity always bore the fruit of calamity, and the calamity always fell on the poor laborers first.

The laborers' tools such as shovels, pickaxes, baskets, and carts were all made crudely and literally from scratch, by various teams of workers. To make shovels, a team of workers had first to go and dig iron ore. Next, a team of blacksmiths had to strike the hot iron. Then, a team of carpenters had to cut trees to make wooden handles. As the nature of the work varied, different teams of masons, stone workers, or other laborers were needed.

The strain of building the bridge was worse than that of besieging a city during a war. As ten of thousands of people busied themselves around the clock (they were seldom allowed to sleep more than five hours a day), digging the channel, driving the stakes, making the abutments, etc., it seemed like so many ants struggling in a hot frying pan. The difference was only that uphill or downhill, on this bank or that bank, near or far, wherever the "criminals" worked, there were leaders standing nearby ready to flourish their whips or clubs on those suspected of laziness, whereas ants, as far as we know, never undergo forced labor.

Death, again, was a frequent occurrence among the bridge builders. As snowstorms came, many froze. As food supplies ran low, many more starved. But the most direct cause of death was overwork: So many simply passed away from exhaustion. Some became desperate and committed suicide. Others had a stronger will to live, but a careless act often ended their lives, too. Chen Fu-sheng, a gentle fellow on our team, was carrying a big stone down the hill one snowy day when he suddenly slipped and rolled down a steep path. He was severely injured. His face and limbs were bruised and broken. The Communists, upon seeing his bloody face, simply put a bullet through his head. They said later that Chen was trying to escape. And according to the Communists' practice, all those who were caught escaping were shot immediately no matter how young or useful they were.

Some people who went into the mountains to cut wood or carry stones were bitten or even eaten by wild beasts. Originally the mountains had been a rather safe place, as far as wild beasts were concerned. It is believed that thousands of years ago, when the mountainous area was covered with dense forests and sparsely inhabited by people, the wild animals there—leopards, bears, wolves, elks, and monkeys—had no fear of humans. When we began to build the road at White Skeleton Beach, in fact, we were used to seeing beasts and birds mixing harmoniously with human beings. They would take food from our hands. Occasionally they would stand staring at people working near by, like spectators watching a fascinating stage show. Now and then on a dark night, we heard the howls of fierce animals and became frightened, but in the daytime, when no such sounds were heard, we thought of the wilderness as a peaceful place. Deer, hares, goats, oxen, and monkeys also saw us as friends. They approached us, smelled us, licked our hands, or touched us gently with their horns.

The harmony between us and nature was soon destroyed by the Communists however. When shortages of food became frequent, they started to hunt wild animals on a large scale, and great tension and hostility developed in the originally peaceful land. At first, only the hunters who had bad aim were madly attacked by wild animals. Later, it seemed as if all humanity was the enemy of nature, and many unlucky men who underwent "labor corrections" in the mountains were killed by leopards, bears, or wolves, and reduced to skeletons in the wilderness.

Notwithstanding the numerous means of death, the building of the bridge continued. After we finished the abutments, we were engaged in placing wooden beams, trusses, rails, and planks, on and over the abutments. Finally, as we had no cement, we ground stones into small pieces of gravel, blended these with sand and soil, and then used the mixture to pave the road on the bridge. Such a structure naturally couldn't last long. As early as a year later it began to show signs of weakening under the pressure of the heavy burdens that it so often bore. One night, with a big rumbling sound, it suddenly toppled down. Fortunately only a herd of cattle, a flock of sheep, and some camels were thrown into the river; the pedestrians and the owners of the stock who had followed behind were safe.

Somwhere near the bridge on the bank of the river, we also built a three-story department store in the same primitive manner. The Communists thought it would be permanent, but less than a year after the store was opened, it collapsed suddenly in a rainstorm. The casualties resulting from the accident were heavy; forty-two people, including the Communist leader, some salesmen, and many custom-ers, were killed or injured. After the accident, the Communists investi-gated, and any "criminals" who had had a hand in designing the store and preparing its drawings received increased penalties, along with the masons, carpenters, blacksmiths, and others who had been in-volved in the construction. The penalties were increased such that a death convict on reprieve was executed at once, a life prisoner was given a death sentence on reprieve, and some long-term prisoners were condemned to life imprisonment. These increases caused more than ten of us to die.

Misfortunes, indeed, never come singly. Some years later, the same "criminals" took the responsibility for redesigning and rebuild-ing the Pa Yin River Reservoir, and in 1960 (not long after it was completed and put in use), the reservoir likewise crashed down suddenly one night at about ten o'clock while a violent rainstorm was raging in the region. It was a great disaster. Of the two thousand people living below the reservoir, only about three hundred survived the flood from the broken dam by escaping to the neighboring heights.

By a conservative estimate, four thousand casualties were di-rectly connected with these three great engineering "achievements" of the Communists: the Pa Yin River Bridge, the department store, and the reservoir. The building of the bridge alone caused more than two hundred deaths and about two thousand injuries, including those whose arms and legs were dislocated, those who were seized with apoplexy or had heart attacks, and those who got frostbite or went mad. The sad truth behind these figures is that the injured were never given any rest or special care, with which they might have survived. Later, the "criminals" were sent to Telingha Farm for further "labor corrections."

These three "accidents" also runied Hao Teng-ke. Hao was a so-called "uprising general" (one who formerly belonged to the Nationalist Party but became a turncoat and was awarded a high position in the Communist regime). Originally subordinate to Tun Pao-shan, a Nationalist general, he was made a county executive. When he was sent to Chinghai to take charge of the "labor corrections" there, it was obvious that the Communists were carrying out the policy of "using the Yi to rule the Yi."* And it was also obvious that no matter how flattering he might be and no matter how earnestly he showed his loyalty to the Communist Party, he would never be really trusted by its high-ranking members. Hao was later severely criticized and "publicly prosecuted" for the three ignominious accidents. Unable to stand the shame and torture of the public prosecution, Hao finally committed suicide. The way he ended his own life was very peculiar. With his arms folded across his chest, he plunged himself headlong into a huge crock filled with water. This way of committing suicide was immortalized as "planting the onion upside down."

---

*The "Yi" were the barbarians or foreign tribes in the East of ancient China. Here, the old saying is adopted by the Communists to refer to the use of cadres with the "wrong" political background to control prisoners with the "wrong" political background.

A Tsaidamu Vignette

You might well wonder how I managed to survive so many terrible ordeals to tell such a surprising story. It's a natural question and one I am indeed happy to answer. Among other things, I was saved by a miraculous encounter. Without it, I would have been reduced to a pile of bones like so many others in the secretly blockaded region. To tell the story of this encounter, I must first describe the setting.

After we finished the section through the Touch Heaven Ridge, the number of road-builders (about forty or fifty thousand) was too great to manage. So one-fifth were sent to Hsin Tse Farm, while the rest of us were moved to complete the section through Black Horse Lake.

Black Horse Lake was no longer a lake when we arrived there. It was only a dry bed covered with dense vegetation. The area was such a tangle of primeval trees that it seemed as if you had entered a dungeon completely shut off from the light. To build a road through that place was like groping for a path in the dark. There were gorilla-like creatures, snow panthers, black bears, wolves, and serpents. The hardships we had to endure were as bad as before, but I was lucky; I belonged then to the Chore Section. I didn't actually have to go out and build the road. My daily duty was to boil water for the thirsty laborers.

In our Labor Correction Team, there was an unwritten rule: If a "criminal" did something successfully within his daily duties, he was entitled to continue doing the same thing. Since I never neglected to boil the water, therefore, I was allowed to stay in the kitchen for a long time. My chore was not easy, but it reduced my exposure to the dangers outside, and helped me avoid seeing the threatening faces of the Communists all the time. Sometimes when I was boiling water in the tent, I felt temporarily free from our taskmasters' iron discipline and considered myself lucky.

For the half-year we underwent "labor corrections" in that region of Chinghai, we never washed our faces, not to mention our bodies, because we had only a scanty supply of water. We all deemed it a great pleasure to be able to drink a bowl of boiled water at a meal. What scarce water we had was taken from nearby tarns or ponds, and for the kitchen worker whose job it was, fetching water was a very painful task and, at times, a fatal one.

When you went to a pond for water, you had to crack open its frozen surface. Sometimes the layer of ice was a foot thick or more. You had to drill the ice and break it with a hammer. If you were careless, you might slip and fall into the opening you had made, perishing in a moment. Our former kitchen worker, Hsu Liang, indeed forfeited his life falling into a hole in the ice.

In order to fetch water successfully in winter, one had to learn to walk on the ice first. An inexperienced man from the South would often fall on the icy ground and be injured. A Mr. Tsai slipped on his way to a pond to fetch water, broke his right leg, and fainted away. The leaders, finding him absent that night, sent out some people to search for him. They found him groaning on the ground, unable to get up. Leader Chao immediately took out his gun and shot him dead. Later, when the poor man's corpse was brought back, the Communists said that Tsai was trying to escape and was executed because of his "anti-revolutionary action."

We worked through the forests and eventually reached a prairie. According to the Chinghai Labor Corrections Bureau's plans, the prairie was to be developed into a complex of public highways and large farms. The Communists hoped that the "enemies of the Party," and their relatives living in the coastal provinces and in the provinces along the Yangtze River, could one day be moved to the prairie to develop it.

When we first arrived, the grass was high above our knees. The grass plain extended more than two hundred kilometers all the way down to the bank of the infamous Pa Yin River. Our "leaders" decided that all the grass had to be burned before we could tidy up the land and get logs from the mountains for building houses. For ages, this grassy plain had been the Mongolian and Tibetan nomads' grazing land and the source of their livelihood. All year round, the nomads drove their livestock to the plain for its grass and its water. The government's decision completely ignored the nomads' economic interests, and the nomads swore never to submit to it: "Can we let them burn up the source of our life so easily? Are we cattle too, that they can drive us here or there?"

The nomads' growing protest was, in fact, a sign of impending war. After learning the route of our work, over a thousand nomads carried their tents to the region and put them up all along our intended route. They declared that we had no right to burn the grass or build roads without their permission. They threatened never to move their tents unless their rights were honored. We often saw them riding their strong horses, carrying iron or wooden weapons in their hands, with their guns concealed. From time to time, they drove horses, cattle, sheep, and camels into our path and excited them into a stampede by whistling, roaring, and singing.

The most imposing attendants of the demonstration, however, were the Tibetan dogs. They were all black and seemed as big as small horses. They were normally used to guard sheep, but about two thousand of them were now made to patrol the route. As they moved back and forth at their owner's whistles, they looked like loyal, brave soldiers, ready to die in action. The warlike atmosphere was further strengthened by several belligerent Tibetans, who came to "the front" eager to attack.

All this, of course, was a posture of challenge. And to face that challenge, the Communist leaders had their own studied response. One morning, as soon as we heard the whistles for work, we saw, quite extraordinarily, all of our leaders (about forty of them) come out together and walk menacingly over to us. Then to the three or four thousand of us, Chen Chung-hao, the "Great Team Leader," shouted a warning and some encouragement.

"Dear obedient fellows!" (This greeting was a term of endearment employed especially for this occasion.) "Your job today is different. I hope you will be ready for it. When you set fire to the grass, please be aware of the nomads. They may cause some trouble. But don't be afraid. You know we are armed well enough. Remember. Just go ahead with your tasks. If anything should happen, our strong arms will protect you . . ." He lured us into envisioning a promising future. He said that once we had built ranches there, we would have great rewards, our penalties would be reduced, and we would be able to settle down in the area with our families. The land he described was an Eden, but his honeyed words could not cover up his real intentions.

"Bear in mind. The implements you hold in hand today are also weapons to protect you. Do as you are told to do. Burn all that you are told to burn! Count on us. The Communist Party can even heave up the sky after it has fallen down!" Even as he exhorted us, however, he ended by asking, "Now do any of you have any suggestions?"

To tell the truth, for the last two days we had been thinking that a war between the nomads and the Communists' "Liberating Army" would be inevitable, and that once the war started, the area would be bathed in blood. We pictured a rain of bullets and a field of corpses half concealed by a screen of smoke. We imagined ourselves as observers at the war, gloating over the misfortunes of the Communist Party. But after we heard Leader Chen's "talk," we suddenly realized that this leader of the "Proletarian Pioneers" was killing two birds with one stone; he was trying to persuade us to die for the Party and weaken the nomads' attack at the same time. Chen offered us a gourmet meal, but the recipe was a mixture of menace, allurement, fraud, provocation, and victimization. Seeing his devil's scheme and hearing his question, I suddenly shouted, "Report!"

"What?" Chen stared at me. Thousands of other eyes were also fixed on me.

I went over to him and said, "To do as you told us would very likely lead to bloodshed. You know that some lives are valuable. It might not be a matter of great concern to sacrifice the lives of several hundred criminals. But if the casualties should fall on the side of the innocent shepherds too, don't you think the Supreme Authority might want to investigate and perhaps blame even the Provincial Governors involved?" I asked the question calmly, knowing that my reasoning should have some effect on the "leaders," who, as experience told me, only feared their own "leaders." Then I added, "Has the People's Government ever talked with the shepherds?"

My questions made Chen pause. After a while, he answered, "Yes, we had a long talk with them yesterday. In fact, the negotiation went on until twelve o'clock last night. But they maintained their opposition."

"I think the negotiation should go on through the influence of the Party," Chan Wen-hu interrupted in a quiet voice.

"We did use the Party influence. But their Party members upheld the interests of their side the whole time. They would never accept our view." After the explanation, all was quiet for a while. Then Leader Chen spoke again. "The task handed down by the Provincial Commissar must be completed by any means possible. Do you think we can stop because of their objection?"

"But we cannot help thinking of the aftermath, can we?" I continued.

"The aftermath must be a constructed road and completed ranches. So, our decision must be to sacrifice everything for this goal."

Leader Chao, who was responsible for our instructional affairs, unexpectedly came forward and said with authority, "But can't we make the sacrifice without shedding blood?"

"Do you mean you have a better idea? Speak if you do," said Chen.

We could see the leadership was interested in us. They knew there were many talented men among their "criminals." If they condescended to beg instructions of us, we could help them solve many problems. Chu Tan stepped forth immediately and gave an analysis of the case in his eloquent voice.

"As we all know," he said, "this is a serious problem. If anything should happen, who'd take the responsibility? If bloodshed is unavoidable, it would be better to ask for directions first from the Provincial Commissar. If you make any decision without the superior's directions, you'll have to take the full responsibility for any ill results. Suppose something unfavorable did happen, what would the investigators say? You couldn't very well tell them you made the decision all by yourselves, could you? And you couldn't tell them we pressured you into it either. For who'd believe we 'criminals' ever had any say in the matter? If some Mongolians or Tibetans should be harmed or killed, who'd believe we dared to harm or kill them without your orders? Besides, the minority people have their right to say something, too. They may appeal to the People's Government or the Central Government. When that happens, it may be too late for regrets."

Chu's words really hit home. The "leaders" remained silent for quite a while, not knowing what to say. Then Chan Wen-hu, grasping the opportunity, supported Chu's point thoughtfully but straightforwardly: "We criminals really could die for the cause, but you must consider the nation's tribal policy. To hurt a few minority people may result in a big civil problem."

We had awakened the "leaders" from an impractical dream and exposed their foolhardiness. The "leaders" naturally hated us for this, but they refrained from speaking their minds. Finally, Chao said in a low tone, "On the basis of your consideration, do you mean we have to forsake building the road and the ranches?"

On hearing the question, I thought, "What a crafty guy this Chao is! He's trying to set us up for a fall. If we answer yes, they'll be able to accuse us of sabotage—of intentionally evading our task of building the road and the ranches." Chu Tan was one step ahead of all of us with a proper reply.

"We naturally cannot forsake our task. We need to build the road, and we need to build the ranches. But above all, we need to do anything possible to prevent bloodshed. If we can do that, I believe you, as our leaders, would be rewarded for having accomplished this feat." Chu said this ingratiatingly, but he adopted a severe attitude when he continued, "We cannot rush out to confront them today. No, not today. Otherwise, something unpleasant is sure to happen. If you intend to solve problems, you must face them with the proper attitude. See your future, leaders, in our present. Even one error could make one a criminal like us."

Chu's last remark was the truth, but it was somewhat inappropriate, considering the situation. Chang Hsiao-sung cut in to change the subject. "I think we can delay reporting the situation to the Commissar until we have solved the problem," he said. "If the problem is solved peacefully, I believe you leaders will be highly praised for it."

Then Ling Hsien-yang added, "If, as you said, you had a long talk with the nomads' leaders yesterday but could not settle the dispute, I think we should send some others to talk to them again. If you can trust us, I believe some of us laborers could also work as negotiators. If we should fail to make peace again, it would still not be too late to take other measures."

This was a sensible suggestion. Chen, the "Great Team Leader," looked around at the other disconcerted "leaders" and said, "All right, all of you go back to your tents first. We'll have a meeting and let you know the final decision soon. All section leaders, please come to my office for the meeting. All others, go back to your own tents and remain there until we contact you.

Back at the tents, we all sat on our beds waiting—and thinking, too. We thought that we had possibly averted a crisis. Nevertheless, a second crisis might occur all too soon. When I was thinking of how we could best secure our position, Teng Chung, who was sitting beside me, whispered to me, "Will they machine-gun us and leave our corpses on the field for beasts?"

I answered softly, "If we went out today, we would certainly become fodder for beasts. However it seems the critical moment has already passed. Of course, until the section leaders return, we won't know whether it's good or bad. We have to brace ourselves for any possibility. I know they are most afraid of our contacting the nomads. They fear we might ally ourselves with them. Even if they agree to let some of us go and act as negotiators, they will surely send some of their men to spy on us."

Before we finished the tête-à-tête, our section leader, a "criminal" like us, stepped into the tent, smiling. "Good news!" he said quickly. "We don't have to go out today. They have agreed to choose some of us for negotiation representatives. Among them will be six who are natives of Chinghai, including Ma Ming-su and Ma Chi-wu."

The two Mas were in our group. They both knew the Tibetan language. One was a graduate of the Chinese Political University in Nanking, and was once a secretary colonel. The other was formerly the Nationalist Party Secretary of Minho County in Chinghai.

We were all glad to hear the news. It was our victory; our wisdom and courage had at least temporarily converted an impending battle into a talk of truce. "Did you discuss how to go on with the negotiations?" I asked our section leader, for I was interested in knowing the details.

"We did have some discussion about that. But on the whole, the 'leaders' wanted to do it their own way."

"Haven't they been refused by the nomads already? Why should they stick to their way? Wouldn't it get them nowhere again?" Chen Meng-yu asked angrily.

"I hope for success this time. They accepted some ideas from us. They are going to call the nine representatives [the six Chinghai natives mentioned above and three others, from either Tibet or Mongolia], to another meeting to brief them before they go on their mission. Ah, yes," our section leader turned immediately to the two Mas and continued, "you two brothers, you must be well-prepared for the talk."

The two Mas nodded their heads. Ma Ming-su then said, "Although the matter is complicated, I think talk is feasible as far as we two are concerned. Our relationship with the tribes is based on more than a friendship of only six months or a year. For safety, peace, and love on both sides [the tribal people and the 'criminals'], we will naturally do our best. We will not let the Communists benefit from our mutual loss."

I added quickly, "I hope you can explain tactfully to the shepherd brothers that this negotiation is carried on not for the Communists' good, but, rather, to cripple their scheme. We have no conflicts with them and will not fight each other because a conflict is imposed on us. We are really travelers in the same boat. We care only about our common goal, to escape from the 'Red Disaster.' We cannot let bloodshed pave the way for the Communist Regime." The two Mas and my other fellow "criminals" seemed to be deeply touched. I continued, "Really, we must use our wisdom to prevent this war.

You know, the Chinghai Headquarters is quite near here. Their soldiers may come at any time to make a bloody thing even bloodier."

Half an hour later, the nine representatives were called to the meeting and sent to negotiate with the shepherds. They were "accompanied" (in fact, guarded) by three Communist leaders who did not know the Tibetan language, and who also did not suspect that the representatives were taking advantage of the language difference. In fact, the representatives were very good "accomplices." They talked of one thing to the nomads but quite another to the Communist leaders. They dared to do so because they believed that yielding to the Communists' requests would be worse than trying to defy them.

After the first day's negotiation, the two Mas brought back good news. The shepherds knew how we suffered and they sympathized with us. They had seen us go out very early and come back very late, laboring all day long without sufficient food and clothing. They had also seen our scrawny figures constantly threatened by whips, clubs, and guns. They had witnessed us injured at work, killed in accidents, and tortured with the bad weather. In fact, they had thought of helping us if they could. They did not regard us as "criminals" but as horribly abused men, who deserved only pity and assistance.

At nine o'clock the next morning, the two Mas left to attend the negotiation again. They came back at eleven that night. When they entered the tent, they were smiling very happily, looking as if they had just attended a banquet. The problem had been solved. The shepherds had agreed to let us burn the grass within the boundaries of the intended route for the new road but the width of the route was limited to three meters.

Before we burned the grass on the route, we dug a ditch two meters wide along each side of the road. The ditch was meant to carry water away and serve as a blockade to the grass-burning fire. At the end of each section of road would be a pile of stones or a shallow pond of water so that the fire would stop there. We were so careful in burning the grass that the nomads later agreed to let us burn the grounds for the future farms as well. They were happy to find that our work actually did not ruin the source of their livelihood, but even contributed to the development of "their land."

In the course of the negotiation, the two Mas enjoyed the best food from the tribal people. Over the year of "labor corrections," the Mas had been suffering badly from hunger. But during the talk with the nomads, their stomachs were often filled with Tibetan delicacies. They would have sampled some wine, too, if the Communist Leaders hadn't forbidden it.

After the negotiations, we noticed that some of the Communists had changed their attitudes. Leader Hsu, for instance, became more polite to us. He was one of the few Communists who still had a conscience, who could still take pity on us. He really appreciated our contribution to the peace-making talks. The others who still kept us at arm's length had nevertheless lessened their distrust of us. Now they would pass without concern when they saw tribespeople talking or playing with us in our tents or where we worked. In fact, our tents and the nomads' tents were located on the same grassy grounds, while the Communist tents were pitched a mile or two away. Close contact with the shepherds was only natural, and the Communists could hardly have succeeded in disturbing it even if they had tried. (In addition, the tribal youth were all very tough and daring. Any confrontation could lead to a fight that might get the leaders dismissed or even arrested if they did not act properly.)

A sort of intimacy gradually developed between us "criminals" and the shepherd youth. And it was in this atmosphere that I had my miraculous encounter.

A stroke of luck fell quite unexpectedly on Ling Hsien-yang, Chan Wen-hu, and me. It was at midnight. By then we had seen the two Mas come back with reddened faces, filled stomachs, and an odor of not-yet-digested meat. We had also heard the two lucky ones talk about the entertainment they had with the nomads. That midnight, we felt especially hungry and consequently vicariously attended our own banquet. As our mouths watered and our tongues mentally licked our lips, we imagined before us a ram—the carcass of a whole ram, a ram already dressed and well-boiled, a ram yellowish-white with fat and ready to be devoured.

It really took us some time before we realized that what was before our eyes was the real thing. It was brought to us by four

Tibetans. They said they wanted us to accept it as a gift. But why? Why should they have done that? We three repeatedly said "Thank you" to the four generous men, but we really had no grasp of the situation. We had long ago forgotten about the existence of generosity in the world. It was not until later that we figured it out.

It happened that the three of us were in the Chore Section at that time. Our duty was to boil water for the whole team of laborers. Since the kitchen was some distance from the laborers' working place, we were only casually supervised by the leaders. Besides, our direct overseer was Leader Hsu, who, as I said, was comparatively kindhearted. So we three kitchen workers had a comparatively easy life. When the Tibetans came by, whistling, with their livestock, they would drop in sometimes to chat. They loved to hear us gossip about all the "exotic" things in Shanghai. For them, that metropolis was full of anecdotes, legends, and life. They loved our gossip so much that they often stayed four or five hours at a time, like an opium-eater addicted to his den. Sometimes we simply couldn't keep them away. Once in a while the Communist "leaders" would come for food or drinks and see them chatting with us, but those tough men weren't afraid of the Reds. They chattered on. They even made sarcastic remarks to belittle the Communists and drive them away.

In the winter the nomads often picked out the weak cattle, sheep or camels, and killed them for food. Our ram was killed with two others on the same afternoon. They sent it to us along with the edible organs from the two others to thank us for chatting with them like close friends.

Although the ram they sent us was only about six kilograms of meat, it was like a merciful Buddha come to rescue us! We even fancied that the ram's fat was as white as a Buddha's skin, and its brownish-yellow lean meat was like the color of a Buddha's painted face. We did not dare to eat it at once. We first divided it and put it into two barrels. We watched the two barrels greedily, as fascinated as if we had been marveling at two famous works of art. Occasionally, Ling, Chan, and I would glance at each other and smile. We knew we had something too precious to lose, even if the way to lose it was to gratify our appetites.

When the day's work was finished, we three took turns going

to fetch our six "woh-woh toes" and some boiled vegetables for dinner. We did so because we feared our treasure might be discovered if we were all absent at once.

The dinner that evening was for us as important as a king's banquet, though not as formal. I cut our mutton with vigor while we all held our breath looking at it with love, hate, joy, sorrow, greed, regret: with indescribable emotion. At the time, we could barely understand our own complex state of mind. It seemed we were staring at our hopes and desires, not just at a ram. We knew that with the mutton we would be able to live on for a time without suffering the pains of malnutrition.

With our nerves all strained, we bit and munched, fearing all the time that we might be caught enjoying the extra food. But what a gratifying taste! We felt we had entered the inexpressible enlightened state of Zen Buddhists. For the first time in a thousand days, we had genuinely eaten our fill.

We finished the ram in three days. During those three days we all took pleasure in stuffing our bellies with the godsent meat. In our most gluttonous moments we would not have minded if our bellies had been burst open like umbrellas.

It is ironic that we three kitchen workers should have come to this state, especially considering our personal histories. Ling was formerly president of a famous university in Shanghai; Chan used to be general manager of China's best-selling newspaper; and I was the son of a governor of a Chinese province. In the old days all our food was redolent with spices. But now what we took for divine food was only a mass of bony mutton boiled in water, without any seasoning at all. Later we wondered why we hadn't gagged at the odor of the mutton, as we would have done in days long past, since the meat had been cooked with neither fragrant garlic nor onion. Is hunger a magician that can turn a rank-smelling piece of meat into a sumptuous filet?

"Ah, dear me. . . . What big hotel in Shanghai have I not patronized? What good restaurant food, domestic or foreign, have I not tasted? But how come this lamb chop seems to suit my palate best? Why is it the best appetizer I've ever had?" Ling wondered.

"Yes, old friend! I was an epicure of Shanghai, too. But tonight's dish also seemed to me most delicious." Chan agreed, patting his large belly with one hand.

I added, "I read once of a prime minister of the Ching Dynasty who had eaten some taro root sold by an old peddler in the time before he was an official and was on the brink of starvation. So he claimed the taro root to be the most delectable food in the world. I think we can say our food tonight outdoes that taro root in taste and flavor."

Our conversation eased our digestion a little bit. Later when we remembered how we enjoyed the good cheer by the fireside, how we hiccoughed with stuffed stomachs, and how we chatted with gusto, we really couldn't believe we had dared to do so. Had we been crazy? Maybe. But perhaps it was not so much the result of gluttony as of our desire to survive.

A pair of eyes was gazing at me. It was a bright pair of big black eyes each with a double fold at the lower edge of its upper eyelid, and long eyelashes. The eyes radiated light and grace. The light was compelling and struck me suddenly like a flash of lightning. It attracted my attention to the tenderness suggested by her long curving eyebrows and her white oval face flushed with health. I was suspicious. But of what?

My life so far had been without dreams, flowers, fragrances. She seemed to have appeared in a dream and brought with her all the fragrance of a flower garden. How I would cherish that dream from afar!

Wearing two long braids of ebony black hair, a large black hat, a long black fur-lined dress with a slanting embroidered silk collar and two inches of embroidered silk at the hem, and a wide girdle of apricot yellow, she looked like a big black embroidered butterfly. At that time, I had not been touched by a woman for three years, nor had I given any thought to approaching one. Her sudden appearance certainly surprised me. No woman had ever struck me with such grace and beauty.

"My name is Yelusa and this is my sister Yama." My God, she was speaking fluent Mandarin! I scrutinized her closely. When her eyes met mine, she seemed meaningfully absorbed in me. She appeared not a bit shy.

"And my name is Han Wei-tien," I said. "This is Dr. Ling Hsien-yang, former president of Fuchiang University in Shanghai. And this is Dr. Chan Wen-hu, General Manager of *Shanghai News* in the old days."

"Han was a general. He was chief of a Bureau, too," Ling added.

Yelusa still gazed at me, seemingly sunk in thought. We three kitchen workers, with our past histories and present situation, must have presented a riddle hardly comprehensible to the young girls. In fact, to any of the young Tibetans, the whole crowd of us with our black clothes, forced to labor in the wilderness, were a big puzzle.

The girls, as we later learned, came out of curiosity. They had heard of the three water-boiling "redresses." They had also heard that we were from Shanghai, city of legends. The Tibetans fancied it had gold-paved streets and more gorgeous buildings than the palaces of Lhasa. They may have heard, as well, that two of us had even been to the unimaginable West. So they came like treasure seekers, though the only treasures we could display were bits of lore, a handful of interesting anecdotes, a few pieces of exotic news, and some old wives' tales.

Yelusa told us many things about herself, especially regarding her parents. She said her father was a Han* although her mother was a Tibetan. Her father, Li, had been a brigade Chief of Staff under the command of General Sun Lien-chung. In 1925, when General Sun led his army over the Chinghai Plateau, Li first met his future Tibetan wife and fell in love with her. They had a son and two daughters. Yelusa, the elder daughter, had a Han name, too, Li Hsi-Mei. Yelusa's brother, called Techinpa in Tibetan, was to inherit the Tibetan title

---

*Like Han Wei-tien, Yelusa is probably a descendant of the Manchus of Northern China.

"Thousand Household Chief." Yelusa's grandfather had possessed that title, which was passed down to his only daughter, that is, Yelusa's mother. So Yelusa's family were aristocrats in their tribe, and were respected as such. Yelusa was twenty-three years old at that time, her brother twenty-five, and her sister twenty-two. She and her sister looked very much alike, but her sister was tomboyish and lacked much of Yelusa's softness, attractiveness, and brilliancy.

Yelusa's Han father was the source of her Mandarin Chinese (a Han language); her mastery of the language was largely due to her father's insistence that his children not forget their Han heritage. Her father, Yelusa said, was well-versed in classical Chinese literature. He had been teaching his children to memorize some of the Han poetic prose, Tang poems, Sung verses, and other Chinese literary classics. He had taught his children not only to speak the Han language, but to also live a Han life.

I guessed that the pair of "swallows" did not alight at our sides out of mere curiosity that afternoon. Otherwise they wouldn't have stayed so long gazing at me. Were they just interested in seeing me carry water, search for firewood, build a fire, and boil water with two big iron pots placed on an earthen stove? I turned this question over in my mind long after they left.

Their motive became clearer when they came again three days later with three other Tibetan girls, and a third time at night two days later, this time with some boys. At our tent they talked and laughed, quarrelled and fought with each other in fun. They meant to make merry at our place. Their merrymaking relieved our tension and lightened our hearts.

Thereafter the two sisters came to us almost every afternoon. They became more and more familiar with us; we gossiped and cracked jokes with them. Every five or six days they would bring some mutton, asking us to boil it and eat with them. Thus began a new chapter of my life.

My past had been full of hunger and starvation; now there was plenty of food. Yelusa's sheep often provided us with enough meat for a week. And as we never lost our appetite for mutton, Yelusa never ceased to send us sheep.

With enough meat to eat, we didn't suffer from malnutrition any longer, and we had more strength for work. As I was much younger and stronger than Ling and Chan, though, I seldom let them do the heavy work, such as carrying water or splitting wood. I let them take care of the fire and pour the boiled water into containers to be carried away. They often thanked me for this consideration.

But wasn't Yelusa considerate as well? I thought she was. There were also times when I thought she was more than considerate toward me. Since the first day she gazed at me, there were several times when I thought I detected a hint of love in her attitude toward me. But why? Was it because I was handsome? Maybe. With my tall stature and broad winsome face, I could grant that I might be attractive to girls. But was that it? I had my doubts. I thought the attraction must have been due partly to the pleasant chats I had had with the girls, partly to the praises my fellow workers had piled on me, and partly to the high position I had held in former times.

Anyway, as I became aware of Yelusa's affection, I began unconsciously to pay more and more attention to my outward appearance. I started to wash my face with hot water, to clean my clothes with a hot, wet towel, and to shave more closely in the morning. I even bribed a barber by sending him some mutton to ensure that he would give me a nice haircut. I seemed to have suddenly developed a sense of pride. In fact, Yelusa and her mutton had increased my vigor and zest for life. For the first time I felt our laboring camp had fresh air and good sunshine. Only I did not know yet that it was also to have a romance.

One afternoon, Yelusa and her sister Yama came to chat with us as usual. But this time Yelusa chose to sit beside me and asked me, "Homesick?"

"Home?" her abrupt question caught me by surprise.

"Don't you miss your wife and kids?"

This last question immediately plunged me into a whirl of sorrow. I told her sadly what had happened to my family. My misfortunes seemed incredible to her. But I explained cynically, "You must know we are now living in an incredible age and in an incredible country."

Yelusa sank into thought for a while and then expressed her sympathy to me. She was truly concerned about my family, but later, I realized her question was also her subtle way of trying to determine if I was married.

Her serious attitude toward me became more and more evident. But her affection was still often disguised. She had a passion for Chinese poetry, so she would have me talk about Chinese poetry with her. Once she asked me, "Do you remember the last of the Three Hundred Poems of the Tang Dynasty?"

"Yes, of course," I nodded and replied, "Tu Chiu-niang's Golden-threaded Garment."

"Can you recite it?" she continued.

"Sure. 'Be advised not to put aside ye golden-threaded garment. Be advised to make good use of ye golden youth. Gather ye rosebuds while ye may. Do not wait until they are shed from the bough.' "

"Good," she commented. "You understand the point, don't you?" I did, of course.

Yelusa continued to test my understanding of Chinese poetry for about three weeks. As the days passed her love for me grew steadily and she continued to feed me, sometimes bringing me mutton and sometimes beef. I began to find that I had more meat than three kitchen workers could possibly eat. And I also found that my affair with Yelusa had become known to many of my fellow laborers and some of the "leaders" as well, so I started to share the meat with all of them. In fact, some "leaders" often came by at lunch time for the sole purpose of sharing my mutton or beef. I naturally shared the food willingly, knowing that by doing so I could maintain the present state of affairs safely.

In deep winter the nomads often cleaned out the weak animals in their herds and had them killed, but they ate only mutton and beef. So the meat from the horses and camels was sent to us poor road-builders on the plateau. Their generosity saved many of our lives. We naturally had nothing to send them in return. We could only carry some boiled water to them. I was really very grateful to Yelusa and her family, but what did I have to give? My only possession was a blanket made of goose down, which helped to keep me warm in winter. Could I send her a used blanket? I hesitated. At long last I cleaned it carefully and brought it to her. To my surprise, she said joyously that it was more precious to her than a Tibetan "Hada." (I must confess I still don't know what a Hada is. I hope it is something very valuable to the Tibetans.)

Then, one afternoon, while I was gathering wood on the mountain, I heard the sound of a galloping horse. When I raised my head and looked around, I saw a cloud of red dust with Yelusa flying in the midst of it on horseback. She rode up and dismounted, letting the horse graze nearby, and walked toward me. I couldn't guess what had brought her to the place like that. She wouldn't say anything until she came to me, took my axe, and offered to help me gather wood. I naturally wouldn't let her do it. "Why?" I asked.

"Labor correction, isn't it?" she replied. "Let me be corrected with some labor, too." Then she laughed.

I knew her intentions were good, but I also knew that she had never done any hard work, like splitting wood, before. I continued to refuse her kind help, though I was deeply moved. When I finished the chore, however, I let her help carry some wood back to our tent on Zarba, her horse. Later, Yelusa would sometimes hire some strong Tibetans to gather wood for me. I simply couldn't refuse her help again.

Once when Yelusa came while I was cutting bolago trees (the only trees that flourished on the salty plateau), I said to her, "Thank you so much, Miss Yelusa. I wish I knew how to express my gratitude. I wish I knew what to give you in return."

"In return?" she smiled. "Do you still regard me as an outsider? Don't we share some of the same heritage? Can't I try to relieve your suffering as a proper girl should do? Can't I—well, why should you mention this to me?" She grew uneasy.

I looked into her eyes and said, "I am afraid I'll have no chance to reward you. My life, you know, is entirely hopeless."

"Hopeless? Entirely? Why?"

"Because—" I hesitated, "because I'm a criminal."

"A criminal? Are you?"

"Yes, a criminal condemned to labor correction for life."

"No, listen, Han." She lowered her voice. "You are not a criminal if you have done nothing wrong. In my eyes, you and President Ling and Dr. Chan have never been criminals. You are noble men. Are the Communists better than all of you?"

"But they still consider my status different. They think, for instance, your cheng-fen* is different from mine." I said suddenly, spitting out the stone which had been pressing on my heart.

"Oh, come on," she replied indignantly. "My people believe in Lamaism, which teaches the equality of all people. What is 'cheng-fen' after all? It is just a term invented by the Communists to persecute their enemies. Don't you realize you are just being persecuted? Do you really believe I have better cheng-fen than you?"

I was struck dumb for a moment.

"Ah, Han," I am sorry to have embarrassed you."

I began to shed some tears.

"Oh, Han, I'm sorry to cause you sorrow."

"No, my dear Yelusa, I'm not embarrassed, nor in any sorrow." I calmed myself and assured her. "I'm only moved. I needed you to remind me of my dignity. You are another Baidumu.† I adore you. I really adore . . ."

I felt my heart leap while my face reddened at my words. Yelusa also blushed.

After that, Yelusa came to see me more often and brought me more food. Ling and Chan began to make fun of me, while at the same time predicting my bliss. I really did not know how to handle the situation. Occasionally I would ask advice of my two elders. I

---

*"Cheng-fen" literally means "components, ingredients or factors." The Chinese Communists used the term to describe a person's background or class.
†A Buddhist goddess.

remember Ling once said, "Good brother, It's impossible for you to wriggle out of the affair now. I think you can only let everything develop as naturally as possible. The girl is very sensitive and passionate. If you should let her detect any hint of something wrong on your side, she might become desperate and go to extremes."

"That's right," Chan agreed. "She's only twenty-three. Ten years from now she'll still be young. No one knows what's going to happen in the future. It may not always be that things turn out for the worse for us. If heaven wills, there may be a day when we will be released, and you'll be free to marry her. Time is not always our enemy. You must believe that." With their advice, I accepted Yelusa's love with no qualms.

Some days later, when Yelusa and her sister were leaving at twilight, Yelusa secretly tucked a slip of paper into my pocket. After they left, I sneaked out of the kitchen and took out the paper. On it was written: "Please meet me at the hillside tomorrow morning at nine." I became almost feverish and my heart beat quickly.

The next morning I found that Yelusa had come to the appointed place earlier than I. She insisted on helping me gather firewood. When she took up the axe and chopped at the bolago trees, I suddenly could not resist the temptation I had long been battling. I rushed to her and after looking into her face, seized her and held her tightly in my arms. For the next few minutes I was a wild beast attacking a mild lamb. But the lamb seemed glad of my attack; she remained supple and tender. In the heat of our embrace, I only heard her murmuring, "Dear, yes, dear, I need you . . . I'm yours . . . every breath yours . . . heart and soul . . . forever . . ."

When the storm was over, I really did not know what to do or say next. Yelusa broke the silence first. "Brother Han," she said, "although I've not been long with you, I know I can trust you. I also know what you're thinking now. Please do not let the present situation press too hard on you. You are a conscientious man. You've done nothing wrong. If God so wills, this may be just the beginning of our happiness."

She paused a while and, seeing me still lost in thought, resumed, "I know you are brave, honest, and responsible. I also know you are

a patriot. Now, listen, I have arranged something for our future. I
believe I can help you get out of the fix you are in."

"Really? How?" I was interested indeed.

"Listen," she lowered her voice, "I have thought it over and
over. This road you're building is leading to Lhasa, is it not? Once we
get to Lhasa or near Lhasa, I believe we will be free. I have been there
many times. I know the situation there. I am sure I can take you from
there to India. I can disguise you as one of our men. It is just a short
distance from Lhasa to India. You won't be discovered."

After this reassurance, she told me some of the specific details
of her plan and mentioned some place names in Nepal and India. I
cannot now remember the names, which were all unfamiliar to me.
But have I forgotten her love for me? No, never. I was really moved
by the depth of her love. And I believed her plan, though dangerous,
was not unfeasible. (Before the Dalai Lama escaped to India in 1959,
the Communist control over Tibet was still not very tight, especially
in remote areas. A Tibetan could at that time easily leave his own land
and reach a neighboring country.)

Not knowing how to thank Yelusa for her love and not knowing what would happen if I accepted her arrangement, I just held her
tightly in my arms and wept with gratitude.

Time passed very quickly. The Spring Festival* was approaching. One night after dinner, Yelusa and her sister came again, bringing
us a fat sheep. As they entered our tent, Yama protested: "Those
leaders of yours are real busybodies. They asked, 'Who are you
bringing this sheep to?' and I answered, 'To anyone we please.' You
know, they are no better than bandits. They wear their hats askew
and stare at us lustfully. Yesterday, they came to our house, demand-
ing to buy some sheep. We would not sell them anything. Their
manners were barbaric. Then they forced their way into the livestock
pen. They pointed to the sheep and said they wanted this one and

*The Chinese New Year Festival, usually in February.

that one. In my anger I replied, 'Those sheep are all ours. We have a right to decide whether to sell them or not.' Do you know what they said? One of them warned us that if we decided not to sell the sheep, we would not be allowed to visit the criminals' tent again. On hearing that, I got even angrier. I shook my finger in the man's face and shouted, 'Why, I won't believe it! I will go there today, tomorrow and every day after that! What could you do to me?' He answered, 'We'll have the guards block your way.' 'You would not dare to do such a thing!' I said. Ah, it was a really good fight!''

Yama's heated protests amused us. I knew she needed an outlet for her dammed-up indignation. So to let her exhaust all her anger, I asked her, "How did it end then?"

"I told them that if they dared to cause us any harm or mischief, I would report it to the Ministry of National Affairs and accuse them of oppressing the minority people. As soon as they heard this threat of mine, they made no more remarks and prepared to leave. As they were leaving, my sister called them back. She then agreed to sell them each a sheep."

"So, it was a happy ending, I presume."

"It was. They then said they were merely joking when they said they would make the guards block our way. In fact, they were just bullying and bluffing. I know that. And I despise them for that. They are all cowards in the end. And how can they pretend to 'correct you?' ''

Yama poured out all her dislike of the Communist leaders. Fortunately, of the twelve sharing our tent only one, Ma Chi-wu, belonged to the specially picked group of so-called "positive members,"* and even he was not truly "positive." The Communists used him just because he spoke Tibetan. While he obeyed the Communists, he actually sympathized with us poor sufferers. So Yama's complaint and criticism of the "leaders" did not cause trouble.

Fearing that some day the Communists might accuse us of

---

*Prisoners thought suitable by the Communists to do "positive" ideological work among their fellows.

inciting the minority people to rise against them, though, I hastily tried to change the topic. "Yama," I said, "I know you are just and righteous. But some of your men might not be of the same mind."

"Our men?" she retorted. "Why, it's plain you don't understand them. They all have a good opinion of you. They are all humanitarians of a sort."

"We thank you very much," said Chiang Tie-ming, "but in the present situation we are really not worthy of being your friends."

"How can you say that?" Yama retorted. "We enjoy being with you. Each time we return home from here, we have a long talk with our mother. She thinks that you need some help. She encouraged us to come and see if you would treat us as friends, too."

We knew Yama was sincere and we knew Yelusa also had kind intentions, apart from her affection for me. While everybody was immersed in these thoughts of tenderness and gratitude, I again tried to change the topic.

"The New Year Festival is coming. They say that we shall have three days off for that this year. If it is true, we would like you to come again and play a game with us."

"A game at the Festival?" Yama was fascinated with the idea.

"Yes, a contest of horsemanship, for instance." When I said this, I purposely glanced at Yelusa because I wondered why she had kept silent all this time and also because I knew she was a good horsewoman. Conscious of my attention, Yelusa only raised her head a bit higher and smiled before she said with a blush, "Don't you find us bothersome when we come here?"

"No, of course not," Chu Tan and Chan Wen-hu answered almost simultaneously. Chan continued, "You are always welcome here. Yes, very welcome. In fact, we'd regret losing a chance to welcome you."

"Are you sure you'll always welcome us?" Yama turned to me and asked abruptly. I knew she was referring to my attitude toward her sister. My face reddened at once in my embarrassment. After a short silence, all the others burst out laughing.

Teng Chung then came to my aid. He said slowly, "Well, he is obviously only too glad to have you come. If you were to refuse to come, he would surely become a 'straw man' deprived of all his vigor for work. Understand?" This remark made the others burst into laughter again. Finally, Yama said, "All right, if you are interested, we can arrange for the contest. Masha, Haihsia, Maika, and Kuoshih-chieh are all excellent horsemen. I can have them join the contest and let you see what real horsemanship is."

At this moment, Yelusa pulled me gently by the arm out of the tent. She whispered in my ear: "Mama wants me to invite you to our house for the Festival. You must accept!" Now everything was clear. Her family had noticed my relationship with her. It reminded me of the other day when her mother "casually" dropped over to our tent "to see how we boiled the water." I recalled her mothers' placid, imposing face, which resembled Yelusa's.

" 'Lusa," I replied, "I can't thank you enough for this invitation. But you know I am a criminal here. I have no way of leaving this restricted area even for a moment without permission. How can I accept your invitation?" She fell silent for a time. Before she could reply, I continued, 'Lusa, I'm really grateful to you. We're all grateful to you. You've helped me a lot. You have given us so much. We all wish to have a chance to say 'thank you' to your family. I wish, especially, to see Mama and say 'Happy New Year' to her. But—but you must believe me. We can't go anywhere. We are criminals, condemned for life."

Suddenly Yelusa became indignant. She opened her eyes wide and protested, "Criminals, you always say you are criminals. Well, aren't criminals also human beings? Can't you just ask for a leave of just one or two days?"

"Ask for leave?" I was a bit surprised at this idea of hers. "My dear, don't you know this Communist Party? Do you mean—?"

"I will ask for leave for you!"

"For me?"

"Yes, I don't care what Party it is. And since they can ask us for help, I think I can ask them for help, too."

"Don't be so foolish, dear." Though moved by her steadfastness, I put my hands on her shoulders, looked into her face and tried to reason with her. "How can you ask anything of them for me?

Suppose they ask you what you are to me, won't you be embarrassed?"

This did embarrass her for the moment. But she moved closer to me, lowered her head, and murmured, "I'd say you are—you are my—my fiancé. Will that do?"

Dear God! What a confession! Even if I had been a stone then, I would have shed tears of blood in the face of such a confession of love. But I was still a criminal under Communist control. To console my sweetheart for the time being, I could only promise that I would consider her suggestion seriously.

The next day, right after lunch, the two sisters came again. Yama said, "Mama wants you three to come over for the Festival," meaning Ling, Chan, and me. Then she added, "This morning we killed an ox, three big sheep and eight lambs for the celebration of the Festival. Tomorrow my sister herself will cook for you if you come." I was thinking of what to say when Yama continued, "Mama wants us to send a sheep to your section tonight and to apologize for not being able to invite everybody to our house."

This last made Ling blurt out immediately, "Oh, good sisters, we really don't know how we can ever thank you enough! This time we do appreciate your mother's consideration. But we have difficulty accepting your invitation." Chan added, "Yes, we are very grateful to you, but this time we can only let brother Han carry our thanks to your house." Chan and Ling then explained the difficulty of asking for leave.

"I still won't take 'no' for an answer," Yama insisted. "Mama will say we have not done our best to invite you if you fail to come. As for your difficulty, please don't worry. My sister and I are going to talk to your leaders."

"Don't bother, please." I wanted them to listen. "You don't know them. They'll never approve."

"How can you know they won't?" Yama pouted, stepped toward me, and gave me a sudden nudge. "Do you mean you won't come either? I will tie you to my horse's neck and drag you if you dare to say 'no' again." This brought a roar of laughter.

Finally Chan said, "You two cannot just go and ask for leave for us. It's useless. The only way to solve the problem, I think, is to invite them to be your guests first. If they accept, you can come to fetch them on the day of the celebration. Then, when you pass by us on the way back to the village, you can then suggest that you want us to be your guests too. I believe the leaders will find it hard to disapprove of this sudden suggestion. Besides, they may want to show their willingness to improve their relationship with your people; it would be embarrassing for them to refuse."

This seemed a most promising strategy, and the two sisters agreed to try it. But before they went, Ling added, "Be sure to make Leader Hsu accept your invitation. With him present we can be certain it will go well."

Half an hour later, the two sisters came back with very good news. "Thank Heaven," said Yama, "during the Festival there will be only two leaders on duty. All the others are leaving for their homes. The two remaining are Hsu and Liu. We invited them, and both accepted our invitation."

With this good news, I was so excited that I lay awake the whole night. I kept thinking of what it would be like to spend the Festival at Yelusa's house. Meanwhile, Yelusa's face, her tender voice, and her charming figure haunted my mind.

Yelusa's home was composed of two tents, a big one and a small one. The small one was their kitchen, the big one their living quarters. In this tent we saw a portrait of Kuan Kung. It hung above a table set with various festival offerings, including incense, candles, an ox head, a whole ram, a chicken, liquor, tea, sugar, and some snacks. On either side of the portrait hung two scrolls, both painted by Yelusa's father. The right-hand scroll read: "Chih Tsai Chun Chiu Kung Tsai Han" ("With a will for history and deeds for Han"). The left-hand scroll read: "Hsin Tung Jih Yue Yi Tung Tien" ("With hearts like the sun and moon and minds like the skies").

I stepped on the carpet in bare feet; it was exceedingly white and clean, and I was glad I had not come earlier, when my feet were still scarred with frostbite and cuts. To bring such feet onto that carpet would have been like driving a pig through a flower bed: cruel without any sense of beauty.

There was also a small emerald carving of a Lamaist Buddha placed on a red-painted table. It was their heirloom. In front of the carving were a couple of emerald vases and eight jade horses in red, yellow, white, black, and multicolored, vividly caught in various postures—recumbent, standing, galloping, and so on—and so finely carved that one could clearly see the horses' manes, tails, hoofs, and eyes.

The four of us were seated around a large table near the fire. We were first served tea in an elegant teapot, another heirloom. We thanked our hostess and extended our new year greetings. Yama came in wearing a new dress. She looked charming and urged us to have some liquor. 'Lusa was in the kitchen busily cooking, and after a while she came out with two plates of mutton, hot and aromatic.

Before we started in on the main course, Yama brought in a two-day old lamb and put it in my arms, saying, "Take good care of this baby. If it cries, we will fine you by making you drink three bowls of liquor." I held the little creature gingerly. Its white fluffy pelt was indescribably soft. Its two little eyes looked steadily at me. I loved it. As I glanced from the "baby" to 'Lusa, I saw she blushed.

We had an incredible feast that night, more than ten courses of meat, each so wonderfully prepared that it seemed a work of art. Our conditioning simply would not allow us "laboring criminals" to drink in the presence of our overseers, but leader Hsu made an exception that night by allowing us to drink. In fact, he himself got so drunk that at the end of the meal he fell fast asleep on the carpet.

Ling, Chan, and I did not drink so much. We remained quite sober throughout the evening. After the meal, many of the neighbors came by, urging us to tell stories about "the outside world." Four lovely girls—Anco, Rema, Haya, and Malisa—sat beside Ling and Chan and kept pressing our arms and asking for stories.

"Quick, quick, we're impatient!"

"All right," Ling said. "Have you ever been on a train?"

"No, never seen any," one of the girls replied. "How many people can it hold?" another asked.

"At least six or seven hundred. Sometimes over a thousand." Chan smiled as he answered.

"Woo-ah! what a marvelous vehicle!" The girls and boys present all gasped, opening their mouths and eyes wide.

"You also never took a plane or a ship, did you?" Chan asked.

"Of course not," some of those present replied at once. "Aren't they only for the leaders, the exploiting class?"

In this remark we sensed a strong hint of anti-communism. We decided that this was a good opportunity to engage the Tibetans in our communal protest against the ruling regime. When our conversation drifted to the topic of woolen fabric, Chan purposely told the youth that our clothes were made from the same wool gathered from their sheep. The youth then asked, "What is the price of woolen yarn?"

"Eighteen to twenty yuen per jin," Chan replied.

"Why! When they buy our wool, they give us only eight chiao per jin," the Tibetans complained.

"Yes, that's a difference of twenty times," Chan continued. "Who is buying your wool, by the way?"

"The People's Government. They set the price and do not allow us to do business privately. When they come to gather the wool, they often tell us that it must undergo a very complex and expensive process to become woolen yarn for making cloth. And they say they usually sell the yarn for two to three yuen per jin. So they are obviously cheating us! We are being exploited, are we not?"

"No doubt," Chan said. "And the Communists are always saying they are against any kind of business exploitation!"

"The merchants in free-trade countries would not have done so," Ling added, meaning to rouse the Tibetans' anger to a higher pitch.

But I quickly changed the topic of our conversation for fear that we might excite the youth and bring about some unnecessary mischief. "President Ling," I said, "why don't you tell them of some of the interesting things you've seen abroad. I know they love exotic tales." At my cue, Ling began to talk about the animal husbandry and livestock industries he saw in America. His stories fascinated the Tibetans and made them reflect upon their present situation.

"They do not live like you. You are forever at the mercy of the weather. Your only hope is the health of your livestock. The herbs that grow around you are your only cure for illnesses. How poor your condition is, compared with that of the American cattle raisers! They have their own pastures. They have enough hygienic and safety equipment. They have electrified everything from the water supply to wool cutting . . ." After this comparison, Ling gave a general description of the American way of life. The skyscrapers, the factories, the department stores, and Hollywood movies were among the things most interesting to our audience. Afterward I continued with stories about the people of Shanghai and their life, knowing that urban culture was an everlasting attraction to our frontier friends.

Finally, we told them that to enjoy a life like the Americans, one should have freedom first. "Aren't we Chinese but slaves at the command of the Communists? Do we have any freedom at all?" Ling grew more indignant as he posed these last questions.

"You're right," Yelusa observed. "We are the Party's slaves. We must all struggle for freedom, or all die!"

"Yes, right, freedom or death!" chorused the other youths.

I knew we had said enough for the present. We only dared to agitate the Tibetans that way because we were certain they had long harbored a hatred for the Communists and would never tell on us. Besides, we felt we were obliged to enlighten them as to the true nature of our oppressors.

As we became familiar with Yelusa's neighbors, they also invited us cordially to be their guests at their homes. Their hospitality was sincere and moving. We could not accept it, though, because as "laboring criminals" we really had no freedom to mix so freely with others.

The next night Techinpa, 'Lusa's brother, insisted on our going over to his house for dinner. We knew he was in earnest, but we still hesitated to accept his invitation. Finally, clever Yama saw our difficulty and went straight to Leader Hsu and said, "Come on, let's all go, okay? On this New Year's Day, all the leaders have left except you and Leader Liu. Mama said we'd invite Leader Liu to our house tomorrow. So, Leader Hsu, please accompany us to my brother's and have a nice evening there." Asked this way, Hsu was unable to decline. We were soon on our way to Techinpa's house.

Leader Hsu, to be sure, had been kind to us. Whenever the other leaders were absent he would talk with us, and we could gather that he was nostalgic about "the old society." And that, we surmised, might originate from some personal burden of the heart.

That night at Techinpa's, Yama again urged us to drink, and Leader Hsu was again beginning to get drunk. Grasping the opportunity, we made bold to ask him about his personal background. "Why didn't you bring your wife here?" Yama initiated our inquiry with this embarrassing question, which to our surprise brought forth a long, pathetic, and most incredible story.

Whether or not Leader Hsu was really drunk we did not know, nor was it important. One thing we did know was he became not a bit afraid to speak that night. It seemed that he already trusted us, and was not afraid to speak confidentially.

"Why didn't I bring my wife here? How easy it is for you to ask that question!" he said. "Don't you think I would if I could? How ignorant you are of me!"

Then he sighed, bit his lips, and continued, his voice quivering with indignation. "Have you ever thought how much it would cost me to move my family from the South to this forsaken place? Don't you know my wages come to just over fifty yuen a month? Let me tell you. I have five members in my family, all dependent on me. Here, I have to spend some twenty yuen a month on food, two or three yuen on daily necessities such as towels, toothpaste, brushes, and soap. Though I have stopped smoking and drinking, the most I can save for my family is only twenty to thirty yuen per month. And that is not enough. I know my children are often hungry, my wife doesn't have enough clothing to cover her back, and my whole family cannot cover all their expenses. I am not complaining. But it's true. My father has long been laid up with an illness, but has no money for a cure. My mother looks better, but has a heart disease. I have a little sister, still too young to earn money. My wife makes some money by working as a washerwoman. But the little money she earns isn't much of a livelihood. As a result, our eldest son, who is eight now, cannot go to school but has to go out every day to gather dried-out branches or unclaimed coal for fuel. You may not believe it, but it's true. They often pick up vegetables that have been discarded on the roadside or in garbage cans for nourishment."

By this time Hsu's voice had become hoarse, and his eyes red with tears. But he went on in earnest. He told us that he originally came from Chu-chi, a thriving city in Chekiang Province. His father had been a businessman. After graduating from primary school, he helped his father with the family business. "But in 1950," and here he paused a while before he went on, "the Korean War broke out. The call of 'Against America for Korea' came to my county. I was among the youth summoned to the front for the cause. I pleaded with the government to spare me on the grounds that my father was sickly and needed my help. I was his only son. Yet the plea was futile. They said I should be proud to be chosen for that 'mission.' They also told me that the government would take special care of my family in my absence. In a word, I had to join in the 'sacred war.' I remember the day when I left my hometown, my mother accompanied me to the station. Before we parted, she clasped my hands tightly and cried out, 'Son, Heaven bless you. May God bring you back safely. I must see you again.' Then she fainted. Later, when the train was moving, I wanted to jump off and escape back to my mother's arms. But the 'leaders' had prepared against such incidents. I could not help crying as the train rushed on. But I was told that it was forbidden to cry. They said it would affect others . . ."

His sorrow was indeed contagious, but we urged him to continue. "I certainly did not want to die for the Korean cause and prayed that I could return safely to my mother," he continued. "But after arriving at the front, I found everything to be hopeless. Our weapons were no good. And we had no tactics. The soldiers were mostly people like me. We had no fighting experience and no training. We all shuddered at the sound of the shells exploding. We had a regiment stationed at Height 501. It was bombed by American planes, and more than half of the soldiers there died or were wounded. One day I was wounded and was sent back to a hospital. After I recovered, I was to be sent to the front again, but before I set out, the war ended. After I returned from the war, I was considered one of the 'heroes' and so was promoted to lieutenant and sent to the Wuhsi Airfield to work as a police guard. Then do you know what happened?"

"What?" we all wondered.

"After some months in Wuhsi, I found that every Saturday afternoon several buses arrived loaded with girls. They were either factory workers or students. They were sent to certain places to spend the weekend with the Russian airmen, engineers, or other staff members then stationed in the area. When they were sent back on Monday, every girl looked sad and tired. Some were crying, some had disheveled hair. At first, I imagined they must have just had a weekend of dancing, drinking wine, and hugging and kissing their lovers. Later, I learned it was much more than that. Oh, my God, what a shame! It's too shameful to mention!"

"Do you mean they were cheated?"

"Cheated? Yes, you could say that, and raped!" he said heatedly. "Dragged in and raped! By the high-nosed ones! Sometimes three or four took turns raping one! And do you know what?! The girls said they had no choice, they could not even protest against it! They were sent to the Russians under the direction of the Party chiefs. They said they were purposely sent to promote friendship with our 'Big Brothers.' They said that if they protested against such 'sacrificial glory,' they would be accused of 'anti-organization, negative sabotage, and unreasonable disobedience!' And as a result, they would be transported to remote areas for labor reform."

"Are you sure about this?"

"Why, of course. I had heard about it and then saw it myself. In fact, it was just because I had witnessed it and talked about it so angrily that I was later charged with the crimes of 'lacking a sense of international cooperation,' 'lacking a friendly spirit,' and 'wavering in the support of Party policies.' Consequently, I was asked to write a report criticizing myself."

"That's really incredible!" we all seemed to shout at once.

"But you must believe it." Hsu clenched his fists and went on most indignantly. "One day I was called to my aunt's house, and there, saw my cousin crying bitterly on her bed. I asked why. My aunt told me that she had suffered a horrible disgrace. I knew my cousin was working at the Yung-An Textile Mill in Wuhsi. She was nicknamed 'silly Hsi Shih' by her co-workers because she was as pretty as Hsi Shih* but as naive as a little girl. When I asked further about her misfortune, my aunt told me how our beauty was sent to entertain the 'Big Brothers' over the weekend with some other factory girls, and how she was raped several times by two Russian high-ranking staff members in one night. My aunt also told me that the shame had almost driven her mad, and she had been trying to kill herself. I knew what I should do. I tried every way to console her. I promised to avenge her. I even advised her to report it to the Party leaders. But some days later—can you imagine what happened?"

Hsu paused a while and then resumed, "She had been sick in bed for a few days when the Party chief of the mill sent some men to my aunt's house and dragged my cousin by force to the mill. There they began to accuse her of being 'anti-Party and anti-revolution, of having betrayed an international secret, and of lacking communist spirit.' And as a result, she was sentenced to 'labor corrections' and sent to an unknown remote area. Since that time, we have not been able to find out what has become of her."

At this point, Hsu realized that we had all become as indignant as he. He raised his voice and began to appeal for our sympathy. "Please judge this case with me. A seventeen-year-old girl, pure like a pearl, frantically ravished by two beasts in one night, and then penalized for fabricated reasons. What sort of world is this?"

"The world of communism, of course," Ling commented sarcastically.

"Yes, you're right," Hsu said, apparently glad of our sympathy. "After this shame to my cousin, I questioned my commanding officer angrily, 'Does communism mean raping together? Is Communist 'love' just communal lust?' My severe questioning naturally brought

---

*The most famous beauty in Chinese history.

me severe consequences. I was publicly prosecuted for my rashness. And because I refused to admit that I was at fault, they sent me to this plateau. Here, I am a 'leader' in name only. In truth I am like you, condemned to 'labor corrections' for some secret reason. Now I guess you can understand why I have no family with me here, can't you?"

Leader Hsu's story penetrated our hearts and remained poignant in our minds. To us "criminal laborers," the story was more evidence of our innocence and another reason for our anti-communism. To the Tibetans, the story was a sort of initiation, ushering them into the horrible world of the Communists. By the time Hsu was finished, it was already after nine o'clock. We knew Hsu was already drunk. But we also knew that his story would have the far-reaching effects of any wise remark from a sober philosopher.

For three days we celebrated the New Year Festival with Yelusa's family, their relatives, and neighbors. We entertained ourselves with various jollities (including a contest of horsemanship), and almost forgot our present status as "criminal laborers." Yet I knew my romance with Yelusa would still be fraught with dangers and difficulties once the celebration was over.

How earnest 'Lusa's love was for me! To smooth our way, she had managed to bribe many of the Communist team leaders with meat from her household. She believed that bribery was always efficacious in silencing the Communists' fault-finding mouths. She was not wrong, but the Reds, as I understood, were never content with bribery. Besides, they were suspicious, too wary to forget that "the history of mankind is a continuous process of class struggle," in which any dominating class is liable to fall if it is merciful to its subjects.

As my romance with Yelusa became more and more public, the Communists paid more and more attention to me. They remembered I was one of the first to object to burning all the pasture grass for the road construction. Now that Ling, Chan, and I had become close to the Tibetans, it was increasingly obvious that the Communists were beginning to doubt our single purpose of befriending the minority people. They were afraid that any solidarity between the nomads and the laborers could overthrow their sovereignty.

It was under these circumstances that a conflict arose between Director Chao and me, which gave the Communists an opportunity, they thought, to lay their hands on me. Director Chao was one of "the Ten Rascals" among the leaders. He came from the northeastern part of China and was short, with a sunburnt face, a large mouth, two protruding eyes like those of a goldfish, and an air of wickedness. He was the one who had shot a laborer just because the poor fellow broke a leg on the ice and consequently could not catch up with the rest of his team. He also often came to my tent to demand a share of meat which 'Lusa or Yama had brought over. It was during one of these visits that the confrontation occurred.

One day 'Lusa brought us a lot of camel meat, including the hump, which was, to us Chinese, the most delicious and nutritious part. The hump had been intended for my two elderly fellow kitchen workers, Ling and Chan. Director Chao was with us, however, when the rare delicacy was delivered. Chao widened his protruding eyes, laughed a hideous laugh, and snatched it from 'Lusa's hand. "A pretty thing, isn't it? Not easily available I think. How lucky I am to have come across it. My wife needs it. She's just had a baby. We must give her some nourishment." After this, he pointed to us three men while looking at 'Lusa and her sister and said, "They're strong fellows. They really don't need such nourishing stuff. Besides, are criminals entitled to such delicacies? Think of their past. They bullied our people, deprived them of everything precious. Are we to pay them a tribute?"

I found myself shaking with anger and growing more and more bitter by the moment. "Yes," I shouted sarcastically, "actually you'd better keep it for yourself. I can see you're in poor health. A strong wind might even blow you down. I know you need some tonic. But I am afraid no tonic can ensure longevity. One needs to live virtuously, too. We were condemned to labor here because we were not virtuous enough. I hope your virtue always brings you a good return. As to the hump meat, may it do you or your wife much good and not ruin your appetite."

Chan was equally indignant. He thanked Yelusa for having thought of sending him and Ling such a nice present, then observed, "But this hump is indeed too precious a gift for the likes of us criminals. We're not used to such delicacies. I think Director Chao is indeed a much more proper recipient." He turned to Chao and remarked, "But my dear Director, please be careful when eating it. I wouldn't want you or your wife to choke."

Chao flew into a rage. For a moment he could not find words, but then he bellowed, "What do you mean? Do you know who I am? Who you are? What do you take me for? You want me to blow your heads off?! How many heads do you think you've got?! Oh! If only I had a gun with me!"

At this, I lost my temper and my sense of fear as well. "You're lucky. If you had brought a weapon with you, you would have known us for the undauntable men we are."

Chao leapt at me like a mad dog. As he raised his fist to strike me, I stood motionless, thinking that I had the right to kill him since he proved to be the initiator of the fight. But at that moment, Yelusa stepped forward, pulled back Chao's hand, and said in a pleasing tone, "Please stop. Please blame everything on me. I did not mean to cause any trouble here. Dear Director, I'm glad to hear your wife has just had another baby. If I had received the good news a little earlier, I would have brought you some extra gifts. But it's not too late. I still have something for you. If you care to have some lambs, for instance, you can come to my house tomorrow."

These soft words from 'Lusa quelled Chao's fury. He continued more calmly, "Thank you, girl. You do talk a lot more sense. Not like this Han. He, I had suspected, fostered quite an unsound attitude toward our Party. Now I know he is hostile and refuses to repent. Do you think we can let such a malcontent alone? Never. I am going to suggest that he be transferred from his present position to the big team of laborers. There he might develop a good grasp of our Party policy."

This threat didn't scare me, but it did scare 'Lusa. Although she knew the Communists often used such bluffs, she couldn't tell this time whether Chao was in earnest or not. Anyway, she thought she had to prevent Chao from taking any real action, for she could not bear to think that I would be sent elsewhere. So she appealed to him to forgive our improper speech. Meanwhile, she promised to give him a satisfactory "reward" provided he forgave us.

I resented 'Lusa's appeasement, but at the time I did not know how to show my resentment. While I was thinking, Chao realized that he couldn't gain more by staying longer, so he pretended to accept 'Lusa's reconciliation and left laughing scornfully.

After Chao was gone, my resentment turned into despair. I hated myself for being powerless to destroy the devils that persecuted us. After a while of silent thinking, tears ran down my face. 'Lusa then gestured to me to follow her out of the kitchen.

We went to a small sand hill nearby. There, for the first time, she reproached me seriously. "How could you be so indiscreet?" she said. "You know it's always better to bend than to remain rigid and break. You know we are not yet in a position to defy the Communists. Suppose you killed that dog just now, what would have become of us? Don't you see you need to live, to care for me? My darling, I adore you. And I hope you will always love me. So please control your temper, for my sake. Besides, have you forgotten your duty to your nation? Don't you want to save your life for our future plans?"

I knew I was wrong even without her reminding me. I admitted I had been too rash in trying to challenge Chao's authority. I promised that I would henceforth be more discreet in my speech and conduct. I was determined to act wisely from then on for her sake, and for the cause I had been struggling for. But I feared that this resolution might have come too late to save me from further troubles.

After the incident with Director Chao, I expected some sort of retaliation from him. But for some time, nothing happened. One day Leader Hsu came by and told me that Director Chao had never mentioned his quarrel with me, and he was only too glad to have me stay in my present position. This information naturally gave me some comfort.

So I continued to boil water for the laborers while winter

seemed to set in deeper and deeper instead of leaving us. For two weeks snow fell incessantly around us. The hills, the valleys—everything that we could see was covered with snow. In the lower places the snow was as deep as two meters. On our usual paths, the snow lay at least knee-deep. The trees with their ice-wrapped branches looked like white giants or dragons and the white-faced rocks were hung with icicles like veils, or the crystals on chandeliers. The scene was beautiful, but we hardly ventured out on those days.

The wind was so cold that we felt it could freeze everything instantly. The drafts that blew through our tents were still able to nip our ears and noses. The wind swept everywhere with such violence that anything lighter than a rock might easily be blown away. On those stormy days, we ceased working and hid ourselves in our tents. Only occasionally would a few men venture out to clear away the snow that had accumulated on the tops of the tents, so they wouldn't collapse.

But during those stormy days people had to eat and drink. Consequently, we kitchen workers suffered the most. We had to strain every nerve to fetch enough water and boil it in time. In addition, we had to gather enough fuel to cook the meals as usual. Sometimes, when the food was not prepared well enough, we would be blamed. In those days many died from hunger and cold. Such deaths were natural, but we were often taken to task for such inevitabilities.

On one especially stormy day, Leader Chu, who led our branch team, came to me very early in the morning. He ordered me to go out immediately to gather wood for fuel and ordered Ling and Chan to stay behind and continue boiling water. We knew that there was more to this than a sudden desire for fuel. The Communists were taking advantage of the weather to get me out of the way. But what could I do except obey the command?

I went out immediately after breakfast. But before I left, I told some of my fellow team members that I was afraid I might either be frozen to death or eaten by animals while outside. "You know me," I said. "It's not that I want to go on living so miserably, it's just that I would hate to die as a result of a grievance." They understood what I meant, but we all knew they couldn't help me in any way.

I chose to walk along a familiar path. As I trudged on, the snow made it harder and harder for me to tell my way. My feet disappeared into the snow in most places. I also stumbled a few times, partly because of my difficulty in navigating the tricky ground, partly because of the sweeping wind which chilled my bones, numbed my limbs, and threatened to carry me away.

As soon as I managed to reach some bolago trees, I took out the axe and, digging into the snow, began to cut their roots as well as branches. I knew I couldn't go any farther. I could only gather wood from the nearest trees.

As I wielded the axe, my body started to warm up. I fervently thanked Yelusa and her family for having fed me so well that I had the strength for this difficult job. After two hours or so I began to feel exhausted. I rested a while and measured the quantity of wood I had gathered. It was still far short of what was needed, but I knew I could not work any longer. My sweat began to turn into ice. The chill penetrated my bones. I started to shiver. I knew I had to get back soon to save my life. But where was my strength now? I had hardly moved a few steps when I felt dizzy. The world around me went dark as I passed out.

When I regained consciousness, I found myself lying on a bed, surrounded by Yelusa, Yama, and some other friends. They told me I was found unconscious in the snow. "Who saved me?" I asked. "My sister, of course," said Yama. "How did you know to look for me?" I murmured again. "Your friends told us about what happened this morning." Later I learned that Yelusa had asked some Tibetans to search for me after she heard about Leader Chu's command.

For several days I remained in bed. When I had first awakened, I found they had brought me to Yelusa's house. I was lying on a warm bed padded with two thick quilts; I was covered with another quilt made of silk and cotton, a cape made of fox fur, and a blanket.

I was very carefully nursed by Yelusa and Yama during the few days of my convalescence. They made me eat ginger soup, kaoliang liquor, and mutton soup. They felt my pulse, rubbed my back, fondled my hair, and talked to me affectionately. I could see they were overjoyed that I was still alive.

I knew Ling and Chan were quite concerned, but they were not allowed to visit me. In fact, even if they had been permitted to see me, the violent snow storm which was still raging would have prevented them. I really never expected anyone from the camp to come to see me. My only concern at the time was that I would soon have to leave Yelusa. On my second day at Yelusa's, Leader Chu payed a visit. Yama immediately spat, "Well, Comrade Chu, are you here to see whether he's still alive or not? Are you prepared to bury him?" To this, Leader Chu replied, "I come only to express fraternal love." This reply was as unexpected as his coming.

"Thank you, comrade," Yama continued. "We appreciate this Communist humanitarianism of yours, but please excuse us. We have brought him to life again. This wasn't against your wishes, was it?"

"Of course not. We've never meant him any harm."

"Then why did you choose weather like this to send him out in?"

"You know we are badly in need of fuel."

"Then why didn't you send out a company instead of a single man?"

Leader Chu was not able to answer this question. He remained silent for a good while. Then he apologized, "We are really sorry that things turned out the way they did. But my command was issued under the direction of my superior. I really had no intention of harming your beloved one. If you won't believe me, you can ask Leader Hsu."

Later we learned from Leader Hsu that Leader Chu was acting under the orders of Director Chao. This information made Yelusa and me realize that Director Chao still bore me a grudge. But what could I do? For the time being, I thought, I could only watch out for more schemes.

Thanks to the love and care of Yelusa and her family, I recovered quickly. My love for Yelusa and my gratitude to her family soared to great heights, and their ensuing consideration touched me even more deeply. Fearing that I might meet further malice from the Communists, Yelusa's mother and brother decided that from then on they would pack up their houses and follow our team of laborers. Fortunately, wherever we camped, there was enough pasture for their grazing stock.

The two big tents of Yelusa's family and her brother Techinpa were now always pitched a very short distance from the kitchen where I boiled water for the team. The distance was so short that they could reach me in half a minute, and easily see what was happening at my place. This closeness facilitated the love affair between 'Lusa and me. Hardly a day passed now without her staying a long time with me. In my imagination her two big eyes shone constantly to light up the many dark corners in my life.

To make my protection more complete, 'Lusa began to bribe all the Communist leaders with handsome gifts. The gifts were mostly cattle, sheep, and camel meat. They were worth a lot, to be sure, but for a family like 'Lusa's (who had in their possession more than two thousand sheep, five hundred cattle, two hundred horses, and fifty camels at a time), the bribery was never an economic burden. The bribery worked. As time went on, the Communists ceased to care about my love affair. In fact, they wouldn't have considered making me leave my present post. That was how I escaped from the life-threatening labor when we were constructing the Pa Yin River Bridge.

Still, there were times when I realized I was enjoying love in the shadow of death. Although I was happy with 'Lusa, the news of deaths (from beatings, shootings, starvation, diseases or accidents) infringed on our blissful peace. Though we were sure the Communists would no longer bother us, we were afraid envy might still arise in unexpected places.

Yelusa asked Ling to be her "kanpa."* Ling looked out for us carefully. When he saw that 'Lusa was pampering me by employing servants to help me gather wood and carry water, he warned her not to, since such extravagance might incur the envy of others. 'Lusa took Ling's advice, though she still tried to lighten my load secretly. At

---

*Roughly equivalent to "foster father" or "godfather," but without the religious or legal implications.

times she herself would gather wood for me. If she came across any Communist leaders on the way back with the wood on horseback, she would take it first to her house and store it there until she had a chance to send it over to me without being noticed.

'Lusa's charm did not lie in her figure, her flesh, her wisdom, her knowledge, or her attitude alone, but mostly in her "volcanic style" with its lava of tenderness and love, which poured out when I most needed warmth to melt a frozen heart.

If 'Lusa were indeed a volcano, she never ceased to erupt, and I never ceased to burn with her love. The more brightly I burned, the more remarkable her pristine freshness appeared to me. Every fiber of her body was fraught with the native strength of the high plateau, even though her speech and behavior were softened with Han civilization. Every look, every gaze, every glance from her was a dart shot into my heart, causing not pain but a keen thrill of pleasure. My intimacy with her was bliss. My desire for her grew unstoppably in its intensity.

There were times when I could not help but make love to her. In the height of pleasure, however, I would become suddenly panic-stricken; not because of her strong embraces at the peak of passion or her gentle murmurs afterward, but because I was doing something forbidden by the Communists, something for which I could die.

Despite my panic I felt certain that I would not be caught in the act. Nevertheless, our intimacy would become very hard to conceal if I were not always careful. I always took the necessary steps to protect her from becoming pregnant, though these "strategic retreats" were frustrating to both of us. Fortunately, nothing occurred during those amorous months.

Soon May came. The snow stopped and the icy ground thawed. We felt the breath of spring everywhere. I would occasionally take a walk with 'Lusa in the warm sunshine. As we walked arm in arm, we enjoyed gazing out over the meadow, whose withered grass had turned green again.

Both 'Lusa and I liked horses. In the spring I decided to have a good look at the great variety bred on the plateau. Looking at the glossy red, white, or black coats of the horses grazing and galloping,

I imagined they were the legendary steeds from the great stories of China's history. When they neighed, I was tempted to shout my heart out in reply.

Besides horses, there were herds of yellow and black cattle, single- and double-humped camels, flocks of sheep, and goats of varying colors. The livestock, together with the nomads' white or gray tents, were colorful and lively. I am not a poet, but I was inspired by the hopeful spring scene between the blue sky and the green meadow. I remember saying to 'Lusa, "Dear love, amidst such beauty and peace, I dare believe I am a man again."

"But we are not going to linger here, are we?" 'Lusa reminded me. "Have you forgotten our plan? Once your construction of the road is extended to Lhasa, my family will help you to escape and realize our dream." "Yes, I know," I replied. "Judging from the speed of work now, we will reach Lhasa in two years. Our freedom is not too far away, it seems. Let's hope for the best."

Ling and Chan had become participants in our plot. The three of us were to be disguised as shepherds and concealed in a Tibetan house as soon as we reached Lhasa. Then 'Lusa's family would seek a chance to send us across the border of Tibet into a foreign country. This plan presented us with very promising prospects, and we were happy to see the Pa Yin River Bridge was about to be completed, a signal that we were soon to move on toward Lhasa.

At last the bridge was finished! The entire team, or rather army, of us "criminal laborers" was excited, though we knew yet another difficult task must be waiting for us. Ling, Chan, and I were especially excited, for we thought we were moving toward our target as planned.

One sunny morning on a huge piece of land adjoining the riverbank, Hao Teng-ke called a rally of ten thousand of us. It was an especially hot summer day. We felt like so many loaves of bread being baked or toasted as we stood there listening. Sweat dripped from every pore in our skins. As usual, we waited with foreboding for bad news, though we could not guess what it might be. Hao was to die six years later, inverted in a big water crock. But at that time he was the Chief of the Chinghai Agricultural Exploitation Bureau and vice-chief of the Labor Corrections Bureau. Therefore he was entitled to call the rally, and roared at us like a lion.

"Comrades! The completion of the bridge is a victory for our Party," he began. "It is also a victory for our people, and a victory for Socialism as well!"

We really could not understand why it was not a victory for us "criminals." In our anger, we saw him as a blackfaced dwarf disturbing us with noise only a little more insignificant than firecrackers. We decided not to listen too closely, but suddenly, we heard something that caught our attention.

"Let me give you all a bit of news: We originally wanted the seventh branch team to continue the construction of the road leading to Lhasa. But the plans have changed. The Provincial commissars have given us directions stating that the seventh branch team should stay and help complete Telingha Farm. I believe this change is sensible. And I believe the seventh branch is lucky to have received this new assignment."

On hearing this news, I almost fainted. I was conscious only of a buzzing sound in my ears. After a while, my consciousness returned, but my ears were still vibrating with the words: "The seventh branch should stay and help complete Telingha . . . " My God! These words exploded in my ears and pierced my heart!

I don't know how I managed to return to my working place that day after the rally. I was so numb that I was like a drunkard on his way home after a long night of heavy imbibing. I couldn't walk steadily, nor could I think clearly. I felt like something was gnawing at my heart, but I couldn't spit it out. When I saw Ling and Chan, I sobered instantly. They were buried in sorrow just like me. We three remained silent for a long while, looking at one another, too depressed to talk. Finally I broke the silence. "I'm going out to gather some wood," I said very softly. I wondered if they had even heard me. Anyway, they didn't bother to ask me why I was going out without eating lunch.

As I came to the hillside, sadness seized me completely. I threw down my axe, sat on a rock, and began to cry out loud. I simply could not accept the fact that my dream was so easily shattered by some words from the Communist Party. I also refused to accept the Labor Correction Farm as the place to end my life in unceasing slavery. What was worse, it was not I alone who would become desperate after hearing the bad news. How could I, and the ones I loved, pass the remaining hopeless days? In my imagination, each year, each month, each week, even each hour and minute were already a thicket of brambles through which I, and they, must suffer without dignity.

How horrible it was! The heaven 'Lusa and I had made in those months had been turned into a hell so very unexpectedly! What could I do to prevent it from happening? I thought and thought and thought, still with the same result. "What could I do?" Agony became a dull knife using my heart as its whetstone. I wanted to end my life.

"If to suffer is my share of life, what then is 'Lusa's?" I thought. "Yes, I could go through every level of purgatory. But could she? She is as fragile as a rosebud. One blooming on my fragile branch. One that could not withstand a mild storm, not to mention this hurricane. And one that would break easily, and be swallowed easily by the mud once it fell off." I sat there, a melancholy poet brooding over his possible future. Finally I came to the conclusion that I could blame only myself. I repented and wished I could spit out all my blood and die in remorse for everything I had done to 'Lusa.

Right at that moment, I heard the sounds of a galloping horse. I lifted my head and looked over. It was 'Lusa! She had heard from Ling and Chan that I was out gathering wood. So she came immediately on the horse, fearing that I might take a desperate step. As soon as she dismounted, she rushed to me and plunged headlong into my arms. I noticed she had not combed her hair, and had dressed hastily. We cried together for a long hour. Then Yama came, too, to join our sorrow. We all approached hysteria in our mourning. Then suddenly 'Lusa leapt up on horseback and galloped away.

I saw she was going up the top of the mountain toward the brink of a precipice. I was afraid that she was intent on some desperate act, but too frightened to take any action. Fortunately, Yama saw the danger too. She screamed and pushed me at once onto her black horse. I then beat and kicked the horse into a fierce gallop as I started the chase after 'Lusa.

When I came within a hundred meters of 'Lusa, she had already gained the mountaintop. I yelled to her, pleading with her to turn back. But she would not listen. Lost in my desperation, I suddenly heard myself shout out these words: "All right, dear, come! Let's die together! Come! Let's die like man and wife! Come! Before I test this head against the rocks!"

Those words stopped her. She turned her horse, came slowly down the slope, and when she reached me, leapt down from her horse, plunging again into my arms.

Another long hour of communal lamentation ensued. As we grieved, it suddenly dawned on me that we were being foolish. We were forgetting what was most important in such a situation. I knew, then, that we all had to preserve our lives so that we would have a chance to struggle against our fate. I hugged 'Lusa tightly, kissed her again and again, and said consolingly, "My dearest, we'll love each other forever. We should become man and wife. We must stop our sorrow and show our strength. I believe Heaven still supports our cause. If only we can calm down, we are sure to think out a solution to our problem. Let's come here again tomorrow afternoon. I think I can devise a way out by then." 'Lusa was comforted, and Yama added, "Yes, let us be hopeful. Let us go back and get a good rest first. And don't shed tears for goodness sake! That would easily arouse the Communists' suspicions."

So our sorrow turned into a strong determination. We went back, hopeful once again. The next afternoon 'Lusa and I met as we had planned. Before 'Lusa became sorrowful again, I explained calmly, " 'Lusa, dear, I thought it over and over last night. I am afraid we really have no chance now to reach Lhasa. But according to Hao, once the Telingha Farm is completed, all the laborers there will be allowed to have families. Perhaps I can marry you then. It won't be long. One or two years later, maybe."

"But isn't something sure to happen again during that tedious wait?" 'Lusa had become doubtful of anything connected with the Communist Party.

"You're right." I answered understandingly. "Something might happen in the interval. But that something must be good for us. Do you think such a regime can last long? If I am not wrongly informed, they say that Stalin has died and the United States has become very hostile toward Russia because of Russia's aggressive policy in Europe. They also say that the Third World War might break out any time. I believe the Chinese Communists will necessarily be involved in the warfare once the fighting starts. When the war comes to the East, the ROC army in Taiwan may counterattack the mainland. American soldiers might even land on this plateau, helping the minority people in this area to rise up at the same time. If that happens, don't you think we might find a chance to escape?"

'Lusa was pacified and started with me another hopeful stage of our lives that I had constructed out of hearsay. The days that followed saw us growing even closer. Our tête-à-têtes often went on for many hours at a time, punctuated only by kisses.

Then, for the last time before I left for Telingha, I made love to her at her house. It was not so much a satisfaction of carnal desire as a farewell guarantee of our mutual affection. Into that act we cast all our regret at having to part. For me we seemed to have both fallen into a whirlpool, too dizzy to feel the pleasure of the motion. As she gave me a long last kiss, I had almost sunk into the depth of oblivion, though I still struggled to assure her that true love must have a truly happy ending.

After the Pa Yin River Bridge was finished, the construction of the Telingha Farm began immediately. We were first made to build the cabins and the irrigation system, whose main channel was to be fifteen meters deep, thirty meters wide, and 150 kilometers long. To dig such a canal required the blood and sweat of tens of thousands of laborers.

When Ling, Chan, and I first arrived at the farm, we were assigned to boil water as before, and I still could find time to meet Yelusa. But her family could not move close to me because there was no pasture near the farm. If they were to set their tents close by, they would have to drive their livestock miles away in order to graze them.

So now 'Lusa usually came to see me every other day. Often she came with Yama and they brought us meat as they had done before. Whenever she came, I would take her five or six meters away from the kitchen. We would sit on a rock there and talk privately. We did not dare to display too much intimacy, however, because, in this new place, the Communist leaders seemed more attentive. Besides, the farm was much more densely populated than our former camp, and the kitchen was only about fifty meters from the main working site where a large crowd of workers was always looking for the slightest distraction to provide an excuse for them to slacken their labor.

In such circumstances I could only communicate with 'Lusa non-verbally. On her face and mine were written long letters of love, poems of lament, and the movements of pathetic symphonies. I stared at every ripple in the waters of her eyes. She was fascinated by my gestures, which seemed to possess for her a rhythm of despair and hope. Her facial expressions varied with my moods. A cloud seemed to have covered her face when my melancholy was reflected in her eyes. Sometimes her cheeks were veiled with a tearful shower of joy when I tried to squeeze pleasure out of pity and fear. Occasionally she would hold my hands tightly, making palm kiss palm most suggestively. I could feel the arch, loop, and whorl of the patterns on her fingertips revealing her innermost secrets to me.

When we spoke, 'Lusa often recited classical Chinese literature. Po Chu-yi's "Unending Lament" and some of Li Ching-chao's verses expressed her state of mind:

> *Over the throne flew fireflies, while he brooded in the twilight.*
> *He would lengthen the lamp wick to its end and still could never*
>   *sleep.*
> *Bell and drum would slowly toll the dragging night hours.*
> *And the River of Stars grew sharp in the sky, just before dawn,*
> *And the porcelain mandarin ducks on the roof grew thick with*
>   *morning frost,*
> *And who'd share with him his cold quilt of emerald blue?*
>
> *"By the east hedge I held up a cup after dusk,*
> *While fragrance stole out to pervade my cuffs.*

Do not say I was not losing my soul over it.
Just see how the bamboo curtain was rolled up and the west wind
was blowing.
Then see how much more withered I was than a yellow flower.

I could not help but lament, " 'Lusa, why do you remember such sad verses? A little too ominous isn't it?" She just laughed at me, glad perhaps that I was a good listener.

Three months passed, then all the farm laborers were reorganized into new groups. As a result, I left the kitchen and entered the First Production Team of the Third Working Station. By that time the first laborers' prison house had been built on the farm. So I moved with others from the tents into the prison house, which had strong walls and was heavily guarded. When we walked out of it to work, they called it "to be released from seclusion," and when we returned after work, they called it "to receive safeguards."

Later I learned that those who were "privileged" to move first into the prison house were those considered most liable for severe penalties for "having especially aroused the people's rage." These "privileged laborers" were mostly formerly privileged members of society, including college presidents, school principals, generals, government officials, and business tycoons. They "especially aroused the people's rage" because they "were stubborn in their opinions." They "received safeguards" because they needed "concentrated re-education" and "specified inculcation."

I was told to leave my position as a kitchen worker quite abruptly, though I had had some warning from Leader Hsu some time before. Consequently, I did not have time to inform Yelusa. What was worse, I learned that Ling, Chan, and some other friends were leaving for different groups, too. (Chang Hsiao-sung was sent back to Sungchiang Province and later beaten to death during a "public prosecution" by representatives of the "outraged people" gathered by the Communist leaders.)

I could not bear to part with Ling and Chan after two years of working together and sharing the same hopes and fears. Fortunately, however, they also lived in the prison house and so we could still see each other occasionally, especially when we met in the prison house clinic. My greatest regret was that each time we met, we could exchange only a few words. My relationship with my friends was like that of so many fish caught in the same dried-up riverbed rut: one consoling another merely with the bit of froth remaining on their lips.

Telingha Farm was some fifty kilometers from the Pa Yin River, and covered a wide basin surrounded by hills. Two mountain ranges, each about a hundred kilometers long, served as prison walls. Within the farm, about 150,000 "criminals" were made to live and labor according to strict rules.

After I was moved into the prison house, I didn't see Yelusa or her sister for three months; this caused us constant worry and pain. One Tuesday morning at about ten o'clock, while I was laboring with others in the field, (engaged in "spring sowing" as they called it), I saw two horses galloping toward us in clouds of yellow dust. The sight made me put down the spade I was holding and focus all of my attention on it. During the next few moments I saw the two horses stop by the "discipline room," and two girls dressed in black leap down from their backs. Then a man mounted one of the horses and spurred it toward where I was standing. Before long I recognized the man and the horse. It was Disciplinarian Chou riding Yama's black horse. Before he reached me, he called me over to him. At this unusual sight, Leader Teng, an amiable southerner, also came over.

"You can rest a while. Come to the discipline room, quick!" Chou said vehemently. He was from Shanghai. He had a square face, a fair complexion, and was rather tall. But what was more important to us was that he was a man of culture and thus had compassion for us poor laborers.

In the room, I saw, as I had expected, Yelusa and Yama waiting. But the sight of 'Lusa instantly caused me pain. She seemed much changed and had lost her vivacity. Seeing me, she just cried. We both seemed to have become dumb after three months' separation.

Chou then came to our aid. "Comrade Yelusa," he said, "please don't cry. And listen to me. It's against the regulations for the two of you to meet today. So if you would like to come again, please come on the second or fourth Sunday of any month. Those two days are days when I am on duty. If the prisoners are allowed to rest as usual on those holidays, I believe I could give you some time alone. As to this first visit, I think I can only let you have a good talk."

Chou and Teng left the room. Yama told me that originally the "criminal laborers" were scheduled to meet their families once a month, but now for some reason the plan was not going to be carried out, which was why they hadn't been able to see me for three months, although they had come three times for that purpose. This was the fourth time 'Lusa and Yama had come to the farm to see me, and they had finally succeeded because they had appealed to the "political commissioners" and obtained special permission. Yama had also sent the "leaders" a handsome gift of dried roast beef. With that okay from the high command, Chou and Teng naturally could treat us magnanimously by leaving us to ourselves. I could be with 'Lusa for an hour and a half without any disturbance (the normal time limit for a criminal laborer to see his guest or family was thirty minutes).

Yelusa came to see me as my fiancée. Ling had suggested this because he knew the commissioners could not give permission unless the visit was with a family member. So, in part, I owed this reunion with my sweetheart to Ling's good advice.

It grieved Yama that her sister and I, though left alone, could not utter even a word of joy to mark our reunion. She found us both buried in deep sorrow and deprived of lovers' eloquence. To ease our awkwardness, she rushed to us and advised, "Dear sister and dear brother-in-law, you can't just cry away your time. Shouldn't you take this opportunity to pour out your hearts? I know you must each have accumulated a lot of tenderness. Come on, be sensible. Make yourselves like lovers anew."

But how could we when we were in despair? If we had been standing on a precipice, we would probably have hugged each other tightly and thrown ourselves into the abyss without trying to break the sorrow with false eloquence.

Yama must have sensed our feelings, "All right," she said, "if you can't be romantic, then be practical. What can a poor couple like you do, if there is no hope of going to Lhasa? Do you mean just to meet once or twice a month here by the favor of Disciplinarian Chou?"

A good question indeed. But 'Lusa and I were too sad to think, so Yama continued. "Why, have you forgotten? Leader Hao once proclaimed that the laborers of the farm would be allowed to have families. Don't you think you can apply to the commissioners and obtain permission to marry each other and live together here?"

"He did announce that," I found myself replying. "But they have yet to decide to honor their words. They say we have to wait until the farm is fully constructed and all the working stations are well settled."

"And how long will that be?" Yama asked.

"Two or three years, perhaps."

"My God, you'll be an old couple by then!"

Yama's joke attempted to break through our frozen sorrow. I saw her intention, and replied, "Yes, two or three years here are enough to make an old couple out of us. But beware, as we get old, you'll grow no younger."

Our bantering lightened the atmosphere instantly. I grasped 'Lusa's hands and consoled her in a low tone, "My dearest, let us be patient. We can't be otherwise for the time being. But believe me. I'll marry you sooner or later. Nothing except death can break this promise of mine. We must hope for the best though we must prepare for the worst."

Hearing this, 'Lusa quickly held out her hands, stopped my mouth with them, and said, "Yes, darling, you are right. But please don't expect the worst for us. I believe our merciful Goddess Baidumu will protect us and bless us until we are happily married. Meanwhile, please take good care of yourself. Yes, take the best care, for my sake." With these words she hugged me and I bent over her face and gave her a long parting kiss. Yama took the hint and went out of the room, saying she wanted to see Chou and Teng. In the ensuing moments, I really wished I could gulp Yelusa down and possess her forever.

When our time was up and I was told to leave the room, 'Lusa and Yama drew a number of packages out of a big canvas bag they had brought with them. The packages were loaded with food, mostly dried roast beef and butter, which I thought could last me over a month. Besides the food, the two sisters also brought me a vest made from a leopard's skin, a pair of trousers made of sheep skin, a pair of leather stockings and a leather overcoat. These articles of clothing naturally could keep me warm. But more important, they would remind me of Yelusa, who I dreamed would never really part from me, no matter how cold the weather was.

For three years I met 'Lusa regularly on the farm. In the spring-time, grasses grew lush and the nomads were encouraged to drive their cattle and sheep to the outskirts of Telingha to graze. During that season, Yelusa's family came with the others and set up their tents near the farm. But during the summers they left for faraway meadows because the farm leaders were afraid the nomads' cattle, sheep, and horses might eat the farm's early grain. It was not until we had finished harvesting in the autumn that the nomads were allowed to come back with their livestock. As a result, I could see 'Lusa more often during the spring and fall (usually twice a month) than during the other seasons (sometimes only a single time in three months). During a long period without seeing me, 'Lusa would write me letters, real love letters. I could read passion and warmth in every word she wrote. But regrettably, I could not answer her letters because, as nomads, her family had no permanent address and their temporary addresses were of no help to the delivery service.

When 'Lusa came, we would meet in the "discipline room," or at a secluded place near our work site. If it was Chou who was on duty when she came, she would be able to stay longer with me than usual. Once she asked the director of my work station to permit her to stay overnight with me, but the request was denied.

At first both 'Lusa and I were in anguish over having to depend on the Communists for our occasional short unions. But as time went on and the situation never improved, we gradually came to accept it. Thus, when later we heard that there might be no hope of our getting married after the farm was fully constructed (because, they said, I was condemned to life imprisonment and a "criminal laborer" with such a sentence would never be allowed to get married while still serving his term), 'Lusa as well as I were resigned to our fate.

Deep down in our hearts 'Lusa and I constantly prayed that the Communist regime would not last long. We were convinced that such a tyrannical rule would soon collapse. Something had only to happen to initiate its downfall. One year, 'Lusa managed to obtain a very good shortwave radio set, with which she could hear messages from places as far away as Taiwan and America. We listened regularly to international news, hoping that the Third World War would break out and all of China would be delivered. It was with this hope that we followed excitedly the news of the Suez Canal crisis of September 1956, and the Hungarian coup d'état in October of the same year. It was also with this hope that I sought every opportunity to read the *People's Daily News* and the international page of the *Chinghai Daily News*. But the Third World War never broke out and we finally grew impatient. Our hopes never died, but our frustration was keen.

Occasionally 'Lusa would become so desperate that she even suggested committing suicide together. On such occasions I had to put forth my greatest effort to comfort her and exhort her to be brave. Once, to console her, I said, "I've found a way out. If only you agree to this idea, we can end all these long and painful expectations."

"What is it?" she was more than eager to know.

"You know I am one of the strongest laborers here, and have a reputation for wisdom. I've also developed very good relationships with the other laborers. The Communists are trying to approach me."

"To approach you? What for?"

"To make me one of their 'positive members' of course. If I am willing to obey them, to become their minion, to become a Communist, I believe they would reduce my sentence to only fifteen years, or even ten. And you know I have already served almost six years."

"But will your conscience let you do that?"

"I didn't think so. But for your sake I might do anything."

"Oh no!" 'Lusa protested. "Don't say that! I won't have you sacrifice your dignity. I can't let you ruin yourself. Let us retain a good conscience. Let us not talk about the idea again."

"Very well then. I'll be a righteous man throughout my life so long as you stick by my side."

Her nobility made me revere Yelusa even more. From then on, I was determined to show no sign of compromise to the Communists. And that is why nine years later I was imprisoned for two years in the well-cell for "purposely being the stubbornest unrepentant member on the farm."

In April 1958, I met 'Lusa again. It was an unforgettable meeting during the time of spring sowing. She wore an apricot-yellow satin blouse with a big red flower pattern, and black breeches. When I first saw her, I sensed something strange, although she talked and laughed in her usual manner. In the past I could easily have detected any sadness or bitterness under her outward happiness. But this time was different. I felt in her tone, her attitude, and her posture a sort of resolution. But I could not guess what it was. At first I was happy to see her determination, but gradually this unusual comportment filled me with misgivings. She had become a riddle to me.

During our usual heart-to-heart talk, I tried to guess her state of mind, but it was not until she was leaving that I got some inkling. I remember she grasped my hands tightly, her wide open eyes staring into my face, and said to me resolutely, "Dear, I'm leaving. You know I have loved you and will love you forever. Although we are not formally man and wife, I have experienced more happiness than most married couples. I won't regret having loved you these five years. I am only too happy to belong to you always, so I have been willing to share your fate. I know you have been disgraced, ill-treated, wronged and tortured. I can share your hatred, too. Don't you see? This is a world unjust and unfair. I feel I cannot love you without doing something to change it. I feel pure love in this world must be protected, and actively . . ."

When she came to the word "actively," I was still thinking over everything she was saying, and didn't realize that she meant the word literally. When she finished that speech, she suddenly shook off my hands and "actively" dashed off without looking back. Then I began to realize that something painful was happening. Puzzled, I ran and called after her, hoping she would stop and listen to me. But she got on her horse, kicked it to a gallop, and was quickly gone. I imagined

at about ten o'clock that evening the Dalai Lama and some of his retinue, as well as family members, escaped to India. It was a sensational event worldwide. Further report had it that on March 20, the Communists shelled the Dalai's Lobulinka palace and all the temples near Budala. After twenty-four hours' shelling, the palace and temples were reduced to burning and smoking ruins. The Tibetan "rebellious army" was defeated, they said. At that time, we could read about the event in the *People's Daily News* and the *Chinghai Daily News*. The reports in those papers were, of course, biased, representing only Communist views, but I still understood what was really going on. Before and after the Lhasa Event, anti-communism was prevalent in Southwest China. It was said that the Kangpa tribes had gathered an army of more than one hundred thousand people to take action along the banks of the Yalutzangpu River.

The Lhasa Event did not end with the defeat of the Tibetan army in Lhasa by the Communists. We knew then that rebellious Tibetans were still scattered all over Tibet ready to attack the Communists. And it was at this time that I came to realize fully what Yelusa had meant by "doing something actively." It suddenly occurred to me that 'Lusa might have gone to join the "Rebellious Army."

We couldn't be sure what exactly happened to the Tibetans, but after the Lhasa Event thousands of captured nomadic people arrived at Telingha Prison to add to our "labor power." Our working station was reorganized into a "big team" comprising several "middle teams," each consisting of several hundred people. (The leaders of the rebellious army had been shot much earlier, without being tried and sentenced. Those who came as criminal laborers were only ordinary soldiers.)

I thought the newcomers to the farm could be good sources for information about Yelusa. I questioned every newcomer I met about her. Fortunately, many had heard of her, which meant she might still be alive. Unfortunately, no one could be sure of her present situation. They all agreed that she had become a heroine by leading a guerrilla band against the Communists. But some said she and her followers had retreated into the Kunlun Mountains while others said she and her family had escaped to India with the Dalai Lama. Later, still others said that she had probably died in action. This last speculation stunned me. I hoped it was only a rumor. But news or rumor, it left me no peace. I mourned and shed many secret tears. And I determined to seek out the truth about 'Lusa before I died.

In 1962, the Communist administration began to show "leniency" toward the Mongolian and Tibetan criminals. Consequently, many criminal laborers on our farm were released. I thought it another good chance for me to seek out the truth about Yelusa. So whenever possible, I would ask the released Tibetans to take my message to Yelusa, or Yama, Kuoshijie, Kese, Chienmei, or any others who had some connection with Yelusa's family.

Meanwhile, I kept laboring, and waiting for further news. My health deteriorated. After twelve years' menial life, I had developed heart disease and stomach ulcers. After being hospitalized twice, I was grouped into the "Senile and Sickly Section," apparently to ready me to accept the end of life.

One spring day I was busy sowing as usual on the farm when Disciplinarian Chou suddenly called me to the discipline room. Before I reached the room, I saw two horses in front of the gate, one of which was none other than Yama's black steed. At the sight of the horses, I felt my heart start to beat wildly.

"Where is 'Lusa's horse?" I asked myself when I saw that the other horse was not her Tsaoliu. On entering the room, I was surprised to see Yama's face so lean and yellow, not a bit like the Yama I knew in the past. I was also very disappointed to find Kuoshijie there instead of Yelusa. As soon as she saw me, Yama flew into my arms and started crying bitterly. Kuoshijie also began sobbing. I knew that they were bringing bad news. I felt dizzy but I tried to compose myself and demanded to know why 'Lusa was not there.

Kuoshijie then sobbed out the story. After the Lhasa Event, the Communists put their so-called "Democratic Renovation" into practice, during which all rich men's properties in Tibet were confiscated. The victims of that Renovation naturally rose up with the rest of the Dalai Lama's faithful followers to revolt against the Communists.

Yelusa emerged at that time as the leader of several hundred Tibetans. She fought in the Numohung area. The civilians there, they said, all supported her with water and food. But after fighting ten or more days against a Communist battalion, 'Lusa's band was defeated because her enemy had better weapons and was better trained.

'Lusa withdrew her band into the Kunlun Mountains, hoping to regroup there. Quite unexpectedly, however, over a thousand men attacked her band from the north. It was another Communist force with even better weapons and supplies. 'Lusa's band was surrounded and, after fighting desperately for two days and two nights, all her men were either killed or injured. Yelusa herself was hit with several bullets and was captured. Yama, who always accompanied her sister, was also injured, though less seriously than 'Lusa.

"Injured? Where is she now?" I could not bear their slow unraveling of the truth.

Instead of answering me right out, Yama showed me the scars on her neck and feet and told me she had just been released from Kermu Prison, where she was kept as a criminal laborer for three years after she was captured. Kuoshijie also told me a similar story about himself.

Still I demanded to be told of Yelusa's present situation. Yama then handed me a cloth parcel. I did not know what it meant, but I opened it at once. Enclosed in the parcel were two long braids of black hair and a pair of silk pillow cases, on each of which were embroidered four red characters signifying: "Good Mate, Love Match." Obviously, these were to be, for me, 'Lusa's legacy.

How can I describe what I felt then? A thousand knives rending my heart? That was the least of it. I wanted to abandon myself to tears and howling, but I soon collected myself. I was aware that I could not mourn for an anti-Communist in a Communist "discipline room," even though the bemoaned was my beloved. To do that proper act in that improper situation would cause trouble, not only for myself, but for Disciplinarian Chou, who was doing me a favor by allowing me to see my guests then and there.

Then Yama sobbed out her sister's story: 'Lusa's wounds . . . beyond cure . . . Mama could not go and see her . . . she was dying . . . cut the braids . . . told me to bring them . . . back to Mama . . . and asked Mama . . . to send them . . . and the pillow cases . . . to you . . . wishing you to . . . to cherish them . . . for memory.

For memory! Yes, all was memory only! My love for her and her love for me. What else could I expect? Yama added that 'Lusa had thought she had somehow avenged me by killing some Communists. But did I need that vengeance? I looked again at the four Chinese characters she had embroidered on the pillow cases. I began to imagine each character was a spirit. And each spirit was saying, "No, she was not born for vengeance. Yes, she was born for love, for a good mate, for a good match."

I picked up the pair of braids. I stared long and hard at them. I stroked them, caressed them, kissed them, and hugged them fast and firm. "Yes, good mate and love match, love mate and good match," I heard myself murmuring almost hysterically. Yama and Kuoshijie saw that I was failing. They each held out a hand to me. If they had not done so, I might have fallen down on the floor immediately.

After a while, I came back to myself, and it was time for my guests to leave. I took a last long look at the unhappy messengers. Their faces, I saw, were both inscribed with the two characters denoting "woe" and "disaster."

But they also brought dear gifts. They brought me a big bag of dried roast beef and butter. They brought me their families' greetings and blessings. And above all, they brought me my sweetheart's remains, which I would forever hold precious for her memory. I have forgotten how I bade farewell to my guests that day. But that meeting with them is burned in my brain. Even now it seems as if I have not yet said good-bye to them, and they are still sobbing with me in the discipline room.

Thirteen years later I was set free. But I felt as though I was still imprisoned, and as though a heavy burden of sorrow was still weighing me down. I sought to find Yama, but no news of her or her family could be had.

After I returned to Shanghai, I was lucky enough to become

familiar with a man who was the brother-in-law of one of my sister's students. He was a disciplinarian from the Chinghai Kermu Labor Correction Farm, and a native of Shanghai, though he had lived in the Northwest for more than ten years. As he had a gentle manner and I knew he was returning to Chinghai, I suggested to him that I go with him to have a tour of Kermu. He approved, and we departed. We first arrived in Hsining, the capital of Chinghai. From Hsining we had to travel four days to reach Kermu. After we got to Kermu, I spent a day walking about the town and two nights resting on the farm. Then I left Kermu for Numohung, my real destination. I did not tell my friend the purpose of my trip. As I bumped on a bus along the Chinghai-Tibet Highway bound west for Numohung, he was likely thinking I was on my way east again.

After about 150 kilometers, I reached my real destination. Numohung was a big town compared with other towns in the West. It had more than ten stores on its main street and some fifty or sixty houses. All the houses were built with thatched roofs and earthen walls. A "Labor Correction Farm" and a "Stationed Regiment's Farm" were located not far from the center of town.

Early the morning after my arrival, I took a sheet of paper out of a plastic bag. On the paper was a map drawn by Yama for me before she parted with me at Telingha. The map, she told me, showed where I could find traces of Yelusa in her last days. I had taken great trouble hiding that map the last thirteen years, lest the farm leaders should discover it. In those days, the Communist leaders searched every prison house once every two months. They searched every prisoners' trunk and every corner likely to hide weapons, documents, or other forbidden items. I can't remember how many times I was compelled to change the map's hiding place.

I read the map closely and memorized the route. Then I went out of the town, heading north toward the Chilian Mountains. It was already after eleven o'clock on a sunny morning when I ended my fifteen kilometer walk at the foot of the mountains.

I was in a wide expanse of craggy terrain. This was where Yelusa's band first fought against the Communist army. As I understood, Yelusa's strategy was to attack Numohung Farm and deliver the three thousand criminal laborers there first. If that plan succeeded, she would organize them into a new band and lead them in an attack on Kermu Farm to release the ten thousand prisoners there. If the plan again succeeded, she would have become the leader of an enormous rebel army which could have attacked Telingha Farm next so that the fifty thousand criminal laborers there, including myself, might be set free.

It was a reasonable strategy. She might have guessed that the Dalai Lama and his military counselors also had had the idea of liberating the hundreds of thousands of imprisoned laborers in Chinghai and arming them to form a strong anti-Communist force to protect the freedom of Tibet. But as we know they never succeeded.

I lingered there a good while. I imagined it was here that 'Lusa received two bullets, one scratching her arm, the other slightly injuring her leg, and causing her to call her band to withdraw into Kunlun Mountains.

I looked around and far into the distance. I saw one mountain range after another, each, I knew, more than three thousand meters high, and each a different shade of green. Didn't these include the same Sun Moon Mountain and Touch Heaven Ridge upon which we risked our lives to build a road? The distant scenery called me back to the days before I had met Yelusa.

All of a sudden, I thought I smelled 'Lusa's hair. It seemed to be coming from the distant mountain ranges. I imagined the different shades on the mountains were the shades of 'Lusa's hair; 'Lusa had become the Goddess of Mountains.

I had become a pilgrim. In climbing those mountains I was journeying to visit her holy shrine.

I trudged over one sandhill after another until I came to a lofty eminence. I surveyed the height and then climbed to its top. The eminence commanded the hilly plateau beneath. It was where 'Lusa had commanded her band, I imagined.

Standing there and looking all around, I recalled the scenery of Black Horse Lake and the Pa Yin River. In my imagination, the scenery was no longer tinged with ugly spots where criminal laborers toiled under the threat of death. The scenery, instead, was that of

Arcadia, in which 'Lusa and I had walked hand in hand and recited our favorite lyric poems.

That eminence became a holy place for me. I had to pay homage to Yelusa then and there. I folded my hands and bowed three times toward the north. Then I knelt on the ground, again bowing my head three times in the direction of the Kunlun Mountains. Lastly, I prostrated myself on the ground, kneeling with my head touching the yellow sand, and kissed the earth again and again, shedding tears and praying repeatedly: "Saint Yelusa! Saint Yelusa!"

Nobody was watching me. A few birds flew by—eagles or larks or sparrows. Perhaps only the Kala chick—a native bird as big as a dove, with a red head, yellow body, and blue tail—noticed my strange behavior there, for it stood on the sand near by, and took wing upon hearing my repeated prayer.

After I finished my prayer, I dug the sand with my fingers and put some handfuls of it into the plastic bag in which I had kept the map. Then I stood and bowed my head again three times toward the north. I brought my ceremony to an end by saying a silent goodbye to my beloved saint: "Fare thee well, my love. You'll forever live in my heart."

Back in the Communist world, I knew it seemed a bit sentimental to have gone on that pilgrimage. But I deemed it not sentimental at all to keep the handfuls of yellow sand, 'Lusa's two braids of hair, and her two pillow cases, to be buried together with my body when I die.

In the Barrens

I was sent to Telingha Farm in the fall of 1954. From that point, I led a life of "labor correction" for nearly twenty-six years. If one's life could be compared to a piece of music, mine in those years was a "Symphony of Hell," to which my earlier tortured life was a simple prelude.

Communist society in China, especially in the secretly block-aded area of Chinghai, was like the most terrifying fantasy. It seemed the Communists did nothing but study how to improve their skill at treating people cruelly. They whipped, flogged, cursed, insulted, per-secuted, and killed innocents suffering from hunger, cold, and disease. They created a "Land of Terror," in which every tick of the clock could bring an unthinkable incident in a daily life-and-death struggle. The following is an account of my experiences during the "Three Years of Great Famine" and the "Great Cultural Revolution," as well as how I was eventually set free. But let me first describe our general life on the farm.

Monotony was the first characteristic of our life on Telingha Farm. We were made to talk, behave, work, and rest according to rules fixed with the purpose of reducing us to machines. We had no ability to exercise our free will. We acted always with predictable regularity. We weren't even allowed to think or believe as we wished. We became mere bodies without souls. As machines, we developed the same facial expressions, the same gestures, the same speech patterns. It was only in our shared hatred of the Communists, that we were not fully reduced to automatons. Our environment, also, was utterly monotonous. We worked the same ground, used the same tools, saw the same fierce eyes in the faces of "the leaders," ate the same things, and slept in the same places every day for more than twenty years!

The farm was located at the east of the Tsaidamu Basin, an area of over one hundred thousand square kilometers which covers a large part of the province of Chinghai. Telingha had once been one of the twenty-nine Mongolian chis.* It was some fifty kilometers away from the Pa Yin River, the river in which Chu Pa-chieh or "pigsy," companion of the Monkey King in the story "Journey to the West," is said to have bathed.

We on the farm were called pioneers as well as "criminal laborers." Upon our arrival in Telingha, we found only a few shabby houses. We thought the place must have been an uninhabited wilderness since before the Stone Age. It is said that the Mongolian or Tibetan nomads came to this place only in recent centuries, and never for permanent dwelling but only to water their livestock in the Pa Yin. The place was then an expanse of yellow sand covered with straggling weeds. As "pioneers," we were to turn it into a farm. Our first task was to build an irrigation system leading to the Pa Yin. That project began in 1954. After it was finished, we started to prepare the ground for growing crops.

The farm was about one hundred kilometers square, and surrounding the large area were Communist guards, who patrolled the grounds day and night. Within the bounds some 150,000 "criminal laborers" had been put to work, or rather, put to torture. A few minutes before we laborers were to go out to work in the morning, the "leaders" would blow whistles to rouse us. After we had each wolfed down two loaves of black bread, we would start. Usually, a "middle team" had four hundred people divided into twenty sections. Each team was overseen by fourteen guards carrying whips, cudgels, and guns. In the winter, we toiled under this "heavy guard" from six in the morning to six at night. In the summer, we worked for one more hour, that is, from five in the morning to six at night.

---

*A Mongolian chi was basically equivalent to a county.

I heard her crying loudly from where I stood. I never saw her again. Even today I still cannot believe she could have left me that way.

For more than ten days after that, I suffered the most acute anguish I had ever known. I simply could not believe that this was to be our end. I kept thinking of the past, especially of the way she had parted with me in former times. Then I began to consider the reasons she might have acted as she did. I thought of every possible reason. One possible cause was the policy the Communists had adopted to carry out their "Socialist Economic Revolution" in every corner of China. According to the new policy, many private enterprises were forced to become corporations run by both private and public managers. It was tantamount to confiscating private property. This policy was followed by the implementation of the so-called "redeeming system," which was similar, and the "Three Red Banners" movement, which was also an extreme step, aimed at confiscating private enterprises. But what directly affected 'Lusa's family was the implementation of the "Collective Ranching System," which required that all nomads' livestock be confiscated. Perhaps Yelusa just couldn't bear to think that she had to suffer a double tragedy in terms of love and property. And so she had gone to do something "actively."

Anyway, after that day, Yelusa never visited me again and never wrote me any letters. She became for me an insoluble mystery. Although I have since learned what became of her, and have reconciled myself that she is just a cherished memory, I have yet to understand exactly what was in her mind at that time. Needless to say, after her departure I was very anxious to hear from her. But year in and year out, I found no way to satisfy my yearning. I could only pray for her health and safety. Whenever I prayed, I would recall her tender love for me. I remembered she had saved my life three times: once from starvation, once from the freezing cold, and once during the last few years from debilitating hard labor. I knew she had saved the lives of Ling and Chan, as well.

One year after she left me, the "Lhasa Event" happened in Tibet. On March 17, 1959, a fierce battle was fought in Lhasa between the Tibetans and the Communist army. It was reported that

A coal factory and an infirmary were located not very far from Telingha. Those who worked there had to suffer through sandstorms in the spring. They often complained that they had to grope about blindly while outdoors. We who worked at Telingha suffered from another sort of blindness. In clearing the fields, we first burned the grass. The resulting clouds of smoke were often blown against us, choking and blinding us. Even under these conditions, the "leaders" wouldn't allow us to slacken in our work.

It is said that millions of years ago, Tsaidamu Basin was a sea, but the water dried up, leaving only a great quantity of pebbles to mark where it had been. Whether or not it's true, we found millions of pebbles of various sizes, colors and shapes, and after we burned up the grass, we had to remove them. Beneath the pebbles, we often found larger stones, which we removed with pickaxes. This was made more difficult because our tools had very short handles. In using them, we were bent over all the time, and when we returned from work, we had difficulty standing up straight. We lay on our beds like so many dead lobsters. Our night's rest gave us barely enough time to cure our hunched backs.

A group of twenty was required to prepare a field of four to five mu.* To achieve that goal, we labored strenuously twelve hours a day with only a thirty-minute recess at noon. Our efficiency was largely due to the fact that we worked with the constant threat of bullets, whips, and cudgels. When we came back from work every evening, our bodies were suffused with pain. We wished we were the machines they would make of us so that we could perform super-efficient work without fatigue and pain. But, alas, we were only flesh and bones! And we had been deprived of our souls! We never had the guts to strike.

We did not dare to fall behind our schedule of work, not to mention attempt a strike. If any group failed to finish its assigned task

*1 "mu" = 733.5 square yards.

at any time, the "leaders" would look into the matter and seek out those who were to blame. Usually the unlucky ones would be accused of "willful slackening of efforts" and publicly prosecuted in the evening.

The "public prosecutions" on the farm proceeded in the same manner as in other places. They usually started right after dinner time and ended at around ten o'clock. The prosecuted were reviled, cursed, kicked, beaten, and otherwise humiliated by all present, especially by the "positive members." Such "prosecutions" went on for six years, until 1959, when the Great Famine made it unnecessary to torture the laborers by such cruel measures. In the fall of 1962, however, the "prosecutions" began again, though not so frequently as before. The Communists thought that these "activities" were a good way to discipline us, and a nice means of creating conflicts among us so that we would be divided and thus easier to control.

Reducing rations was the Communists' other way of taming us. Every two or three weeks, or at most every two months, our rations would be "reallotted." In the reallotment, we were classified into three groups, judged on both our loyalty to the government, and our recent ability to carry out our tasks. The laborers in Group A might have three normal-size, or two large-size loaves of bread for a meal; Group B, two normal-size loaves; Group C, one-and-a-half normal-size, or two small-size loaves.

To get a better allotment, all except the "stubborn ones" strove to increase their labor output. An exceptionally good laborer could even become a "positive member," or a section leader, and thus enjoy some special privileges in addition to better meals. There was always a keen competition among the "loyal laborers." Not infrequently, one person accused someone else of "not really being positive." Hearing such accusations the Communist leaders often replied, "That's all right. We don't mind whether you are truly or falsely positive. You could be false one or two years. But in the third year you'd become true." This was a basic tenet of the Communist political philosophy. Because I refused to subscribe to it, I could never become one of their "positive members," even though my labor power often surpassed others'.

In the autumn, we had a harvest time of about twenty days. During those days every laborer was required to go to the field before dawn, at half past three, and work until nine o'clock in the evening. Many sick or weak people died from exhaustion during that time. Even the strong ones couldn't stand such labor. But guns, whips, and clubs were constantly aimed at those who tried to evade work in any way. So we worked incessantly, like machines. Sometimes when a poor wretch fell dead on the ground, the "leaders" would go over and examine him to determine whether he had really ceased to breathe, but they wouldn't allow death to provide an excuse for malingering. When the harvest time was over, many survivors felt that one couldn't leave a Chinghai labor correction farm without being short at least two layers of one's skin. None of us left the farm without some brutal emotional or physical wound.

We undertook a wide variety of work on the farm. Besides working in the coal processing plant, we were employed to turn wilderness into arable land, to make flat fields for cultivation, to plough fields, to sow seeds, to weed, to apply fertilizers, to irrigate, to harvest, to thresh grain, to store grain in barns, to convey grain to other places, and do many other things that were considered "agricultural." After we started to grow crops, we continued to build the irrigation system. We dug three different sizes of irrigation ditches. The biggest was thirty meters wide; the middle, two or three meters; and the small one, less than one meter. The task was difficult because we had no modern machines. We had only spades, shovels, pickaxes, and carrying baskets. We ourselves served as the machines.

We labored in all weather. No matter how windy, rainy, or snowy it was, we went out every day as usual. Occasionally some conscientious leaders allowed us to suspend work and squat in the rain during a storm, or even let us come back early if the storm hit when we were about to finish. But more often than not, we were made to continue in the rain or snow after the leaders had hurried away to seek shelter. While working, we usually wore only a single layer of clothing. Our cotton overcoats were laid aside, and we were often chilled to the bone even in the summertime. But none of us dared to leave work unless the leaders noticed our drenched condition and suggested we use our coats as raincoats.

The quality of work they required of us was simply absurd. For instance, they required we make the surface of the field as smooth as a mirror, turn the dried manure into a powder as fine as dust, and make the field ridges as straight as rulers. Such requirements could never be met, of course, when we had only simple implements to work with. In fact, they made such high demands on us largely in order to make it easier to find fault and to punish those with whom they were not pleased.

The most odious work we had to do was to grind dried manure into a fine powder. You might not know that in China night soil was the primary fertilizer used on farms. Therefore, no bit of it was allowed to be wasted. We were normally required to empty our bowels over pits specially designed to accumulate the night soil. The filth in these pits froze in the winter. When spring came, we were asked to break the dry lumps of filth into pieces and grind them into powder so that the fertilizer could be easily absorbed into the soil. When we broke the night soil into dry lumps, we could use shovels or hammers. But when we ground the dry lumps, we had to use our bare hands. Here I may mention, by the way, an interesting event called the "Single Discharge Movement." To accumulate feces for use as fertilizer, the leaders asked us to carry baskets of earth to convenient places, and demanded that each laborer make at least one contribution of "human fertilizer" to the earth in the baskets. All the baskets of night soil–enriched dirt were then put together, creating a big fertile pile.

The Telingha Farm had two branch farms: the Gobi and the Kehai Farm, both of which were built by us as well. In addition to the labor correction farms, we built a brick and tile factory, a sewing workshop, a coal plant, a carpenter's workshop, a car factory, a flour and oil processing plant, a farm implements works, some storehouses, offices, lodgings, and prison cells. Once we were sent to work in a sulphur ore and coal mine. We were "criminals," engineers, and omnipotent laborers at the same time.

And indeed, we achieved something. We cultivated two hundred thousand mu of farmland and produced at least three hundred million jin of grain, one third of which was turned over to the government. Within six years we saw Telingha change from a wilderness to a productive farm. The two hundred thousand of us made Wulan, a city on the Pa Yin River, and the entire Wulan county a very prosperous place. The city became densely populated, and boasted blocks of offices, all kinds of shops, and recreational centers.

But for all we did in Telingha and Wulan, we were never rewarded. In the years before 1962, we received no wages. After that, we were each paid two yuen per month as pocket money, a sum equal, at that time, to less than one U.S. dollar. Nor were we fed well enough to keep up our strength and health. For ten years we were allowed only six "woh-woh-toes" a day per person. It was not until many people starved during the three years of famine that our food allowances were increased a little bit, and we were occasionally granted some meat on holidays to gratify our palates.

A civilized state is one governed by laws, not by individuals. By that measure China has returned to a barbaric state since it fell into the hands of the Communists. No civilized laws have been observed since 1949; the people seem to abide only by the law of "natural selection." In this lawless state, we "criminal laborers" in Chinghai suffered the most. None of us was ever formally tried in court before being declared guilty and sentenced to "labor corrections." As a secret agent of the Nationalist Party, I was guilty in Communist eyes when I was arrested and thenceforth cruelly treated. But there were many people in Telingha who were wholly guiltless, and wrongly persecuted.

In 1953, a certain Niu Chin-yi, a newly arrived "criminal laborer," increased the number of prisoners on our team. He was tall, handsome, and amiable. He was a specialist in meteorology, a graduate with honors from the Central University of Nanking. He was the founder and had been the chief of the weather stations in Lanchou and Hsining. His achievement had contributed greatly to the welfare of the Northwest. Nevertheless, he was arrested one night in 1951 when he was fast asleep at his house in Hsining. The secret police took him directly to the prison. He was sent to the "labor correction camp" without trial or sentencing. Those in charge at the camp took him in without questioning the nature of his guilt, and without inquiring after his background. They just accepted him, in a gesture of obeisance to their superiors.

In order to justify his stay in the camp, the Communists declared that he had to serve thirteen years with us, on the grounds that he once resisted contributing his labor power to his fatherland by malingering. Thus the poor fellow underwent all sorts of torture and hardship with us: building roads in foul weather, attending "public prosecutions," and sowing and harvesting under the threat of guns and whips.

Once he was sick and could not keep pace with the others. A Director Chao beat him soundly with a club, swearing that he was deliberately slackening his efforts. Knowing the accusation to be wrong, a section leader and I went to speak to Chao. We said we had seen Niu spit some blood that morning before coming to work.

"Is that so?" Chao wouldn't believe us. "If he is so seriously ill, why didn't the doctor say so? Don't try to take him under your wings! You just want him to be your protégé, don't you?"

"Why should we?" I replied. "Just call the doctor now. If he isn't ill, accuse me of whatever you like. But if he is, I hope you'll talk sensibly and act like a human—"

I knew I had spoken beyond prudence. So I stopped suddenly, expecting a threat or retort from Chao. But before Chao responded, the section leader affirmed that we really expressed no ill will and begged Chao to show mercy toward Niu. Since the section leader was a "positive member," Chao naturally believed him. But instead of sending Niu back for treatment and rest, he just released him from further labor and let him lie on the ground.

Then came the snow. Niu's inadequate clothes simply could not keep out the cold. When, toward noon, they were sending bread to every laborer, we found him laid out like a dead dog on the cold ground. We went to Chao again, entreating him to show some real mercy. He said, reluctantly, "All right, let him go." By then, Niu was too weak to walk. We suggested he be sent back on the cart that carried our lunch to us. That evening, when we went back, we learned that he had a high fever, but according to the doctor, he was not mortally ill and still had a chance to recuperate.

Niu did recuperate eventually, but his life with us didn't change for the better. The family he left behind suffered, also. It was said that he had a very smart daughter who was often scoffed at and punished for no reason at all at school. After she finished her primary school education, she did not wish to go to school again. She wandered off and became a drifter, earning money whenever she had the chance. After she had accumulated some funds, she decided to make the trip to see her father at the camp in Telingha, but found herself entangled in red tape. She was made to run back and forth between the Provincial Commission of Chinghai and the Provincial Department of Common Security, as well as the Labor Correction Bureau. When she finally received permission to see her father at Telingha, he had been away from home for almost thirteen years. That is, he had almost finished his term of "labor corrections."

Yet the happy reunion of father and daughter did not bring about a happy ending. For fear that Niu, once released, might reveal the Communists' lawlessness and cruelty, the officials at the farm suddenly declared him an anti-revolutionary who had worked as a secret agent under the direction of his sister, Niu Hui-ying, a legislator of the Nationalist Party. (In fact, he hadn't been in touch with his sister since she fled when the Communists took the Chinese mainland.) So Niu was sentenced to seventeen more years at Telingha. This second sentence ended in 1967 when he became seriously ill, and was sent back home to die. Pathetic stories like this were abundant among us.

As early as 1959, when the "Three Years of Great Famine" had not yet begun, stories of starvation were already circulating around Telingha Farm. Tuan Cheng-te, a "criminal laborer" who belonged to the Fifth Big Team, told us a pathetic story: "My younger brother was a peasant. He raised a family of seven. But each season the rations he received were barely enough for five. When his youngest son was born, he went repeatedly to the police station to have the newborn baby registered. But for five years, the household registrar refused to make the registration for him. As a result, the child never had a ration ticket to his name. And his parents and brothers and sisters each had to spare a bit of their already insufficient rations for him. When the sixth year came, the family felt they couldn't stand the situation any longer. So my brother went again to the registrar. He knelt down and bowed to him, pleading, 'For mercy's sake, please let my child be registered!'

" 'Why?' The registrar replied, 'Can't you just manage as others do? You're not the only one suffering in this manner.'

"My brother was thus forced to speak his saddest words. He said, 'Sir, if you won't do this for me, I will have no other recourse than to kill this child. I cannot let the whole family starve for his sake.'

" 'All right, kill him then if you dare. I believe there are enough prisons to hold those guilty of such crimes.' The registrar seemed deaf to any threats.

"On hearing that, my brother turned his head and came home without giving any reply. He immediately went into the kitchen and fetched a knife. Then he rushed to his youngest son, caught him by the shoulder, made a violent cut in his throat, and ended his life without giving him time to know what was happening.

"My brother was blind with rage then. After committing that horrific murder, he held his dead child in his bloody arms and carried him to the police station to prove that he had dared to do as he had threatened.

"That event was the talk of the town for a time. But strange to say, most of the townspeople who witnessed or heard of the tragedy didn't blame my brother. They only cursed the Communists who were astonished at my brother's foolhardy audacity.

"After recovering from his astonishment, the registrar reprimanded my brother for his inhumanity and took him into custody. Not long after, he was sentenced to five years' imprisonment. The sentence was lenient. Maybe the Communists became suddenly conscious of the fact that they were the real murderers."

Tuan's story was too incredible. Knowing that some of us doubted its truth, Tuan then told us how he came to know it. He said he had learned the story from his wife when she had come to see him at Telingha, to where he had been transported as a "criminal laborer" because he had had an illegal love affair with a woman.

Buddhists believe that east of a place called Yenfuti is Mount Tiewei, under which are hidden eighteen big hells and hundreds of small hells. This belief describes perfectly our situation. In those years we prisoners experienced the sufferings of endless hells. We were like so many "hungry ghosts" spitting out fire to devour anything edible. The peak of our suffering was in the three years after 1959 when famines plagued a large part of China. According to the estimate of an American scholar, more than twenty million Chinese died of starvation during those years. The province of Anhui alone witnessed ten million deaths. Later, during the period of "Cultural Revolution," the Communists admitted that the total number was around seventeen million. The great famine caused a colossal wave of refugees to break on Kowloon and Hong Kong in May 1962.

Although the great famine was something almost all Chinese experienced, the Communists still tried to block any report of it. Consequently, it was quite some time before most starving wretches dared to spread any "rumor" of the real situation, for fear that they might be arrested and tortured by something worse than deprivation of food. The more desperate, however, began to talk and act boldly. They not only protested the Communists' irresponsibility in such severe times, but also dared to rob the granaries. In our prison house on Telingha Farm, there were some newly arrived "criminal laborers" from Anhui Province who revealed to us, on occasion, what they had seen in their plagued homelands.

They had witnessed whole families, even whole villages, starve to death in Anhui. They claimed that in many villages, after people ate up all the animal feed, they began to eat grass, roots, tree bark, and twigs. They were able to eat such things by hammering them thoroughly first, removing all the hard "husks," and grinding the remnants into a powder, which they cooked with the more tender shoots of trees or weeds. Such "natural food," they added, was not only unpalatable but indigestible. Many got sick or were poisoned from living too long on that diet.

They were most impressed, they said, by the sight of a hungry multitude, frantically striving to eat the young shoots of beans, corn, and vegetables. They asserted that the greed and the speed the "hungry ghosts" manifested in eating the shoots far surpassed that of locusts.

While famine was ravaging Anhui and other provinces, we "criminal laborers" in the remote areas were hardly unaffected; we were sharing the "task" of starvation with millions of other Chinese. I say "task" because at that time starvation seemed to be a daily duty imposed on us by the Communists, just like any piece of hard work. You know our allotted rations were insufficient. Now, under the pretext of famine, the Communists had our rations reduced every month: from 25 to 20 jin for a "healthy" prisoner, and from 20 to 14 jin for a sick one. To make up for the loss of grain, we also had to eat weeds and wild herbs.

During the three years of "natural famine," I was transferred nine times from one unit to another. The units I labored with included the Third, Fifth, and First Big Teams of Telingha, the First Big Team of Gobi Farm, and the processing plants and the sanitariums at both of the farms. According to my observations, over twenty thousand people must have died of starvation in the nine units during those years. If we extrapolate using this ratio, over a hundred thousand people must have suffered the same fate in the whole Telingha area, and over two hundred thousand in all the labor correction farms of Chinghai.

The second half year of 1960 saw the greatest number of deaths from starvation. Every day, from every Big Team, more than thirty corpses were conveyed to a yard by cart. That yard became a horrible place. When passing it, we experienced a spine-chilling gloom. We did not even dare to cough in the presence of that "graveyard of cadavers." At night, if a queer sound was heard from that direction, we would imagine that ghouls were feeding on the corpses, or that the starved were still groaning for food even after death. Every week, every day, every hour, one corpse after another, each stiff as a tree trunk, fell before our eyes. We could not believe that death could come so easily. The dead bodies were like raindrops, and we stood in stormy purgatory for three years on end.

In those years, starvation became a sort of mental manacle, depriving us of our freedom to think. We could not for a moment forget its threat. It seemed to be continuously putrefying the air and making it difficult to breathe. How we longed to swallow that sinister word along with the morsel of food allotted to us! During the slow torture of starvation, we became sick enough to imagine a fire burning our bodies, or a pump forcing out every bit of liquid.

If you saw us, you would find each face starved into a pale mask, without flesh or life. Such faces were little different from those of the departed. No matter its shape, the face of a starvation victim is covered by only a fragile layer of skin. The eyes are hardly eyes but rather the pits of nuts fitted into sockets of bone. Such eyes shed no light. Yet, they bespeak the urgency of their owner's case. Although ghastly, they are more serviceable than the mouth, for they plead better than any words.

Some fellows were still alive when they lay down at night, and at dawn they were dead. They had become icy bodies with stiffened limbs. Nobody knew the exact time they had yielded up their last breaths. If you went close enough to examine the corpses, you might find the eyes of some of them wide open, while others still clenched their teeth. These phenomena occurred so frequently to the dead at the farm, one wondered if they were significant gestures. We speculated that a man who died with his eyes wide open had died somehow unsatisfied or unavenged, and a man with clenched teeth had not yet ended his hatred. Or, perhaps, the starved were still straining their eyes to find food, and, finding none, could only bite their teeth together tightly.

The search for food was everybody's priority in those times. The kitchen became a magnet. On our farm, many stronger fellows gathered there to rob the food senders. It is hard to believe that men on the brink of death could still be so energetic, but they struggled out of their beds, staggered up to the kitchen door, and lay in ambush there, waiting for the moment when the bamboo hampers of loaves were carried out of the kitchen. They were all prepared to steal. One day these starving plunderers snatched the loaves away, and afterward many suspects were imprisoned in special cells, and kept constantly in close custody until they died. Strife was inevitable among these men. Three to five people died every day fighting one another for food at the kitchen door, or in the yard. They did not fight with clubs or fists, but merely pushed each other with their remaining strength. That push was often enough to knock down one's opponent and deprive him of his life.

Death took a great variety of forms among the starved. In addition to those who were pushed in fights there were those who simply stumbled and fell, shattering their fragile bones while happily biting off their first pieces of "woh-woh-toe." There were those who, having finished their own meals, took quick, shy glances at others who were still eating, and found their mouths watering profusely and their hearts straining a little too much. They didn't recover from these strokes.

The starving criminals still had to labor, but the weaker and more miserable tried to save their energy by evading hard work. They actually did not toil as much as they rested, and their tasks were often not completed. At the end of each day, when they were walking back for the night's rest, they had no strength to walk steadily, and each wanted to rest his hand on someone else's shoulder while they walked in line. But no one could allow such a fatal burden on his weak shoulder, and all staggered along alone.

Back at the tents, no one felt he was still himself. It is strange that hunger can cause so much pain in your body. It seems like a vise pinching all your bones, which feel dislocated for lack of flesh and sinews. Your head, hands, feet, even your belly and bowels, are no longer where they normally are. You are tempted to cry out loud but haven't the strength. When experiencing extreme hunger, one can barely utter an audible sound.

Before dinner time, some of the prisoners gathered outside the kitchen. They were not allowed in but could stay outside for a short while watching the preparation of dinner. They watched with their dull eyes sunken in their big sockets. They watched attentively the way the kichen workers mixed together flours of different colors (usually white and black), made it into dough, shaped it into loaves of bread, and steamed the loaves in a tight basket and sieve of bamboo. Occasionally, a breeze might blow some of the escaping steam out of the kitchen. The steam, with its accompanying smell of food, became a treat for the "hungry ghosts" waiting outside. They inhaled it with avarice. And they deluded themselves into believing that some form of food had already entered their bodies.

At last, one kitchen worker would strike an iron plate with a stick, giving the signal that dinner was ready to be served. At this everybody was cheered, though each would be given only two loaves as small as one's fists. The two small loaves were swallowed down quickly by each "gluttonous criminal." If someone were slower than his peers in devouring the bread, he would be watched and envied. His neighbors would stare at him greedily, hoping that some crumbs might fall unexpectedly onto the ground so that they could snatch up the godsend for themselves. But such a thing never happened. When anybody swept the ground with his eyes, the best he could grab was perhaps a discarded rotten leaf of Chinese cabbage, and that leaf was regarded as a treasure. When the lucky finder thrust it into his mouth, he probably believed it was his savior, too.

The threat of starvation, like any other prolonged frightful threat, is liable to cause insanity. But how can you believe the insanity I saw in our famine-stricken area? Hunger drove many men so mad, they took their enamel basins to the fertilizer pits, and fetched back basinfuls of night soil. They then washed the dirty stuff with water again and again in order to pick out the undigested grain that remained in the excrement. Strange to say, they did find a lot of such grain and ate it for supper.

How did they come to know that such "treasure" was there to be found? The criminals were divided into different classes, allotted different tasks, and treated quite differently. The first-class prisoners were those party leaders, officials, or officers who had committed "errors"—Communists were seldom said to have committed crimes, and they were seldom openly called "criminal" although they could become prisoners. Such prisoners, when undergoing "labor corrections," were often assigned to work as kitchen managers, prison doctors, carpenters, masons, ironsmiths, tailors, cleaners, keepers of grain yards or barns, and members of watering teams. Since they were engaged in such "lighter and nobler" work, they were said to be undergoing "great labor corrections." And those "great laborers" often enjoyed privileges unshared by other classes. They were not guarded by armed men, they had bigger allotments of rations; they were often free to take a walk inside or outside the prison house; when they worked outdoors, they had more freedom; they were not followed everywhere and watched over by guards. Thus, they often crept to the grain yards or barns and stole grain. The keepers of the yards or barns normally overlooked their pilfering, for they were pilferers, too. The pilferers often had no opportunity to cook the grain before they ate it, however. Whenever they failed to digest the grain because of diarrhea or other diseases, therefore, the grain would be passed out whole and sound. Knowledge of this situation made the grain prey to the insanity of the "hungry worms" who came out clutching their enamel basins.

The "high-class laborers" usually did not dare to steal too much grain at one time, but the more daring ones often had grain to sell or to exchange for clothing or tobacco. The kitchen managers or workers had, of course, food for sale or exchange. They stole flour, bread, and edible oil. They were therefore the patrons of the "rich" starving criminal laborers who could obtain regularly from their families some amount of daily necessities. During the three years of great famine, while the poor and law-abiding prisoners starved, the wealthy ones and the cunning Communists managed to dodge the brunt of the "natural disaster."

As for the miserable ones, their plight was almost too horrible to describe. For me, the most terrifying thing was done by the watering team. They took advantage of the hours they were out working to dig out the newly buried men who had died of starvation. The dead bodies were usually buried in the salty ground within the confines of the farm. In winter the graves were dug to only one meter's depth, while in summer they were dug to two meters. But in all seasons, the bodies were dumped into the graves and covered with only a thin layer of sandy soil. Therefore, it was fairly easy to dig out a newly buried corpse.

Nobody wanted to believe what the watering team did with the dead bodies they excavated, but it was true; they sold them as meat. Although the starved men had little flesh left, it was considered safer to eat than the flesh of those who had died from disease. The watering team cut the remaining flesh from the arms, thighs and breasts of the newly-buried corpses. The meat was then exchanged for clothing, tobacco, and other daily necessities. The transaction was of course, very secret. The "seller" usually pretended to be selling horse meat, camel meat, or the meat of an unknown rare animal. The "buyer" would not inquire into the nature of the meat offered. When you are on the brink of starvation, you don't mind eating mouse meat or lizard meat. In fact, any meat is a delicacy to someone willing to eat even soap or cotton.

So, many ate dead men's flesh cooked or raw, and counted themselves lucky. But such meat was not healthful, although tasty to the eaters, and some time after eating a large quantity of it the eater might swell up and die, only half suspecting he had fed on his former fellow laborers.

The hungry "birds" ("Birds will die for food," goes a proverb of ours) who had no money or barter had no chance to taste the meat offered by the watering team. After they got tired of supplementing their diet with weeds or herbs, they often resorted to theft. If they couldn't steal meat directly, they would steal others' money or possessions to barter for this precious commodity. As a result, loss of money or other valuable things became a daily threat to all the prison laborers. Some people thought that staying in the tent might be a way to protect their belongings, but they were unable to because suspending their labor (even for sickness) would, according to the regulations, cost them half of their daily allowance of food (two loaves of bread would be reduced to one). Under such circumstances, many people decided the only way to protect themselves was to steal. If your jacket were stolen, for instance, you would try to steal one from someone else. This practice naturally added many more cases of theft to the already growing list, and no day passed without quarrels, curses, and despair among the laborers.

The conditions were grim. There was a man named Chang He-lin who was from Hunan Province, where he had been a security officer. He was about fifty, and at Telingha he belonged to the Second Middle Team of the First Big Team of criminal laborers. I was then in the same unit, and I noticed he was absent one day when they called the roll. When they noticed him missing, the leaders sent two malicious men to find him. He was sick in bed, and they dragged him naked (he didn't wear any clothes in bed) to the gate of our camp.

"Why didn't you get out and work?" the leaders asked him. He couldn't reply. He only showed them his pale face and two closed eyes.

"We'll shoot you if you refuse to work."

But he still made no answer.

"All right, take him to the work site!" the Communists shouted.

He remained silent. Some of his fellow laborers laughed at his nakedness while others shed tears for him. Then the two malicious men brought a big basket and pole. They put him into the basket, hung it on the pole and carried him to the place where we were to labor that day. It was very cold then (it must have been several degrees below freezing), and on the way to the worksite, Chang froze to death. That fulfilled the leaders' threat: "Sick or dead, all malingerers must be taken to their place of work."

Famine is, of course, not a calamity peculiar to China. Ethiopia, for instance, is also a frequent victim. Other nations make known the cataclysms befalling them and plead for international aid, as Russia did after the recent Armenian earthquake, but Red China of the '50s and '60s was too afraid to have any of its dirty laundry aired. The "Three Years Great Famine" caused at least twenty million deaths, yet, even now, its seriousness is still little known outside of China. One cannot help but marvel at the Communists' ability to "blockade news" unfavorable to them.

During those awful years, I suffered no less than those I knew. At first, I traded some of my clothes for food. Later, I found my coat, sweater, jacket, even my shirts and trousers—everything that could keep me warm—had been bartered away in exchange for wheat or bread. By that time, I had eaten up all the dried beef Yelusa had given me as a last parting gift. And I no longer had recourse either to Yelusa, or to my former wife. I was on the brink of starvation; every day, every minute, I was haunted by a sense of urgency, seeing that soon I would have practically nothing to put in my stomach. I was worse off than a stableman, who at least had a chance to eat horse feed. I had, in fact, wished to take care of the hogs, for as a "hog tender," you could always steal some peas or bran that were originally intended for the animal. And stealing was no serious crime in a time of famine. As I was neither stableman nor hog tender, I had no chance to pilfer anything edible. I could seek extra food (in addition to my meager rations) only in the great outdoors; I often ate wild herbs and carrots. Sometimes, when extremely hungry, I even munched weeds much like a grazing horse.

At that time there were many eating grass, like me, but also rats, lizards, and other vermin, which I didn't dare eat no matter how serious my hunger. Even rats were very rare during the famine. Formerly, during the harvest time, the fields had been filled with them and to prevent them from stealing too much grain, the leaders had ordered us to catch them on a large scale. We would flood their holes to force them out, and then chase them, catch them, and beat them to death. On a good day, a small team like ours could catch several dozen of them. That meant the whole farm would catch thousands a day. In those days, very few people dared to taste rat meat. But now, even the most squeamish thought of it as a delicacy and would chase any rodent in the field.

I don't know why, but I never dared to eat rat meat no matter how it was cooked and, no matter how hungry I was. Some of those who shared my fear of rats tried to "cheat their stomachs" by drinking water to create a feeling of fullness, and to save their "woh-woh toes" for later. I, myself, usually opted for the tender parts of weeds.

I became not a vegetarian, but a grazing animal. Unfortunately, I didn't have the stomach of a grazing animal. So after I ate some unwashed grass, my stomach would start to ache. And before long I developed gastric ulcers. Once my stomach bled so much that I could no longer labor and was sent to a criminal ward in the farm's hospital. There, for a few days, I was allowed to eat meals made from pure flour and was given proper medical care. I was treated so favorably due to the influence of a certain Dr. Fu, who was from Hunan Province and had known both my brother and my brother-in-law there. While I was recovering in the ward, however, my rations were reduced. The loaves I ate dwindled from the size of one's fist to the size of an egg. After each meal, I was keenly aware that my belly was still empty, yet I was so weak that I had no strength to leave my sickbed and seek food elsewhere.

Thus I simply had no chance to recover, and I became weaker every day. There were times when I sensed I was at last parting from this world. It was not a sense of pain, but only a feeling of yielding. The ache of hunger induced a feeling of suffocation so keen that one day I suddenly lost consciousness. I was later told that after I had passed out they found I had stopped breathing and was stiff and cold. Since they couldn't find any trace of life in me, they sent me to the morgue until the time came for my burial.

Fortunately, Dr. Fu learned of my situation and rushed to the morgue to see me. Apparently, I had lain on a plank in the morgue for half an hour when the doctor arrived. At first he couldn't detect any trace of life in me. But upon examining me with his stethoscope, he detected a very weak rhythm of breathing, and felt there was still some remaining warmth in my breast. He asked some nurses to get me to a fireside immediately and to give me an injection. Afterward, they managed to force some lukewarm thin gruel down my throat. And thus, they said, I was miraculously brought back to life.

Dr. Fu was so concerned about me that he often came to see me after I had revived. He knew what I needed most then was to regain consciousness and strength. So he had me repeatedly injected with some special medicine. It goes without saying that had Dr. Fu not come to save me, I would have died. There were others who were not so fortunate, and who passed away unnoticed and uncared for in their wards or in the morgue.

Starvation is often a quiet death, but it is the most impressive that I have ever seen. While I lay on my sickbed, I saw several others carried to the morgue, and knew that, like me, they felt no pain and therefore made no struggle. As in my case, their consciousness slipped gradually from them, their breath slowed and stifled, and their hearts gradually stopped. They shed no tears. They just waited for the last moment.

Whether it was luckier to survive the famine, I didn't know. After I recovered from my "serious illness" (if starvation can be counted an illness), I was plagued constantly by various ailments. I was easily tired out; there was always something wrong with my digestive system; I developed a heart disease. So not long after, I was consigned to the "Senile and Sickly Group," privileged with more rest. When the time of "spring sowing" came, the senile and sickly had to labor in the field, and, joining in such labor, I witnessed again how the starving "criminals" were worked to death. An employee of the farm was driving a sowing machine round and round in the field, plowing the soil and scattering seeds from behind. We, the senile and sickly, were asked to break up with shovels or spades the earth at the corners of the field that the sowing machine could not reach. Meanwhile, the "young and healthy ones" (in fact, no starving young "criminals" were healthy then) carried bags full of seed and ran after the machine to keep feeding it so that it wouldn't have to stop sowing even for a moment. Even as I watched, some of the poor prisoners suddenly fell down dead while running after the machine. I supposed their heavy burden (each bagful of seed weighed around sixty jin or thirty-five kilograms) and their quick pace consumed their last calories. But I wondered how they managed to keep running right up to the point of death.

As soon as the sowing was finished, crowds of us were asked to shape the field with hoes and harrows. As we did this, several others suddenly collapsed and died. To be sure, they had loyally yielded their last bit of labor power to the "Great Communist country." If the number of deaths that day could be tallied, I believe the result would be a record unbroken in the entire history of "exploiting human surplus value." The victims who made the record did have one thing to soothe their souls; they died mostly in the sunshine on a ground not too wet for the season.

Paradoxically, during the famine, some of us died from overeating. Accidents of that nature occurred in autumn during the harvest when we were awakened at three in the morning and sent to the field at half past three, immediately following breakfast. During the following seventeen hours' labor we rested three times for meals: at ten in the morning, four in the afternoon, and eight at night. Each meal at harvest time was substantial, compared with those in the past. Each laborer was allowed to eat his fill, with no limitations. Consequently, some people just ate and ate and ate, fearing perhaps that this might be their only chance. In fact the policy of the farm was to feed the laborers well so that they might have enough strength to speed up their work and finish the harvest within the limited time—usually twenty days. But this policy was a failure. Many laborers took the harvest time for a convivial festival. After a long period of hunger and starvation, they thought it a good opportunity to build up their health by eating. The opposite happened. When they overate (some were said to have had eighteen loaves of black bread made of pea powder at a single meal) and then rushed back to their heavy work, they more often than not ended up with stomachaches. Some of these greedy eaters simply died in the field from violent stomachaches. Such victims howled with pain while holding their swollen bellies.

There were only about two thousand of these "gormandizing deaths," a small number compared with the number of deaths from overwork. During the harvest time, each normal laborer was assigned to reap one to three mu of wheat a day, and a sickly or senile laborer to reap 0.8–1.5 mu. Such a requirement was equal to a death sentence for many.

The harvest season, I should remind you, was a cold time. We got ready to harvest at the coldest time of the day, and when we arrived at the field, we could see each straw covered with frost. We did not wear gloves while reaping, and our bare hands were pricked by the frozen straw. But worse than the cold or pain were the long hours. What was the use in keeping your stomach stuffed if you had to labor seventeen hours a day without rest? When the reapers cut the wheat with scythes, the "sha-sha-sha" sound was not just the sound of the wheat being reaped, it was the sound of the poor workers being reaped as well. Before long, some unfortunate wretches would fall down in the field, stiff and light as the reaped wheat. They were mostly senile or sickly prisoners to be sure, but there were also some young fellows who we thought ought to have had stronger hearts.

During a famine, everyone is concerned primarily with the result of the harvest, but a harvest should not take precedence over human life. The Communists, of course, never minded forfeiting our lives to guarantee a "successful" harvest, so I have come to realize that famine is not the most horrible of things; brutal policy is even more horrible.

For the ten years following May 25, 1966, Red China was a hell of hells: Its people suffered the most extraordinary and absurd calamity the world has even known. Those ten years of "Cultural Revolution" were indeed the darkest age of China's history.

The "Cultural Revolution" began with a poster pasted on a bulletin board in Peking University. The poster was made by seven people to attack some of the Communist leaders of Peking and Peking University. Who could tell that such a poster would become an H-bomb, causing a destructive chain reaction, ruining the lives of more than ten million people and much of China's ancient cultural heritage?

During that horrible period, I was still imprisoned on Telingha Farm. Therefore I had no chance to witness how the Red Guards ravaged the towns and the people, though I could sense a change of atmosphere on the "labor correction farm." I believe the Tiananmen event in Peking on April 5, 1976, was the most shocking event the world knew of during the whole period of the Communist Chinese "revolution." The Hsining event, which occurred on February 22, 1968, was no less shocking however. It was only that news of it was successfully blocked by the Communists. I was not involved in the Hsining event, but some years after I was released, I traveled to Hsining and heard the details from some important figures who had been.

Since the Communists took China in 1949, their regime has never met the people's expectations. To show their anger and disappointment about this, some people described China (in a phrase that become very popular in 1968) as "a country wholly poor, a country wholly sick, a country wholly imprisoned, and a country wholly guilty." Under these circumstances, slogans such as "We have the right to rebel," and "Down with the Authorities!" appealed to the freedom-loving youth, and to those aspiring to a better life. The Hsining event, according to my sources, was initiated by a worker named Wu Hsin-hua. He had been transferred from a textile factory in Shanghai to Hsining, where he recruited some workers of like mind to organize an "August Eighteenth Rebellious Group."* Within three months, the group's membership had grown dramatically; it included men and women of all ages from all Chinese ethnic groups and social backgrounds. They were following a popular desire to rebel and gain power.

The event occurred on February 22, 1968. The government authorities seemed to have gotten wind of it beforehand, and at dawn that day a good number of soldiers in green uniforms poured into the streets of Hsining. They were all equipped with rifles and machine guns, ready for fierce combat. Tanks and military motorcycles were seen rushing to East Main Street, West Main Street, Seven-one Road, and the area of Yangchia Wan to protect the Military Headquarters of Chinghai, the Provincial Commission Building, the Provincial Renovation Commission, the Two-Fourteen Command, the *Chinghai Daily News*, and the People's Broadcasting Station of Chinghai—all the "important agents" of the Region's Communist administration. But despite the troops, the Rebellious Group continued with their action. At eight o'clock sharp, the rebels signalled their advance with a factory whistle. As soon as this series of "woo-woo-woo" sounds was heard, the waiting rebels suddenly poured out in unison. Their coming was like the furious escape of water from a broken dam. They raged and shouted:

"We have a right to rebel!"

---

*In Chinese, "August eighteenth" is pronounced "pa-yi-pa"; it is quite similar to "pa-pu-pa," meaning "fear or not fear."

"Spare not your skin, be brave and pull down those in power!"
"Rise up, cold and hungry slaves!"
"Rise up, Chinghai slaves!"
"We've been cold and hungry for twenty years!"
"We want food!"
"We want clothes!"
"We want freedom!"
"We want human rights!"

Lines of twenty people wearing bands of yellow cloth painted with three red characters signifying "818" around their sleeves marched arm in arm through the streets, like the waves of a raging sea. This was the first time Hsining, or even the province of Chinghai, ever saw such mobs of people marching uncontrollably through the streets. These people were not without order or aim. While they burned with indignant fire, they advanced threateningly on the Provincial Commission Building to shout their slogans there.

But suddenly from the top of the Commission's concrete building, warnings were shouted through a loudspeaker:

"Do not advance! Halt immediately! Whoever steps another pace shall bear full responsibility."

But the crowd surged forward still shouting.

"We have a right to rebel!"
"We want food!"
"We want freedom!"
"We want human rights!"

The loudspeaker warned urgently:

"Do not advance further! We will shoot!"

Three warning shots were heard, and the entire scene became one of typical riot. Bullets flew and people ran wildly, sounds of guns and human cries pierced the air.

It is said that during the "battle," the rebellious crowd behaved very bravely. File after file of people just advanced, caring not at all about the machine guns, grenades, rifles, and tanks. They continued to shout their slogans, adding: "Chinese do not kill Chinese!" when the slaughter began. If you had witnessed the event, they said, you would have been convinced that the protesters were headless and the soldiers were blind.

In dealing with the rebels, the Communists had neither sympathy nor mercy. Even after vast numbers of the rebels lay injured or dead, the slaughter went on. The Communists were determined to annihilate the entire "rebellious army."

After the situation was brought brutally under control, the Communists set out to arrest all those suspected of complicity with the rebellion, seeming not to care what a bloody scene they had made. They searched house after house, street after street, arresting anyone they suspected, and therefore decided was an offender. This process was arbitrary and horrible; twenty to thirty thousand people, many of them innocent, were arrested and sent away in criminal wagons, leaving their grieving families behind.

The Communists killed so many of their countrymen that the area of the protest accumulated an expanse of blood ankle deep and as wide as a sea. Anyone who walked in the street at that time found the soles of his shoes soaked and plastered with blood. It took two days and two nights to clean the place with water from all the fire engines in Chinghai, and the heavy casualties amounted to seven to eight thousand deaths plus around ten thousand injuries.

As usual, news of the event was blockaded. Very few Chinese outside of Hsining, never mind the people of the Free World, learned anything of it. Details of the event were apparently reported to Chungnanhi, however, so that the "Central Government" could deal with it. Because it had involved such minority peoples as the Mongolians, Tibetans, and Mohammedans, the Communist leaders were afraid the rebellion might develop into a racial or religious problem. It is said that Mao Tse-tung himself analyzed the situation and issued an order to "redress the miscarriage of justice regarding the August Eighteenth Rebellious Group."

So Hsie Fu-chih, then Minister of the Common Security Department, and Liu Hsian-chuan, then a Central Commissioner of the Party, came to Hsining to carry out the appeasement policy. First they declared the arrested twenty or thirty thousand people not guilty. Then they consoled the families of the dead and injured. Finally, after the arrested were released, they even gave orders to arrest Wang Chao, then commander of Chinghai Military Headquarters, as well as Chao Yung-tien and Chang Hsiao-chuan, then Party Commissioners of the Province. During a "public prosecution" that followed, the people became so enraged that they broke one of Wang's arms and cut off one of Chao's ears, despite the guards' attempts to protect their former "leaders." But after the "public prosecution," Wang received a sentence of only fifteen years' imprisonment.

I got these details of the Hsining event when I was consulting doctors in Hsining after I had been released from Telingha Farm. Once I had an occasion to see Wu Hsin-hua, the chief leader of the rebellion. He told me that they had planned to overthrow the Chinghai Government, but they had not meant to seize power immediately. They had wanted to attack the important units step by step, and the demonstration in the street was one of their initial steps. They had not thought that the government would learn early of their secret plan and adopt such bloody measures to suppress them. After the gruesome slaughter, he had expected that his group would receive the sympathy of the whole country, even the whole world. He never knew that their brave actions could be kept concealed so watertightly from the people outside. Therefore, he was glad that, after thirty-one years, he at least had the chance to tell me the buried truth.

In January 1979, it was reported that during the period of the Cultural Revolution, eight to ten million Chinese were killed, while about two hundred million were directly or indirectly involved in its persecutions. This was still a very conservative estimate. From our own observation on the Labor Correction Farms, we "criminal laborers" could guess that the real figures must have been much higher.

The Labor Correction Farms were never exempt from the absurdities of criticism, strife, imprisonment, sentencing, and killing associated with the Cultural Revolution, but they were able to remain out of the grasp of the Red Guards, who carried these absurdities to their extremes. On Telingha Farm, for instance, I saw a succession of "public prosecutions" that continued for three months and involved our big team. We labored in the daytime, and were asked to attend the "prosecutions" at night.

In those days, many seemed possessed by devils, for as soon as night came, they became excited over the prospect of another chance to "prosecute" one or more of their fellow laborers. Once the "play" started, they not only watched and criticized the "tragic hero or heroes," but also stepped forward to inflict all sorts of cruelties on the victims. The "public prosecution" turned into a theater of cruelty and panic, and it was certainly absurd. Its typical acts were curses, insults, slander, and all kinds of violence. There were times when I could not believe my eyes. "How could they treat their fellow men like that?" I kept asking myself. It would be vain to try to give an account of every "prosecution" I witnessed, but one case was unforgettable, and I think it can serve to illustrate the nature of such "prosecutions" on our farm during the Cultural Revolution.

Liu Shih-liang was a "criminal laborer" in our group. He was thirty-eight or thirty-nine, and of short stature, with a square face and big eyes. He was from Ninghsia. Once he made some sarcastic remarks and was suspected of being "anti-movement." He was therefore brought to a "public prosecution" one night. At first he was only "prosecuted" by three or four hundred people, but later, as he would not confess the "truth," it was arranged that he be "prosecuted" by the whole big team, over a thousand people in all. Still he would not tell the group anything "frankly" (i.e., what they told him to tell). The Communists decided to have him "prosecuted" repeatedly until he ceased to be "stubborn." Almost every night he was "brought to trial" by three or four hundred men, but on a Sunday night he would be "generally prosecuted" by the whole big team. The "prosecutions" all took place in a large yard near our prison house. When one of these activities was going on, one could hear from afar the sounds of people shouting "Beat!" or "Kill!" And when you approached the scene, you would see the victim being knocked about and beaten repeatedly while his hair was torn this way and that—his face full of the cruel "prosecutors' " spit, and his dignity trampled under curses and insults.

To Liu this happened almost every night for two months. He was reduced to an ugly black and blue mass. We wondered how he could live on and be made to labor in the daytime, though we knew he was a strong man. The "prosecutions" were directed by the chief leaders who, during the process, usually sat at a long table smoking and giving signals. In one attempt to break Liu's stubbornness they had him bound tightly with a thick cord; the binding was made tighter and tighter minute by minute until the cord almost disappeared into Liu's flesh. But his will survived even this cruelty. By the time they loosened him, his bruised arms and legs had swollen into tree trunks.

This climax of all his "prosecutions" took place on a very cold autumn night. When it was over and we were waiting for some further action, Liu asked for a ten-minute leave. He said he had to go to the toilet. To show their mercy, the leaders consented. He was sent to a nearby toilet. Meanwhile, we waited for him to come back and resume the "prosecution." ("Prosecutions" usually lasted two hours; at that time there was still one hour to go.)

But Liu never came back. We learned later that he had managed to escape from the toilet back to the prison house. There he found a sharp knife and began to cut himself. They said the knife cut open his belly but did not kill him. In his rage, he then took a pair of scissors and used them to cut his own intestines into pieces. Whether this actually happened we didn't know. After we had waited for an undue length of time, some of the prisoners were sent to search for him. When they found him, he was lying unconscious on the ground bleeding horribly.

He was sent immediately to the hospital but as he was "belly-open," and "bowels-broken," and had shed most of his blood, he was beyond cure. The climax of our "prosecution" was an anti-climax, and no such incidents were seen on our farm from that time on, though "prosecutions" of other kinds went on and deaths were still frequent.

Besides being "prosecuted publicly," some suspected of being "anti-movement" were also resentenced, prolonging their "terms of service." Chu Tan, for instance, was resentenced to a term of eighteen years (from twelve) because he tore out a leaf of Mao's book to use as toilet paper. There were others who were resentenced several times and finally got death sentences. I myself was regarded as a "stubborn one" on the farm, so I naturally could not escape from the Communists' "prosecutions." In the winter of 1967, I was accused of being connected with a certain "anti-Communist movement" (I was suspected of planning an arson although I denied it) and was therefore confined for two years in a special prison cell converted from a well, as I've described.

I once heard someone say, "To despair is as vain as to hope." For me this saying rang with some depth, but I had to learn what despair really was before I could really grasp the truth of the saying. In my mind, to despair and to hope had been two entirely different (if not mutually opposing) emotional states. I had been a man who did not despair easily. Since 1950, when the Korean War broke out, I had hoped that I could be released and China could be delivered. But this hope was shattered repeatedly. I had hoped that General MacArthur would lead his army into China and overthrow the Communist regime, but that hope soon evaporated. Later, whenever any important international event occurred, I would again nurture the hope that the Third World War would erupt and overcome the Communists. But the Suez Canal, Prague Spring, the Cuban Missile Crisis, and the Vietnam War all battered that hope. I can't count how many times my hope rose like a balloon, only to burst abruptly and devastatingly.

The repeated death of my hope fostered in me a strong belief in despair as the real state of the world. I dropped into the abyss in the long run and lived by despair.

In 1974, the Republic of China was forced to leave the United Nations. We "criminal laborers" could not but shed tears. News like this was a heavy hammer repeatedly striking our hearts. We were afraid we had lost the last chance to gain freedom through ROC's retaking of mainland China.

At that time I had served my two years' imprisonment in the "well-cell," and my health was deteriorating. I was on the point of losing my eyesight entirely. Partly because of my poor health, and partly because of the bad news I heard from abroad, I was really in no mood for work. I often refused to labor as usual, hoping to be excused. I was never excused; instead, I was often brought to a trial or "public prosecution" to act as a "co-victim" to be "prosecuted" with the main victim.

One night I became so desperate that I decided to commit suicide. I was then sleeping on one of two earthen beds in a prison cell, each of which was intended for five prisoners. In the winter, we would gather wool to make into string to tie our coats closed, so that the strong wind wouldn't blow them open. That night, when I considered ending my miserable life, I thought of hanging myself with the string. So I took out a thick strong piece and tied it to a beam. (I was tall and could do it easily by standing on a pillow placed on top of the quilt on the bed.) Then I tied a loop, and made ready to stick my head into it. But right at that moment, one of my bedfellows woke up and got up to go to the toilet. He saw me and what I was doing, screamed, and roused all the others. I was thus prevented from killing myself.

After that attempt, I was kept in the prison house for a whole month without having to go out for work. (They feared that I might use a farming implement in a second desperate attempt.) During the nights they even arranged for two men to take turns guarding me. I gradually became stable again, in fact, I think my soul was already paralyzed. I was like a plant, I lived without any consciousness or thought. If I had not died physically, I had at least died mentally.

On December 30, 1975, at about nine o'clock, when I was ready for bed, someone called me loudly from outside my door. "Han Wei-tien, come quickly! Come to the Middle Team!" It was a bookkeeper of the Team. Upon recognizing his voice, I was plunged into doubt. "Could they want to 'prosecute' me again?" I thought, with a heavy heart. When I reached the Team Office, more than ten others were already there. Mr. Chai, the team leader, told us to go to the office of the Big Team and receive instructions there. This caused me even greater bewilderment.

At the Big Team office, I found that thirty or more of us had been called to the same place. When everybody was present, Instructor Yueh said, with a smile, "My fine comrades, I have good news for you. As you have been law-abiding comrades, Chairman Mao has decided to treat you leniently. You are to be released . . .''

What delirious news! I really couldn't believe my ears. Released? After twenty-four-and-a-half years' imprisonment? Instructor Yueh said something else to us, but I didn't hear it. He went on, perhaps, to tell us how to behave better in the future, but I hardly cared. What most concerned me was the nagging question: "Am I really free?"

It was true. The same night we were told to pack our bags; the next morning we were to go through the procedures to be set free.

How could I sleep that night? If my last twenty-four-and-a-half years had been a nightmare from hell, could I wake up so suddenly? I thought and thought and thought. I thought of everything. But I also thought I might still be dreaming.

All my roommates congratulated me. I thanked them, but my soul was still paralyzed. I turned on this side and that side in my bed. I wept. I couldn't tell whether I was happy or sad. The next morning at ten o'clock, the thirty or more of us who were to be released were sent to the Common Ground in three coaches pulled by nine horses. There, we made some temporary tents, got our baggage into them, made fires with coal, and spent the last night of 1975 in a happy state of great expectations.

We waited there two days. By January 2, 1976, some three hundred people like us had gathered from all the big teams of laborers. Then Wang Hung-fu, the Political Commissioner, came to speak. He told us what instructor Yueh had told us before. But he made us feel we were the "chosen people" of "God Mao." Finally he had us each fill out a form, and told us we could return either to our native towns, or to other cities in which we had close relatives to support us. He also added, deliberately in a loud clear voice, "You can even go to Taiwan."

This last bit of information was like a bolt from the blue. Yet it brought not woe but weal; it suddenly occurred to me that Taiwan was probably the only place I could go. I had, at that time, practically no relatives left in mainland China who were fit to support me for the rest of my life. My parents had died, and my wife had divorced me.

I might go to my brother or sister for some temporary help. But to live with them was impossible. I had to consider their financial situation and the inconvenience and trouble I would bring them if I stayed for a long time. I thought I might be well received in Taiwan as an anti-Communist even if I could not find any relatives there. In fact, I knew then that I might find a certain Chou Jong-yu, if I were lucky. She was my concubine when I married my first wife, but in 1949 she fled Red China with a daughter, first to Hong Kong, then to Taiwan. Thus I applied to leave for Taiwan.

The day we were set free, we were each given one hundred yuen, a suit of cotton clothes, a cotton quilt, a sheet, a pair of socks and a pair of shoes. We did not leave immediately, however. Most of us were still waiting for further news from relatives. In those days of waiting, we were given better food, and for those who wished to enjoy epicurean pleasures after their long, forced asceticism, provisions of sugar, biscuits, beef, pork, etc., could be found at reasonable prices in the stores of Telingha.

According to Wang Hung-fu, or "Fat Wang" as we called him, all three hundred of us could "go home" at any time, since we were already released. About one third of us had actually left by January 20. One day, a certain Mr. Hsu came to confirm that whoever was sanctioned to go could leave at any time, and that those who had to stay for some time need not worry. "We have already contacted your relatives," he said. "Some of them are afraid that you might become burdens to them. So they prefer you to stay on the farm. In that case, you may well stay on. We shall provide well for you. And you can go to them for a short visit. Anyway, don't worry. Wherever you will be, you'll have our special care." By the end of January only one hundred or so of us were left. Then Hsu came again to announce that those who remained were to work with the forestry team at a monthly wage of 56.78 yuen (about US$28).

There were five of us, including myself, who wished to leave for Taiwan. After working with the forestry team for one-and-a-half months, we were called one day to an office on the Common Ground. There, a staff member named Wang interviewed each of us. When I appeared before him, he said at once, "You can't go to Taiwan."

"Why?" I asked, irritated.

"You have not behaved well enough these past twenty years. We are afraid you might persist with your anti-Communist attitude in Taiwan. That would be bad for us."

"But haven't I earned my freedom after so many years' labor?"

"It's your attitude that counts," Hsu cut in, "Besides, your labor has not been satisfactory."

I suspected that they were cheating me. So I inquired, "Haven't you sent in my application form?"

"No," answered Hsu.

"Why not? Haven't you declared that we can go anywhere any time? Is there any additional policy to prohibit people like me from going to Taiwan?" I found they couldn't answer these questions. So I continued resolutely, "I will write to Peking. I want to inform the Central Government of this matter."

"Don't you dare!" Hsu said loudly. "If you do that, we'll have you tortured."

"All right, let's see who'll torture whom," I scoffed at them. "I'm already over sixty. I know I can't live much longer. So I may as well have a good struggle with you. You can threaten me any way you like. You may send me back to the labor camp. But I will write. I'm determined to sue for my own good."

"Write then!" Hsu replied again, loudly. "As soon as your letter is dropped in the mailbox, it'll be intercepted, I assure you."

Thus the interview came to an end. When I got back to my room, I was so angry, I couldn't get to sleep. I kept pondering the problem of finding a way out. Finally, it occurred to me that Cheng Hsiao-hsien, head of the Chinghai Common Security Bureau, was visiting Telingha at that time with twenty other leaders. "So why shouldn't I report my case to him?" I asked myself.

The next evening, I rushed to the dining room, where I knew Cheng and some other party leaders were eating dinner. As soon as I saw them, I went over and shouted, "Report!" And then I handed my report to Cheng and begged him to tell me whether or not a released prisoner laborer like me was allowed to go to Taiwan. "If it is against government policy," I said, "then I will withdraw my application. If not, I wish you to advise me on how I may proceed with my application and fulfill my wish."

This request of mine surprised everyone present. Wang Hung-fu felt he was disgraced. But he soon called over his two staff members from another table, and bade them "proceed according to policy" and grant me the chance to go to Taiwan.

Thus, later the same evening, Hsu gave me a bus ticket with which I was told I could travel from Telingha to Hsining, where I was to wait for further news about my request.

I rose very early the next morning, at three, I think. I disposed of my baggage and rushed to the station. I arrived in Hsining at about eleven the next evening and lodged at the guest house of the Chinghai Labor Correction Bureau. There I found the four applicants who had been approved earlier; they were also waiting for further news. Ten days later, Tao Ying-su, a section chief of the Labor Correction Bureau, came to tell us that our applications had been sent to the Central Government, but had not yet been sanctioned. He suggested we go back to Telingha and wait for news there.

This was a terrible disappointment. We later learned that about fifteen others who had recently left for Taiwan via Hong Kong, had caused some trouble in Hong Kong (one of them committed suicide there). Therefore the Communists decided to suspend letting us go to Taiwan. Then on April 5, the Tiananmen Event broke out; then Mao died, and the Gang of Four collapsed. The Red rulers were plunged into confusion and dismay and, under such circumstances, who would care about our requests to leave for Taiwan?

Back at Telingha, I took the opportunity to ask for leave to visit my brother in Kaifeng and my sister in Shanghai. I hadn't seen them for almost thirty years, and hoped I could stay with them a good while. Unfortunately I was permitted to leave for only seven days. And since it is a very long way from Telingha to either Kaifeng or Shanghai, I could pay them each only a very short visit; I stayed one night in Kaifeng, and one day and two nights in Shanghai. During my visits I poured out my heart to my brother and sister, and when I got back to Chinghai, it was already the morning of the eighth day.

In Hsining it had not been easy for me to gain permission to go anywhere, and I had stayed away overtime. If I could not give some good reason to the "leaders," I would not be allowed to leave in the future. At that time I had a serious eye disease; I used it as an excuse to account for my delayed return, and at the same time asked for a leave of three months to stay in Hsining to consult some eye doctors. Happily, I was granted that leave, and could continue to stay away from the farm. And I had a chance to meet and talk with Wu Hsin-hua and others in Hsining who were involved in the Hsining event, as I described earlier.

The first month of my stay in Hsining, the farm sent me my wages and ration tickets as usual, but after the second month, they stopped providing for me. So I had to borrow money from my brother and sister. Meanwhile, I thought I might as well travel to Shanghai for better treatment of my disease. So I bribed a doctor in Hsining to write a report suggesting I be sent to a better hospital for further treatment. Then I bribed Tao Ying-su, promising to get him some articles in Shanghai, and thus obtained from him a travel pass.

Once there, I of course lodged in my sister's house. My sister was a retired primary school teacher. She gave me all her sisterly love, and made me feel quite at home. She happened to have a former colleague in Shanghai whose brother was a renowned ophthalmologist. I was able to consult the famous eye doctor, and ask him to produce a statement every two or three months confirming that I still needed to undergo further therapy in Shanghai. Thus I stayed in that international metropolis month after month.

After my seventh month in Shanghai, I began to receive letters from the leaders at Telingha Farm urging me to return. But in Shanghai I was rather free, and the taste of freedom was too good to forsake. I tried every way to delay my departure from Shanghai, but only managed to remain there a few more months. During those months, I fulfilled one of my greatest wishes when I journeyed to Numohung to visit the site of Yelusa's death.

I returned to the farm in the middle of August, not daring to defy any longer the repeated summons of the Labor Correction Bureau. I had by that time recovered my health, though my eye disease was not fully cured. Compared with my former labor, my work with the Forestry Team was not easier, but it gave me a bit more freedom. On Sundays, for instance, I could go and take a good stroll around Telingha Station. Sometimes I was even allowed to go as far as the City of Wulan on the bank of the Pa Yin River. To visit that city was a privilege none of those still "serving time" could enjoy.

The task of the Forestry Team was to plant trees. We also grew vegetables and wheat for our own use. The team had two hundred or so people, who lived independently from the rest on the farm, and worked happily together. I stayed with the team for about a year. In my more than twenty-five-year stay at the farm, it was the first year during which I lived without the fear of oncoming "public prosecutions."

Soon winter came. One morning, at about ten o'clock, we were enjoying beautiful sunshine in the cold weather when something happened to me. We were preparing to store vegetables in the cellar for the spring. I remember I was sitting on the ground, with my head hung down, and I was holding a sharp knife in my right hand to cut a big Chinese cabbage that I held in my left—my job was to cut off the rotten leaves and clean the vegetables before they were sent into the cellar—when I heard someone call my name in a northerner's accent.

"Han Wei-tien, come here!"

I looked in the direction of the voice and saw a tall man standing not far away. It was Chiang, chief of the political section of the team. I rose from my work and followed him into the nearby hut, which was the garden keeper's house. There, Chiang asked me directly, "Haven't you applied to go to Taiwan?" I nodded, wondering why he asked.

"How would you go there? By way of Hong Kong?" he asked abruptly.

"Yes, if possible," I replied.

"No, not by way of Hong Kong. You can get there only by way of Fukien. But that's the front line. You'll encounter shelling there.

They often shell each other. Nationalist forces on Quemoy and Taiwan, and Communist forces in Fukien. It's a very dangerous zone."

"But I'm not afraid of danger. I'm already resigned to my fate."

"Suppose you do meet a shell there."

"Then let me die. I'll leave for Taiwan at any cost."

"All right, then." Chiang stared at me coldly. "Just wait for further news. But before you leave, you must work with the team as usual. Meanwhile, keep it a secret. Don't tell anyone you are leaving."

I naturally attempted to comply with Chiang's request. But my fellow workers were very curious to know what had been said between us. (We were all very inquisitive about each others' private affairs; it seemed that another's fortune could always affect your own.) So that evening after dinner, my fellows swarmed around me like bees, and filled my ears with droning questions.

"What did he tell you?" one asked directly.

I felt I could not lie to them. So I told them the truth. They then asked: "When are you leaving?" "To what place first?" "By what route?"—all premature questions. To such questions I could only answer with a smile, "Please, don't congratulate me too soon! You've been with the Communists for many years, and you know the worth of their words. With them, everything can change radically from one moment to the next. I can't count myself lucky until they really honor their words, can I?"

It was November 6, 1978, when the "something" really happened to me. I confess I did thrill with a bit of joy that day, although I still didn't dare to trust Chiang for what he said. After the fit of joy was over, I again saw myself as a poor laborer, doomed to pass my remaining days working the soil of Chinghai.

I couldn't forget what the Communists had done to me in the past twenty-seven years; I could not but look at them with distrust. For me, the Communist leaders were tricksters, they'd been playing tricks on the people for a long time. Their promises were written on water. Now, I was only surprised to remember that the previous year I had betrayed myself into believing they would set me free.

For the next few days I labored as usual, not expecting any good news. But ironically, I was wrong this time. When I least expected the Communists' favor, it came. Four days later, on the afternoon of November 11, while I was still preparing vegetables for storage, Chiang came to me again. He handed me a ticket, and told me to leave for Hsining the next morning. He assured me that this time I would fulfill my wish.

That evening I packed my bags with some misgiving, but the next morning I did depart for Siling, and I arrived there in time. I rested two nights in the capital, then at six in the morning on the 14th, I boarded a bus to Lanchou. I arrived there at one o'clock in the afternoon, accompanied by the chief of the Instruction Section of the Chinghai Labor Correction Bureau, Chen Nan-ping, and his wife. Chen had been the chief of staff of General Wang Ling-chi, Governor of Szechwan Province. He had undergone "labor corrections" on Gantu Farm in Chinghai for twenty years.

At six o'clock the same afternoon, we boarded a plane for Peking. On the plane I was still plagued with doubt. I hoped they were really setting me free; I hadn't expected that they would treat a "die-hard, never-to-repent, anti-movement fellow" like me so kindly. Was it just a dream?

Anyway, it was true that I was flying toward Peking. It occurred to me that the Communists might want to use me for their political propaganda; three years before, the Communist authorities had granted amnesty to some people like me, and they were treated very kindly. The *People's Daily News* had emphasized their special treatment.

The Bolshevik mode of political propaganda was "a kiss after a bite" when applied to the "die-hard anti-movement fellows." They beat you, flogged you, whipped you, made you faint and bleed, and then tried to cure and console you with sweet words. Their idea was: No matter how bloody their methods, if they won you over, you would be blinded to this bloodiness. They were convinced that one word was often enough to mask the truth, and that because they showed leniency and kindness to some of their dissenters no one would believe they had shed rivers of their people's blood.

During the first few days I was in Peking, the Communist department of propaganda sent their agents to me several times, to try to dissuade me from going to Taiwan (or perhaps to test whether I was resolute in my attempt). They told me that it was truly dangerous to cross the strait to Taiwan; to cross any passageway to Quemoy was equally hazardous, because bloody encounters were still possible between Red China and Taiwan. They told me that if I didn't go, I could stay in Peking or Shanghai, or any other big city I liked. But I refused this proposal. (Only one Mr. Li, a northerner, who used to be a brigade commander, showed interest in staying in Peking. The others who were prepared to leave for Taiwan had also refused to stay.)

On November 15, the Communists held an "introduction meeting" in Hsiyuan Auditorium. There were more than twenty of us, mainly from Chekiang, Fukien, Chinghai, and Kuangchou. Eighteen of us, including Chin Nan-ping and his family, were to leave for Taiwan. (Later a Mohammedan named Tafei joined us and increased the number to nineteen. Before he was imprisoned, he had been a secretary colonel of Liu Ping-che, an army commander; after he was released he had worked at a sulphur mine belonging to Telingha Farm.) The others were to leave for America, Europe or Japan. The meeting was presided over by Vice Minister Pang Chien, a tall man from Shanhsi Province. At the meeting we all introduced ourselves, after which Pang concluded the meeting, saying that, in allowing us to leave, they (the Communist rulers) were just observing the principles of "giving entire freedom, rendering necessary service, providing enough grants, and assigning no tasks," although they still wished us to contribute willingly to the unification of our whole nation whenever we could.

During the few days after the meeting, we were taken to visit several places (the Great Wall, Shih-San-Ling Reservoir, Peking Chemical Plant, etc.) and to the Peking Opera and some movies. Then we attended another meeting, which included quite a few high-ranking people who had been Nationalist generals, but who were captured by the Communists and converted in the '40s. Among the renegades were Tu Yu-ming, Cheng Tung-kuo, Sung Hsi-lian, Huang Wei, and

Tung Chi-wu. Tu and Sung were invited to speak to us. They spouted propaganda, and we made no reply to what they said. But a certain Mr. Li, who was to go to America, rose and thanked them for their "good intentions."

On the evening of November 26, Liao Cheng-chih, head of the Propaganda Department, gave us a farewell banquet at Peking Hotel. It was indeed a banquet, and the meal was rich in seasonal delicacies. The next day we flew to Fuchou and were lodged at a Hua-Chiao Hotel (a hotel for overseas Chinese). On the 29th, we took a bus to Amoy and stayed at another Hua-Chiao Hotel. From there we were really to leave the Chinese mainland for the island of Taiwan.

November 31, 1978, is a date I will never forget. On that day we got on a boat and sailed from Amoy toward Quemoy (Kinmen), or rather from slavery toward freedom, ending our horrible lives in the Red land. Needless to say, I was only too happy to have all my doubts and misgivings dispelled regarding the Communists' veracity in promising to set me free. When I was in the boat, I said to myself, "At last, you are to be really free. You don't have to look forward to the Third World War any more. This is not a dream. The Communists have been playing a cruel game with you, but it will soon be over. You'll soon be able to start a new life, a real life, in earnest and in a free land. What a comfort and what a fortune!"

Before I knew it, our boat had started to move toward Kinmen. The distance between Amoy and Kinmen is only two kilometers or so. If it were not sea water but solid land that divided the two places, the distance could be covered by a fifteen-minute brisk walk. But because what lay before us was an expanse of water, I knew we needed more time to reach our destination. And strange to say, I, who had had enough patience to wait more than twenty-seven years to be released, seemed to have no patience to wait one more minute for the coming of freedom.

I kept looking ahead. The sea was calm. The water was light blue. Looking farther, the water gradually turned darker, but, near the boat, all the ripples were bright with sunlight. I thought of every legendary stream that is said to connect this world and the under-world; I thought of Charon of Greek legend, carrying passengers to the land of shades, and of the legendary sirens who caused so many sea wanderers to perish.

I turned my attention back to the world before my eyes. Our boat was a two-ton wooden boat; we were being dragged by a motor-sailboat into Nationalist waters. At that point our boat would be set to drift toward Tatan Isle, the nearest island controlled by the government of the Republic of China.

Our wooden boat had drifted within two-hundred yards of Tatan Isle when I heard a series of shouts from ahead.

"Halt! Stop! Advance no more! Wait for orders!"

The nineteen of us in the boat suddenly became aware that we were face to face with "our enemy," as they were labeled by the Communists. Although we knew they weren't our enemies but our saviors, we all froze at their yell. We cast anchor and waited for further directions.

For half an hour we waited for nothing. Then suddenly, we heard a succession of banging sounds. "My God! They're shooting at us!" I was then sitting on a water barrel. I saw a bullet hit the barrel, missing me by merely twenty centimeters, and ducked by instinct. Sun Shui-yun, the oarsman, immediately shouted, "Don't shoot! We're your men! Nationalists! Sent back to you!"

At that moment I began to think maybe the Communists had purposely arranged for this to happen, maybe they were tricking the Nationalist Party into killing its own loyal Party members. But what-ever the truth, we soon found a white cloth which we tied to a string and lifted to the top of the mast. We believed the Communists had prepared the cloth for us, but wondered why they didn't tell us beforehand to use it.

As soon as we hoisted this sign of surrender, the Tatan soldiers stopped shooting at us. We waited over an hour in our boat before they sent a boat of theirs to take us to land. On the isle of Tatan we waited for directions from the main island of Quemoy. The next morning the vice director of the Political Department of the Quemoy Defense Area, General Yang Tzu-chieh, came with three motor-sailboats and took us all to Kinmen where we were well received. We were lodged at a guest house for loyal countrymen, had a good rest and enjoyed the best food we had had for more than twenty years.

On the first day of 1979, we flew to Taipei. The Gobi Desert, the Pa Yin River, the Telingha Farm, the Tarim Basin with its rugged mountains and cold weather, as well as the Labor song ("Good days are rainy and windy days . . .") haunted my memory. There were times when I started nervously from my nightmarish reflection in which cudgels, whips, bullets, and curses came from all directions to attack me. But each time I comforted myself with the fact that I was now not flying to Peking. Instead, I was flying to Taipei, where my wished-for freedom and happiness surely awaited me.

I looked out of the window at the sky and the clouds. No sky and no clouds had ever seemed so beautiful. And wordlessly, I thanked God from the bottom of my heart.

Epilogue

by Pu Ning

I lived in Red China for thirty-three years. During that time I was in a concentration camp at Hangchou Bay, made to undergo "labor corrections" in a barren countryside, and put in the Hsiao-che-Chiao Jail at Hangchou. In those places I came to know the cruel nature of the Chinese Communist regime, the better to understand the experience of Han Wei-tien in that anguished land, and to help the world better understand the often-overlooked "labor corrections" system of Communist China.

Before I knew Han Wei-tien, I had heard little of the "reform through labor" farms in the Chinghai area, although I knew they were places for such "anti-movement" criminals as Wei Ching-sheng, the now famous champion of democracy. I was eager to know more of them, but it was not until 1987 that I met the person who could provide me with such information.

I first met him in Yunghe, a satellite city of Taipei. He was then living in a small, second-floor apartment. The inside of his house impressed me with its display of Buddhist carvings and caged birds. He was tall, with a big head, a broad face, big eyes, and thick eyebrows. He wore glasses and spoke in a loud, self-confident voice. He had spent twenty-eight years in Chinghai and had now been in Taiwan ten years. He had the deportment of a hero.

I interviewed him in the presence of three of his friends; they were released prisoners from Communist China and had come to Taiwan on the same ship. During the interview Han brought out a thick manuscript for me to examine, full of neatly written Chinese characters. It was a sort of journal in which he had recorded his past life of coping with the Chinese Communists—a description of his life frequently interrupted with sentimental cursing of the Communists. From the slogans he used, I understood his loyalty to the Nationalist Party and his extreme hatred of the Communists. As I read further, I found the volume contained a touching series of episodes concerning his past struggles against the "Scarlet Predators," as he called the Communist leaders. I thought these episodes were worth making public, and I suggested that he rewrite them into a story. But he said, humbly, that he had no talent for writing and wouldn't presume to try. I suggested that I rewrite them for him. To this he instantly agreed.

I brought his manuscript back to my house and began to read it carefully. In the fall of that year, I started to write his story. During that time I always had a great number of questions to ask him; I often called him on the phone, and I paid him frequent visits. He had a very good memory and was able to answer most of my questions clearly. I think this was due to his former training as a secret agent.

Now I have turned his experiences into *Red in Tooth and Claw;* I think I have succeeded in recording what he wanted most to say about the Chinese Communist regime.

Seeing his story in print has brought him great joy, as he believes this book can serve both as a testimony of his loyalty to the Nationalist government now based in Taiwan and as a protest against it. As I learned from my repeated interviews with him, he was thoroughly investigated by R.O.C. security officials in the first few months after he arrived in Taipei. And to his great disappointment, they seemed not to accept him as a true anti-Communist hero. Instead, they decided to keep him in another sort of prolonged custody. He was placed in Lungtan Custodial House for four years and then moved to Tucheng Experimental Training House, where he spent another year in custody. Now he is free to live in Taiwan, but he feels he has not enjoyed the freedom he had anticipated before he came to Free China, as Taiwan is often called. He is sad that in crossing the Taiwan Straits, he seems only to have fled from one jail to another.

I understand his sadness, but for the time being I can console him only by telling him that the political climate necessitates suspicion. An honest, meritorious person is likely to remain victimized once he is trapped into politicized actions. Perhaps that is why I think a book like this is worth publishing.

About Han Wei-tien

Han Wei-tien can trace his family's origins back to Yung-chi County in Chilin Province; he is therefore very likely a descendant of the Manchus who populated China's northern territories. In the Ching Dynasty, Han Wei-tien's great-great-grandfather, Han Tien-pao, was elected to the Han-lin National Academy* by the emperor. After the Academy, Han Tien-pao was sent to Ninghsia to assume the office of Tao-yin, or governor, of the province. When he was informed of his appointment, Han Tien-pao decided that his family would move to Yin-chuan, the capital of Ninghsia Province. In Yin-chuan, they were assimilated into the race that makes up the majority in China, and whose members still consider themselves the most cultured—the Han. During these years, Han Tien-pao amassed a very respectable amount of property in Yin-chuan.

Han Tien-pao's daughter-in-law, Shih Chun, Wei-tien's great-grandmother, was originally from Peking; she was a very good writer, and well-versed in the Chinese classics. She assisted her father-in-law in reading documents, and was highly praised as the most distinguished woman of the clan. Her son, Wei-tien's grandfather, Han Chieh, married a woman named Yen Shih, also impressed with the value of education, and herself a scholar. As the women of the Han family lived within the tight bounds of tradition, the men lived within a code of behavior with equally strict confines. Opium smoking,

---

*Equivalent to the present-day Chinese National Academy of Science, whose members are elected by the government.

drinking, gambling, or frequenting brothels—pastimes that were all too common during the decline of the Manchu Dynasty and the early years of the Republic of China—were frowned upon by the Han family.

Wei-tien's father, Han Chin-jen, attended a private village school as a young boy and went on to study at the prestigious Ching Hua School in Peking. After graduation, in or about the year 1921, when General Men Chin-jen was Governor of Ninghsia Province, Han Chin-jen was commissioned to be Chief of the Civil Office. He served a three-year term and then entered into mercantile pursuits, gradually accumulating a great deal of wealth. By the time Wei-tien was born, the Hans owned a huge estate. It is said that two whole city streets were lined with hundreds of buildings belonging entirely to the Han family. Wei-tien's mother, Wang Ying, was a highly gifted woman with a head for business and an innate managerial sense. After the death of her husband, she was able both to care for her prodigious family and to keep the enormous Han estate intact.

Han Wei-tien was born on March 1, 1918, in Yin-chuan, when his family name was still associated with most of the real estate in that city. His family lived in a house that boasted nearly one hundred rooms, including a number of spacious living rooms, several boudoirs, a palatial garden, and more than twenty servants. At that time, motor cars were yet to be seen in Yin-chuan, but the Han family's luxurious horse-drawn coaches and mule-drawn sedan chairs were a common sight. The district within Yin-chuan where the Hans lived was originally called "Stockade West of the River." As the family's prominence grew, however, the place was renamed "Stockade of the Hans." At the time of Wei-tien's birth, the Hans had over one thousand head of cattle in their domain and were nicknamed by the people of Yin-chuan "The Ten Thousand Cattle Hans." Although a slight exaggeration, the Hans did have incredible wealth in cows, creatures as precious as children to the average Chinese peasant.

Wei-tien had five siblings; an older brother, two older sisters, one younger brother, and one younger sister, not all of whom were the children of his mother. In keeping with the social mores of the time, Han Chin-jen, Wei-tien's father, had one wife and two concubines, all of whom enjoyed fairly equal treatment under the same roof.

At age five, Wei-tien was enrolled in a private village school and taught by a scholar specially employed by his family. Soon he was reciting, at this very early age, passages from the Chinese classics, The Four Books: *The Confucian Analects, The Writings of Mencius, The Great Learning,* and *The Golden Mean.* At seven he entered primary school, and at eleven a middle school, where he remained until graduation five years later. Immediately upon graduation, in 1933, at age sixteen, he was married.

Wei-tien's wife, Jen Hui-ying, was also his cousin and his elder by three years. The marriage was contracted shortly after Wei-tien and Hui-ying were conceived, a common practice at the time. Wei-tien and Hui-ying had been schoolmates. They went to and from school hand-in-hand, and in childhood expressed great affection for each other. In the year before his marriage, suffering from insomnia one sultry, summer evening, Wei-tien slipped out of bed and into the back garden, where, to his surprise and joy, he heard the sound of someone singing and softly playing the lute. Searching for the source of the sweet sounds, he realized they came from the room of his betrothed. This taste of Hui-ying's beauty filled Wei-tien with passion for her, and not long after their marriage, she bore him a daughter. But his passion never obstructed Wei-tien's search for a glorious future, and in the summer of 1934, the seventeen-year-old Wei-tien was accepted into the Training Corps of the Fifteenth Army Headquarters, the commander of which was the Governor of Chinghai Province, Ma Hung-kuei.

Wei-tien thought, as many did during the early years of the Republic of China, that to be a soldier was the necessary first step for anyone with political aspirations. In keeping with the political traditions of the time, most high-ranking civil officials—including, up to the time of the Sino-Japanese War, most of the governors of China's various provinces—began as officers in the military. After Yuan Shih-kai,* in fact, several of the presidents of the Republic of China were generals prior to taking office. The brevity of Sun Yat-sen's first term as President of the Provisional Government of the Republic of China may have had something to do with the fact that he was not a military man.

General Ma Hung-kuei was a Muslim. He was nicknamed the "Lord of Chinghai" by the people of that province, though his power, at one time, was probably far greater than that enjoyed by any common monarch. The peasants of Chinghai later told tales of how any attractive girl in the province was in constant peril of being taken by Lord Ma to be his concubine—whether or not she was already married or engaged, and with or without her consent, or that of her husband or parents. Lord Ma wished to have all the beautiful women of his "kingdom" under his sway, even if this meant his entourage would include hundreds upon hundreds of concubines.

Ma Hung-kuei's passion for women was surpassed only by his lust for power, and he established the Training Corps of the Fifteenth Army Headquarters to secure a host of officers under his personal command; his ultimate aim was to establish a military power base for his own ends. For this corps, he wanted only cadets with schooling and ambitions to match his own. This was perhaps why Wei-tien was so readily accepted.

The central government, however, did not approve of General Ma or his schemes. His corps posed a real threat, even though his interest in fast, large-scale recruitment resulted in his cadets going through a comparatively simpler course of study and a much less rigorous training program than the national army. In an attempt to dilute Ma's power, the Central Government incorporated the Training Corps into the Lanchou Division of the Central Military School. The Central Military School was originally the Huang Pu Military School, the Nationalist Party's officer training academy. Its principal

---

*Yuan Shih-kai (1859–1916) was the first president of the Republic of China; he died shortly after he proclaimed himself emperor.

was Chiang Kai-shek. The main campus was in Nanking proper, but there were several divisions located in other provinces, the Lanchou division being one of them.

Wei-tien remained at the Central Military School for three years and graduated in 1937. His graduation coincided with the Marco Polo Bridge Incident (July 7, 1937), which was followed, a month or so later, by the Rainbow Bridge Incident (August 13, 1937). Together, these triggered the Sino-Japanese War, and Wei-tien had an unexpectedly early initiation into real battle.

During the war, Ninghsia and Kansu provinces belonged to the Eighth War Zone, under the command of General Chu Shao-liang. In 1938, Wei-tien was a lieutenant in Company 3, Battalion 1, of the Transportation Corps of the Seventeenth Army in this same War Zone. The headquarters of the army was in Lanchou Province, but Wei-tien's battalion was stationed along Liangshih Street in his home city of Yin-chuan. The next year, he was promoted to captain of a unit within the same corps, and in only December of 1940, transferred to the Eighth Army to serve as a major in the Staff Office.

In January of 1941, he was again transferred, this time to the Twenty-eighth Army to serve as a vice-commander of the First Regiment of the Second Cavalry Brigade, at the still tender age of twenty. At this point, he was promoted to the rank of lieutenant colonel, and left Yin-chuan for Tao-lo County. According to his own memories of the event, in 1942 he joined an attack on Pao-tou, the capital of Suiyuan Province (modern Inner Mongolia), where he received a bullet in his left arm and was forced to leave the battlefield. He was subsequently sent to Sichuan Province, where he was Chief Executive of the Thirty-second Nationalist Party Office of the Plane Repairing Works at I-pin County, and where he taught politics in the local military school.

When the Japanese finally surrendered in 1945, the twenty-eight-year-old Wei-tien went to Shanghai to be Section Chief of the Shanghai News Agency for the Investigation Office of all Central Military School graduates. In March of 1946, Wei-tien left Shanghai to take a new appointment as co-commander of the Seventeenth Team of Officers, which was at that time stationed in the city of

Wu-hsi in Kansu Province. A full colonel, he returned to Shanghai in July as Director of Military Instruction at the Kuang-hsia Technical and Middle Schools, and in February of the next year he was appointed Chief of the Shanghai Office of the Seventeenth Army.

Wei-tien also married for the second time while in Shanghai. Jen Hui-ying, his wife from his first, arranged marriage, seldom accompanied him on his travels, preferring to stay at Yin-chuan to take care of their family estate and her mother-in-law. As his time in Shanghai lengthened, Wei-tien fell in love with Lu Shu-chen—or Chen-chen, as her close friends called her—a twenty-six-year-old student in the Economics Department of Ta Hsia University. They married, had a son, Han Yue-chun, and bought a Western-style house with a garden on Haige Road.

Two years after marrying Shu-chen, Wei-tien became involved with another woman, named Chou Jung-yu. Jung-yu, a native of Suchou Province, was soft-spoken and very pretty. He met her when he was the Director of Military Instruction at the Kuang-hsia Technical and Middle Schools, and she was a teacher at the Kuang-hsia Primary School. She accepted her situation as Wei-tien's concubine because he was wealthy, powerful, young, and handsome, and an alliance with him offered endless prospects. Jung-yu bore him a daughter, and Wei-tien, who was quite wealthy at the time, rented a small house for her in Shanghai.*

Wei-tien's advance was rapid and seemingly unstoppable: lieutenant colonel at the age of twenty-four, full colonel at twenty-eight. This had much to do with his family background and his father's position as a prominent political figure in the Northwest of China. In addition, Wei-tien himself was very ambitious and very smart. In his ascent through the ranks, he put all of his energy into securing

---

*Regarding Wei-tien's polygamous conduct, some explanation should be made: In the deep-rooted Chinese matrimonial tradition that governed much of the social conduct of the time, it was not unusual for a man, especially a wealthy man, to marry as many as three wives and still take four concubines into his home. Wei-tien's father had one wife and two concubines. There was no legal interference with this practice; in fact, at that time, the place of the concubine in the Chinese family was protected by law.

positions that granted him ever greater authority. His return to Shanghai, to be the Chief of the Seventeenth Army Office, was all part of a long-conceived plan. Shanghai was at that time, and still is, the largest city in China. All of the country's political officers and leaders of industry and business met in Shanghai. Wei-tien moved there knowing that such an atmosphere would yield opportunities to meet many important people, and to secure an even more promising position. Indeed, before the Communists attacked, Wei-tien's prospects were impressive.

The years from 1946 to 1949 were a golden time for Wei-tien; he lived like a pasha and wanted for very little. A small part of the rent from the hundreds of buildings belonging to his family was more than he could possibly spend, and he was meeting people like Chiang Ching-kuo, the son of General Chiang Kai-shek, who later became president of the Republic of China.

When Shanghai fell into the hands of the Communists in 1949, Wei-tien sent Jung-yu and their daughter to Hong Kong. A year later, he accompanied mother and daughter to Taiwan, helped them settle into a house, and gave them some gold and U.S. currency. After he returned to mainland China, he regularly sent them financial assistance, until he was captured and imprisoned by the Communists. *Red in Tooth and Claw* is the story of his imprisonment; it ends with Wei-tien's release and eventual return to Taiwan. From the time of his release to the present day, Wei-tien has had no news of either mother or daughter (Jung-yu may have remarried long ago), but thanks to this marriage, Wei-tien was able to claim his wife was living in Taiwan. Otherwise, the Communist officials would never have allowed him to return when his imprisonment ended.

After the Communist takeover, Shu-chen was imprisoned for two years. While Wei-tien was still lying in his cell, she was forced to divorce him and was sent back, with their son Yue-chun, to her native Yue-ling County, in Shantung Province. As a young man, Yue-chun decided to search for his father; after a trek of thousands of miles, Yue-chun found him, still a prisoner. Upon seeing the son he had known only as a child, Wei-tien embraced him and sobbed violently.

After Wei-tien was released in 1976, father, son, and Wei-tien's daughter from his marriage with Shu-chen were reunited in Yin-chuan, the Han family's ancestral home. The grandeur of the Hans' "Stockade" was destroyed, and the buildings had long ago been confiscated by the state. Only a few rooms were left them, sufficient shelter from the elements.

Wei-tien was indeed an extraordinary man, strong in body and mind and possessing unusual vitality. It was not only luck that saw him through the tortures of "labor reform." He had an unbreakable will to live, which was undaunted by the horrors and insurmountable obstacles that confronted him.

A Chronology of

Han Wei-tien's Years

of Imprisonment

March 23, 1951   Han Wei-tien, working for the underground
                        movement of the Kuomintang, is arrested
                        by Communist agents and imprisoned by
                        the interrogation division of the Bureau of
                        Public Security in Shanghai.

End of June 1951   Han is transferred to Tilan Bridge Jail,
                        Shanghai.

August 1952   Han is sentenced to life imprisonment; later
                        that month, he is sent by train to the city of
                        Hsining in Chinghai Province.

September 1952   Han is imprisoned in the district of Huang-
                        yuan, Chinghai, the starting point of the
                        main road leading from Chinghai to Tibet.

October 1952   Han begins working on the construction of
                        the main road between Chinghai and Tibet.

February–April 1953   Han participates in the construction of the
                        road leading through the Sun Moon Moun-
                        tains.

May–July 1953   Han participates in the construction of the
                        road through the Touch Heaven Ridge.

August 1953– spring 1954	Han participates in the construction of a road on the banks of the Black Horse Lake and a road through the surrounding plains.
Early fall 1953	Han first meets Yelusa, a woman of Chinese and Tibetan blood living with a tribe of Tibetan nomads, and falls in love with her.
Winter 1953	Han and Yelusa are lovers.
Spring 1954	Han takes part in the construction of a bridge over the Pa Yin River.
Summer 1954	The Pa Yin River bridge is completed. The Communist leaders announce that the seventh team (Han's) of the Labor Correction Bureau of Chinghai Province will not continue work on the road into Tibet but will stay and build the Telingha Labor Correction Prison Camp. As a result, Han will be separated from Yelusa. She attempts to commit suicide and fails.
Fall 1954	Han is imprisoned at Telingha Farm and separated from Yelusa.
Winter 1954	Yelusa visits Han at Telingha.
April 1958	Han's last meeting with Yelusa.
1959	Yelusa organizes a division of Tibetan guerrillas to fight the Communists. She is wounded and dies due to lack of medical treatment.
Spring 1963	Yelusa's sister Yama visits Han at Telingha to tell him of Yelusa's death.

1966	The Cultural Revolution in China begins.
Early winter 1966	Han is accused of setting a fire that destroys between four and five million pounds of Telingha Farm's wheat grain. He is tortured and questioned several times. Because he does not confess, he is imprisoned in the well-cell.
Fall 1968	Han loses his eyesight in the well-cell and is sent to the prison hospital for emergency treatment.
1970	Han regains his eyesight.
December 30, 1975	The Telingha Prison Labor Camp announces the rehabilitation of Han Wei-tien and several other military prisoners, but Han's desire to go to Taiwan prevents his immediate release.
1976	Han travels to Kaifeng to see his brother, then to Shanghai, where he spends two months with his older sister. He returns to his sister's later in the year for an extended stay to be near eye specialists in Shanghai.
Summer 1977	Han returns to Hsining and travels to Numohung, where Yelusa died. He is free now, but he returns to Telingha to resume his agricultural duties for a small salary, and to wait for clearance to go to Taiwan.
November 6, 1978	The Telingha Farm authorities inform Han that he is free to leave for Taiwan.
November 14, 1978	Han flies from Lanchou to Peking.

November 15–26, 1978   Han, along with a number of other rehabili-
                       tated former military personnel on their
                       way to Taiwan, is received with confer-
                       ences and dinners by Communist party
                       members in Peking.

November 27, 1978   Han flies to Fuchou with the others.

November 29, 1978   They drive to Amoy.

November 31, 1978   They travel by boat to Kinmen, where the
                       military leadership eventually agrees to re-
                       ceive them.

January 1, 1979   They arrive in Taipei.